STAND UP AND BE LAUGHED AT

Over 4,000 gags for comedians, speechmakers and everyone else who wants to make their friends and colleagues exercise their chuckle muscles.

An essential book for anyone called upon to say a few amusing words.

Copyright © 2014 by Brad Ashton

All rights reserved. This book or any portion thereof may not be reproduced or used in any manner whatsoever without the express written permission of the publisher except for the use of brief quotations in a book review or scholarly journal.

The moral right of the author has been asserted.

First Printing: 2014

ISBN 978-1-326-04933-1

Brad Ashton,
7, Abbotshall Avenue,
Southgate,
London N14 7JU
em : ashtons@email.com

Previous published books:
The Dalek Outer Space Book
How to Write Comedy
The Funny Thing About Writing Comedy
The Job of a Laughtime

STAND UP AND BE LAUGHED AT

by

BRAD ASHTON

FOREWORD
by Ken Dodd.

Some years ago I received a letter from a certain Mr. Bradley Ashton offering to supply me with humorous comedy material at a reasonable price. At the time I was endeavouring to secure a small amount of money from my Punch and Judy shows, at garden fetes, etc. Sadly I had to decline the offer. How he obtained my address I don't know; possibly he had a mole or some other access to my personal details held by the Social Security or MI5.

Down through the years I have observed Brad's rise through the ranks of writers, notably his success in writing wedding speeches for best men, funeral eulogies, devising railway timetables for British Rail, TV recipes and political wit used by leading Cabinet Ministers. Brad has spent a lifetime seeing the funny side of things. The gagmeister, a guru to a lot of aspiring comedy writers. Also speeches made by certain entertainers and lecturers on cruise ships. Brad has a joke for every occasion which is what this book is all about.

Both of us have risen to a high point of obscurity and now he has done me the honour of asking me to introduce his new collection of funny stuff. "Fifty shades of embarrassment."

What is a joke? It's a quip, a wisecrack, a story, a humorous happening. You may ask "Where do these wonderful things 'jokes' come from?" They are discovered by intrepid heroes — adventurers — explorers in the realms of imagination. These marvellous jokesmiths, gag men, scriptwriters, they're often a bit odd, eccentric. They find these gems — these jewels of laughter in odd places, they mine them and then polish them until they glow and sparkle.

In this tome of titters — this cornucopia of comicalities — you will find a wealth of wit and laughter to tickle your fancy. You may ask 'who is this marvellous man who has brought us these delights from far off the wall?' He is of course Brad Ashton and this gagopaedia of mirth should activate all types of chuckle muscles. This collection of japes is his latest exhibition for which he should be knotted

or at least decorated!

I have known Brad for a long time — but I forgive him — As long as he keeps writing and cruising all over the world. if laughter really is a great medicine, this book is the perfect prescription. Brad's fun-filled fertile mind has put together a quality quip quotient of over 4,000 gags.

May I wish you, dear reader, lots of Laughter and Happiness.

Ken Dodd.

Subjects covered

Age	12
Animals	16
Art	19
As The	20
Automobiles	27
Boxing	40
Children	41
Christmas	46
Clothes	49
Computers	49
Cooking	52
Courting	54
Cricket	56
Crime	56
Cruising	64
Darts	65
Dentist	66
Diet	67
Divorce	70
Education	76
Exercise	82
Fashion	84
Films	88
Flying	91
Food	95
Football	99
Gambling	100
Gold Diggers	101
Golf	101
Hollywood	104
Homosexuality	106
Husbands	107
Income Tax	107
Insults	109
Law	114
Marriage	117
Medical	130
Miscellaneous	144
Money	146
Music	159
Obesity	161
Politics	167
Puns	186
Questions	193
Religion	196
Riddles	198
Royalty	199
Royal Mail	199
Rugby	201
Sex	201
Shopping	215
Show Business	217
Signs	224
Ski-Ing	231
Sport	231
Stingy	232
Television	235
Tennis	242
Theatre	243
Things You - hear	244
Travel	265
Ugly	267
Vacations	268
Weather	270
Wives	273
Women	288
Wrestling	290
Jokes	291

Preface

Everybody loves to laugh, or perhaps that should be everybody NEEDS to laugh. We're forever experiencing doom and gloom on the news, so anyone who can break that mood (without offence, of course), will always be popular.

During my half century career as a comedy writer I have written well over 1,000 speeches for a variety of people and occasions. They've included politicians, company Chairmen, clerics, masons and ordinary people faced with the daunting task of speaking in front of a crowd. Whether you're addressing a political rally, shareholders meeting, funeral, retirement party, wedding or whatever the occasion, a little humour goes a long way to making your speech popular and memorable.

I've known people make themselves ill worrying about what to say. They'll hold their written speech in their trembling hand and deliver it as though they were Neville Chamberlain announcing his declaration of war. Give your audience an excuse to smile and they'll love you for it.

You don't have to be a comedian (unless you already are one), to elicit laughter and applause. Nor do you need to spend sleepless nights mentally putting together the few chosen words to earn the respect and admiration you might crave. Leafing through this book's 4,000 gags you will certainly find enough laughs to pepper your speeches with. To make it easier for you, I have grouped the gags into short routines so that each individual laugh can be followed by another.

This book is, of course, not just aimed at speechmakers. It is also aimed at professional comedians and politicians who want to point a humorous finger at the opposition. While topical jibes might be the most potent weapon, I have also gone back to Biblical themes to lay the grounds for a particular point. "When Moses came down from Mount Sinai with the Ten Commandments on stone tablets, it's said that he tripped and broke a few. It set a trend, because many of us have been breaking them ever since." That could lead you into a speech about the proliferation of today's crime figures. "I was recently in New York and didn't realise how bad the crime wave was until I saw the Statue of Liberty had both hands up."

7

If you wanted to make a point about how modern inventions have changed our lives, another reference to Moses would help get the point across. "It took Moses forty years to find his way to Jericho. Just think, if he'd had a Satnav he could have done it in no time." Comedian Red Buttons got one of his biggest laughs saying that Moses was angry when God parted the Red Sea "It was just when I was going for a swim."

Mixing the traits of the sexes can earn you a big laugh. You could say "For years they wouldn't allow women's boxing at the Olympics because of the cost. Once you give them boxing gloves they'll want a handbag and shoes to match." With emancipation rife, women are now insisting on taking part in the same adventures as men. "Can you imagine what would have happened if that Kon Tiki expedition was not conducted by Thor Heyerdahl, but his sister Thora? Whereas Thor would have spent weeks with maps and charts planning his route, Thora would have spent that time planning what to wear during the trip."

Taking a well-known phrase or saying and interpreting it a different way can earn a laugh. Ex-President Bill Clinton famously said "I never slept with that woman." It wasn't funny. But if he went on to say "Or was it that one or that one? I know there's one I never slept with." It's funny. When the newspapers made much of the fact that the Duke of York was getting free flights at public cost it became funny to point out that "Crime doesn't pay. Neither does the Duke of York." When Russia withdrew its tanks from Ukraine's borders it would have been funny to say "It's the first time Putin pulled back since Angela Myrtle tried to kiss him."

There was the famous joke in an old Will Hay film where a message is sent from the battlefront saying "Send re-enforcements" It's passed down the line and ends up as "Send three and four pence." That would be the forerunner of gags such as "The Prime Minister agreed when someone said his party was full of "clones." He thought they said "clowns." Or when they said the majority of M.P.'s are "lawyers" he agreed. He thought they said "liars." Or I could say my wife was excited when the Arsenal football team manager announced he had a new striker. She thought he said streaker. Or "My wife got annoyed when I said her cooking was swell. She thought I said swill."

And of course we have the gimmick originally used by Old Mother Riley and Schnozzle Durante of using the wrong words that sounded similar. Like assembling a flat pack by "following the destructions." Referring to those two evil towns as "Sodom and Tomorrow" And even quoting my old Polish immigrant grandmother who, after having her eyes tested, said "I went to the optimist and he said in both mine eyes I got a Cadillac."

Juxtaposition is another useful gimmick for creating comedy. It's simply taking a normal phrase and placing it elsewhere to give it a different meaning. For instance: If a speed cop giving a driver a ticket points to a 30 mph sign and says "Can't you read?" it isn't funny. But if we then see the man is driving a mobile library, it is. If we hear a woman's voice say I'll wash you dry." It isn't funny, but if we then see it is one Geisha girl talking to another while a man is in the bath, it is. If we hear a man's voice say "Wouldn't you know it? The first chance we get for a holiday in years and it's been raining all the time" it isn't funny. But if we then see its Noah on the deck of the ark talking to his wife, it is. If we hear a woman tell her husband "I bought a pair of towels for us marked "HIS" and HERS" it isn't funny. But if we then see they're dishtowels, it is.

If an Income Tax officer says "Next time you give to charity get a receipt" it isn't funny. But if we then see he is talking to Robin Hood, it is. If a robber with a gun says "Put your hands up in the air" it isn't funny. But if we then see he's talking to a sexy lady who's just come out of the shower holding a towel up in front of her, it is. If one girl says to another "It's hard to tell who the rich fellows are here" it isn't funny. But if you see they're in a nudist camp, it is. If a girl is told her slip is showing, it isn't funny. But if we then see she is heavily pregnant, it is. If a man holds up a sign "Prepare to meet thy doom" it isn't funny. But if we see he is standing outside a marriage registry office, it is. If we hear a doorbell and a voice from outside says "Avon calling" it is not funny. But if the door is opened and we see William Shakespeare standing there, it is.

If a man reaches for a can opener, it isn't funny. But if we see it's a surgeon about to operate on a tin robot, it is. If a woman says "It's a continually changing world" it isn't funny. But if we then see she's the mother of quintuplets, it is. If a man says about his job "The pay isn't too good, but I always praise the boss" it's not funny. But if we then see he's a priest, it is. If, at a boxing match, the announcer says the two fighters weighed in at exactly the same weight of 140lbs, it isn't funny. But if we then see one is short and fat and the other tall and skinny, it is.

Switching is a simple way to increase your range of available gags. Here are some that use the same formula but, with the subject switched, become new gags. "The school drop-out rate has got so bad now it's risen to forty per cent. And that's just the teachers.".... "Fashions are continually changing. I can remember back to the 1970's when they wore high heels, short skirts and a bouffant hairstyle. And that was just Boy George."....."In my first game of golf I clocked up a score of 78. Mind you, I did better on the second hole."....Prisons are so crowded they're now putting four to a cell. And that's just in solitary confinement."

Examples of the "Exaggeration" formula might include "That woman's so fat, when she got married they needed three men to carry her over the threshold."...."She knew she was overweight when the insurance salesman tried to sell her a group policy."...."She's so fat, when she went on jury duty the other eleven had to wait outside."...."She's so weight conscious she even plucks her eyebrows before she steps on the scales.".....""I've got a brother who smokes 50 cigarettes a day. He's got so much tar in him, when he dies he's donated his lungs to Macadam."

If it's true that laughter is the best medicine, then these gags will be cheaper than paying for a prescription. "I asked my doctor what I should do to stop the ringing in my ears. He said 'Get an unlisted number.'"...."I told the doctor I have déjà vu. He said "Have you ever had it before?"....When the doctor heard I suffered from kleptomania, he said I should take something for it."...."The comedian told his doctor he had neuritis. The doctor said "I've heard your jokes, you need them."

With the following four thousand five hundred gags at your disposal you should never be lost for a merry quip. Or perhaps they might inspire you to invent your own along similar lines. Whichever you choose, you will be able to feel much more confident when the M.C. says "Now here's our guest with a few entertaining words....." Good luck!

N.B. At the time of writing this book David Cameron was Prime Minister, George Osborne was Chancellor of the Exchequer and Ed Miliband Leader of the Opposition. And they're all hoping to still be around when you read it.

AGE

As the saying goes "there's no fool like an old fool." You can't beat experience. I've now reached the age where my dreams are all re-runs. My lifetime pen's beginning to run out of ink. I now keep magazines like Playboy and Hustler at arm's length. It's the only way I can get them in focus. I'm so old the phone numbers in my little black book are all doctors. Instead of romantic, I'm now more rheumatic. My sex drive has turned into a putt. The only thing I go to bed with now is a hot water bottle. Nowadays when a girl says "no" to me, I thank her. The last time I winked at a pretty girl she thought I had an affliction. I'm now more interested in my pension than my passion. I still go to see porn movies, but just for the plot. I think the next date I'll have will be on my tombstone.

I'm at that age when all I have to give up is wine and song. But even at my age I have a lot of things going for me. My hair's going; my teeth are going...... I used to spread happiness. Now I just spread. My knees buckle, but my belt won't any more. My ankles crack, my knees crunch, and my stomach gurgles. I'm not just getting old. I'm getting noisier. I'm in such bad shape my health club insists I use their back entrance.

In my younger days it was stairs I took two at a time. Now it's pills. My face is so wrinkled I screw my hat on. I used to spend 20 minutes a day looking at my hair in the mirror. Now I spend half hour looking at it in the sink. And my memory's starting to go. Actually my wife's quite happy about that. So far this year she's had three birthdays and two wedding anniversaries. My wife wants me to get a hearing aid because I came home last week with five parrots. Apparently what she asked for was a bunch of carrots.

By the time they are forty most women have made up their mind what they want to be. Twenty nine. What most women want for their 40th birthday is not to be reminded of it. Dolly Parton didn't find her feet till she was forty. Then someone loaned her a periscope. It's a fact that men age quicker than women. A woman has to be 39 for at least 21 years to qualify for a bus pass.

Now that I'm retired the only thing I HAVE to do is get up in the middle of the night. When you're planning for retirement you have to find activities that don't cost too much while you're doing them and don't hurt too much after you've done them. The good thing about retirement is that if you don't do it well, nobody can fire you. The downside of it is that you have to take coffee breaks in your own time. I'll never understand how I got over the hill without ever being on top of it.

It's rumoured that Mick Jagger, the leader of the Zimmer frame set, was recently served with a paternity suit. The woman claimed he was the grandfather of her baby. I'm not sure how old Mick is. They're still carbon dating his birth certificate. Apparently his last birthday cake had 39 candles....on each slice. The cake looked like a forest fire. His first gig was a tour of the Empire Theatres. The Roman Empire, the Greek Empire, the Ottoman Empire...

I've reached the age when everything starts to wear out, fall out or spread out... Where I not only retain water, I leak it...When I shave each day and look in the mirror, all I see is an old man staring back at me. So I've decided to do something about it. I'm buying a new mirror. I knew how long I was going to live when I was forty. That's when I had a mid-life crisis. Nobody's been able to count the candles on my birthday cake. They get driven back by the heat. At my age, to me David Cameron's cabinet is of less interest to me than my medicine cabinet. I'm so old every time I'm offered a part in a film they hire a stuntman for the love scenes.

On my 50th birthday I took the day off. On my wife's 50th birthday she took ten years off. Actually she's stopped having birthdays now, leaving me to grow old on my own. She was once held in contempt of court because she refused to state her age until they cleared the room

Bruce Forsyth says we should all respect our elders. It's alright for him. At his age he hasn't got any elders. He's so old; when he went to school they didn't have history.

You know you're getting old when you try to change the TV channel with your mobile phone. You go into a room and forget what you went in there for. And that room is the toilet. You appreciate a "Yes" from your bank manager more than your girlfriend. You turn out the lights for economy rather than romance. Your mind retains nothing, but your stomach retains everything. You wake up to find your waterbed's leaked and you don't even have a waterbed. You go to a waxworks museum and they start to dust you off.

ADDITIONAL GAGS

- Most women add years to their life by just telling the truth about their age.
- The closest some women get to a youthful figure is when someone asks their age.
- Old Sarah never tells anyone her real age. She just says she was named after Sarah Bernhardt. Mind you, it wasn't long after Sarah Bernhardt.
- My wife and I have an age difference. I won't act mine and she won't tell hers.
- She's reached the point where it's easier to take years off her age than inches off her waist.
- My wife won't admit to getting older. She says she's just gaining seniority.
- My wife's exhausted. I'm not surprised. She's been pushing forty for the past ten years.
- My wife's growing old is in remission.
- My wife's very age-conscious. Recently she had to fill out a form which had a space for her age. She hesitated for so long, the official leaned over and said "The longer you wait the worse it gets."
- I'm so old now it takes me all night to do what I used to do all night.
- At 80 there are six women to every man. What a time to get odds like that.
- I've reached that age when, if my wife says she has a headache, I'm grateful.
- I woke up this morning feeling like an eighteen year old. So I'm dating one tonight.
- I'm not saying he's old, but on his last birthday by the time they'd lit the last candle on his cake the first one had gone out.
- George Burns says he's so old when he was born the Dead Sea was still alive.

- I visited a town that was so old the traffic lights were in black and white.
- He's so old he has an autographed Bible.
- I'm so old I can remember when a bank was a place you went to to save money instead of borrowing some.
- He's so old the only vice he can still handle is the one on his workshop bench.
- He won't say how old he is, but he admits he's lived through at least six re-runs of Fawlty Towers.
- She's so old she needs three pairs of glasses. One for long sight one for short sight; and the other one to look for the other two.
- She's old, but she can still touch her toes. Not with her hands – her bust.
- He's so old he can remember when Heinz had only one variety.
- You're in trouble when you lose your glasses and you can't look for them till you find them.
- The majority of people over eighty have their own teeth, because by that time they'd have paid off for them.
- I'm at the age where I have reached stage "B" in life. Baldness, bridgework, bifocals and belly bulge.
- As a kid I sold my teeth to the Tooth Fairy. Now that I'm old I'd like to buy them back.
- It seems the people who live longest are rich relatives.
- The trouble with us living longer is that we may have to pay off the national debt rather than leaving it to the next generation.
- Now that I've reached old age I regret all the wine, women and song...I didn't get.
- Whiskey improves with age. The older I get the more I like it.
- An elderly couple decided to get married. He said to her "Where shall we live? With your kids or mine?!
- A crook last week was charged with selling a second hand car that turned out to be four old crocks joined together. He got the idea after seeing The Rolling Stones.
- What with plastic surgery, face lifts, swinging clothes and anti-ageing creams, the big problem today isn't respecting our elders, it's recognising them.
- Frequent naps prevent old age. Especially if taken while driving.

- If you want to live to a ripe old age, stay away from funerals. Especially your own.
- As the 100 year old man said "If I'd known I was going to live this long I'd have taken better care of myself."
- Some people worry about growing old. I worry about NOT growing old.
- The older I get the longer it takes for me to reach the door when opportunity knocks.
- They say there's no fool like an old fool, but the youngsters are catching up fast.
- I must be getting old, now my favourite nightspot is at home in front of the TV set.
- Middle age is when you look in the mirror and wish you'd never looked in the mirror.
- We are always getting advice on how to survive after retirement. But nobody tells us how to survive till then.
- The reason so many older couples find themselves without savings is because the husband's peak earning years coincided with their wife's peak spending years.

ANIMALS

I have a dog that's way too fat. He only knows one trick. How to open the fridge door. He's fourteen years old now and still chases cats. But only when it's downhill. They say Britain's a nation of dog lovers. The Chinese are too. They eat them. Did you hear about the new Chinese cookbook? 101 Ways to Wok Your Dog. My wife did an amazing job of paper training our dog. Now if only he'd wait till I'd finished reading it. Nowadays no one wants to get involved. I circulated a petition to have the dog next door kept on a leash. So far the only one who's signed it is the cat.

A performing dog is nothing new. Unless he's performing something like heart surgery. I actually have a great relationship with my dog. I'm teaching him to jump through hoops and he's teaching me to catch a frisbee with my teeth. He's a German Shepherd. Really big. In fact, he's so big he doesn't beg. He demands. But he's very fond of children. He eats one every day.

ADDITIONAL GAGS

- He's so lazy he not only taught his dog to fetch, but to throw the stick as well.
- I found my wife in bed with my best friend. I'll kill that dog.
- My dog's so lazy he only chases cars that are parked.
- My neighbour asked me to come in and meet his new dog. I asked "Does he bite strangers?" He said "That's what I'm trying to find out."
- As one flea said to the other "Do you want to walk, or should we catch a dog?"
- Whilst dogs are man's best friend, a girl's best friend is a diamond. You can see who's getting the best end of the deal.
- I've got a crazy dog. I'd take him to the psychiatrist but he's not allowed on the couch.
- My dog caught a social disease from using a public lamppost.
- My dog's very religious. Every time he buries a bone he has a memorial service.
- We call our pet Rolex because he's a watchdog.
- I've just bought myself a Rottweiler and I think he's going to have the house broken before he is.
- I took my dog to an obedience school and it worked out great. Now I do everything he wants.
- I taught my dog to sit up and beg. Yesterday he came home with five pounds and forty pence.
- My neighbour's trained his dog to shake my hand....with his teeth.
- My favourite breed of dog is the St. Bernard. I like a dog that can hold its liquor.
- My dog's so lazy he never barks. He waits till the dog next door barks and then nods his head.
- The pet shop owner put this cute little puppy in my arms and said "Try this one for sighs."
- As the little boy said to his mother when their dog had pups "I didn't even know she was married."

- I have my dog trained to bring me the newspaper every morning. The hardest part was teaching him to get it from next door's letterbox.
- My dog's house trained. He does everything in the house.
- I've got a great watchdog. He watches every time a burglar breaks in and steals my stuff.
- Everyone loves my dog, he's so fetching.
- My dog chased two rabbits which separated. Obviously a case of splitting hares.
- Every time the phone rings our dog's ears perk up. I think he's expecting a call from Doctor Doolittle.
- My dog got all excited when he heard someone say I have a skeleton in my cupboard. I think he's hoping to get the bones.
- We've got a very friendly dog. And she's had four litters this year to prove it.
- My cat got ill, so the vet had to put it down…….nine times.
- Seeing a black cat is lucky, unless it's climbed on the table eating your dinner.
- In our house the only one that doesn't cry over spilt milk is the cat.
- I never play cards when my cat's in the room. When the word spade is mentioned it runs for its life.
- As one cat watching a tennis match said to another "My mother's in that racquet."
- The snake charmer switched to playing Rap and that was a big mistake. The snake wrapped itself around him.
- He'd do anything for his pet animals. He even paid for his Mynah bird to have elocution lessons.
- They let me take my pet parrot with me to the library since I taught him not to talk…just whisper.
- Our pet parrot died of exhaustion. He tried to repeat everything my wife said.
- The man returned the parrot to the pet shop because it talked too much. His wife couldn't stand the competition.
- As the angry giraffe said to his mate "I've had it up to here."
- They say an animal's highest form is man. I think they've forgotten about giraffes.
- As the male rabbit said to the female "This is fun, wasn't it?"

- You can depend on a rabbit's foot if you like, but remember, it didn't work for the rabbit.
- I asked the farmer how many sheep he had. He said he doesn't know. Every time he tries to count them he falls asleep.
- Did you hear about the cow that wandered into a dye factory and moo'd indigo?
- The only one in our house guaranteed a roof over their head is our pet tortoise.
- As one skunk said to the other "So do you!"
- As the male porcupine said to the female "I do love you, but I can't stand it when you needle me!"
- A duck went into a department store to buy some lipstick. "Cash or charge?" Asked the salesgirl. "The duck said "Stick it on my bill."
- My local zoo has an elephant that's a big drinker. He wants to forget.
- There was an accident at the circus. Apparently the lion tamer needed a tamer lion.
- It's alright for children to have pets. The trouble starts when the pets have children.
- I put Swiss cheese in the mousetrap. It didn't help. The mice used the holes to play golf.
- The kangaroos were enjoying their hoppy hour.
- My dog doesn't bite, he uses his legs instead. He's a kick Boxer.

ART

One thing I learnt about art. All the people in J.S. Lowrie's time were anorexics. Paintings sell for thousands. I'm surprised Mona Lisa's just smiling. For what they say she's worth she should be laughing her head off. I went to an exhibition of modern art and the only thing on the wall I understood was the EXIT sign. What worries me most about modern art is that I'm actually beginning to understand it. But it does seem as if all someone has to do is vomit on the canvas and they call it art. I've been to lots of those modern art exhibitions where every picture's supposed to tell you something. Mostly that the artists couldn't paint. There is only one way to tell if a modern painting is completed. If the paint's dry, it's finished.

ADDITIONAL GAGS

- Did you hear about the unlucky painter who was born Toulouse?
- When Toulouse Lautrec had a girl model the first thing he drew was the curtains.
- It's easy to recognise a modern painting. It's the one you can't recognise.
- I know artists are supposed to suffer. But in her case it's the viewer who suffers.
- The artist arrested for sexual assault on his model said "An artist is supposed to feel what he paints."
- Artist painting a fat filled wallet says to his colleague "You paint what you see. I paint what I want to see."
- I get the impression that if Picasso had gone to medical school he'd have flunked anatomy.

AS THE………

As the auctioneer said "Gone to the lady with her husband's hands around her throat."

As one astronaut said to another "I've just talked to Mission Control. Our luggage went to Saturn."

As Adam, said to Eve "Now we don't want our species to become extinct, do we?"

As Adam said to Eve "Sometimes I feel I liked you better when you were just a rib."

As the alien flying saucer pilot said when he circled Mount Rushmore "God, these Earth people are tall."

As one angel said to the other "Oh yeah! And just who do you think you were!?"

As the army general said "I owe all my success as a soldier to my wife. I joined the army to get away from her."

As the belly dancer said to her boyfriend "I'll be with you in a couple of shakes."

As the bartender holding an olive and a bit of lemon said to the customer dressed as Charles Dickens "Olive or Twist?"

As the Best Man said to the old man that was marrying a young girl "I know you'll be happy. Exhausted, but happy."

As the man who spilled his Minestrone on his lap said "waiter, there's a soup in my fly."

As the client said to the optician about the eye chart "Haven't you got one in English?"

As the kid said to his pal "Last weekend I went camping with my Dad and next week I'm going to Disneyland with my Mum. Before they got divorced I never went anywhere.

As the Store Manager said to the worried salesman "Either all these goods go, Benson, or you do."

As the chef said to the waiter "How come you get all the tips and all I get are compliments?"

As one lawyer said to another "How are you today, allegedly?"

As the Genie said to his master "You rubbed, sir?"

As the pregnant girl said to her boyfriend "Congratulations, you're about to become a husband.."

As the pregnant woman said to her husband "We'd better go to the hospital now. The pains are just three commercials apart."

As Mrs. Claus said to Santa when he got home "You smell like a chimney."

As the parachute instructor said to the new student "If at first you don't succeed, that's it."

As the nurse said to the patient she was about to inject in his rear "Come now, Mr. Benson, a gentleman always offers a lady his seat."

As the vicar said to his crowded Christmas congregation "This is a time of hope. And I'm hoping to see some of you back here again before next Christmas."

As the client said to the optician about the eye chart "Haven't you got one in English?"

As the prostitute said to the client "It's been a business doing pleasure with you."

As the prostitute said to the prospective client "Yes, I do believe in free love. But there's a small handling charge."

As the prostitute said to the man about to enter the Betting Shop "Want to put your money on a sure thing?"

As the prostitute said to the police officer "I want that man arrested for rape. He didn't pay me."

As the hijacker said to the plane's pilot "Take me to wherever my luggage is going."

As the man said as he stared at Dolly Parton's bust "I've heard about so much of you."

As the Egyptian said when he prepared Pharaoh's body for burial "That just about wraps it up."

As the car salesman said "Don't think of this as a used car. Think of it as a car with years of experience."

As the pregnant girl said to her boyfriend "Congratulations, you're about to become a husband.."

As one critic said about an abstract artist's work "His splatter is impressive, but his dribbles lack conviction."

As the prospective boss said to the ex-discus thrower, "Apart from throwing your weight around, what else have you done?"

As the man said to his date after sex "I had you down as a good girl. I was wrong – you were great!"

As one parrot entering Noah's Ark said to his mate "The one time we're invited on a boat and it had to rain!"

As the knight in armour said to his dance partner "Pardon my dancing, I'm a bit rusty."

As the pregnant lady said to the door-to-door charity collector "I gave at the office party."

As the Sultan said to one of his 15 wives "Happy anniversary – pass it on."

As Superman said to his disappointed wife "You knew I was faster than a speeding bullet when you married me."

As the TV newscaster said "That's all for tonight. We really don't think you can take any more bad news."

As the patient said to the private doctor "Sure I'll tell you where it hurts most. In my wallet.

As one factory worker said to the newcomer "The Boss is only a number here too. But he's Number One."

As the travelling salesman said when he knocked on the door of the brothel "Are the ladies of the house in?"

As the wife said to her hubby as they exited the party "You made a right fool of yourself. I just hope nobody realised you were sober."

As the scantily dressed woman golfer said to her embarrassed husband "But you said the object of the game was to round in as little as possible."

As the husband said to his wife at the milliner's "What do you want another hat for? What's wrong with the silly ones you've already got?"

As the rain-soaked weather forecaster said "I should have listened to my wife. She told me to take an umbrella."

As Methuselah said "I never worry about tomorrow, I live one century at a time."

As the madam told the prospective client "We have a new dominatrix on the team. She's brand spanking new."

As the Boss said to the very pretty applicant for the secretary's job "You must understand the job is just temporary. As soon as my wife sees you, you're out."

As the sports fan said to his wife "If you've anything to say, say it now before the football season starts."

As the golfer said to his mate "You've had some bad lies in this game. The worst are on your score card."

As the theatre critic said "The part I enjoyed most was when I fell asleep."

As the doctor said to the hypochondriac "You're in perfect health and you'll feel fine when you get used to it."

As the shopper in the supermarket told the assistant "I can't remember the brand, but I can hum a few bars of the commercial."

As the cave girl said to the cave man after they'd been out together "I never let a man club me on a first date."

As the woman said when she saw the wind blow the Scotsman's kilt right up "Great Scot!"

As the young girl said to E.T. "It isn't that I don't like you. We live in two different worlds."

As the condemned convict in the electric chair said to those gathered to watch his execution "How about a last game of musical chairs?"

As the mother said to her son about his respective fiancé "She deserves a good husband. Marry her before she finds one."

As the talking parrot said to its owner "I can't keep up with current events when the papers in my cage are a week old."

As the football referee said to his mate "Yes, I DO need them, but I look terrible in glasses."

As the Jewish doctor said to his patient. "This isn't a prescription. It's my mother's recipe for chicken soup."

As the private doctor said to his patient "You're doing fine, but your savings account's on the critical list. I'm going to be honest with you. What you've got you can no longer afford."

As the publisher said to the novelist "I was not only able to put it down, I was able to throw it in the bin."

As the surgeon said to the patient just before the operation "Aren't you going to wish me luck?"

As the Income Tax Inspector said to the clown "Surely you jest?"

As the fat fellow proposing to his girlfriend said "Well, if you won't marry me Gertrude, at least help me get up."

As the teenage girl explained to the police "I socked him on the jaw because he called me a tomboy."

As the lecher said to the good looking woman "If you're looking for a husband, look no further. I'm a husband.""

As the sexpot applying for the secretarial job said to the prospective boss "I don't know how to type, take shorthand or say "no."

As the sexpot confided to her pal "I told him I'd only do it for love. Then he gave me this pearl necklace and I fell in love with it. "

As the waiter said to the very fussy customer "What about the lighting? Do you want candle, incandescent, neon or house?"

As the computer operator said to the sexy girl "I'd like to programme you into my future."

As the golfer said to his wife partnering him "Look, there are enough big traps on this course. Would you mind closing yours?"

As the little boy said to the little girl "Which one of us is the opposite sex, you or me?"

As the pregnant woman said to the chemist "Are any of the pills retroactive?"

As the Tax Inspector said to the client "I'm afraid that tax loophole has become a noose."

As the wife said when her husband came home from work "You're probably wondering why the garage is empty."

As the secretary said to her boss "You never tell me something's important till I've lost it."

As the pregnant woman said on the phone. Great news, mother. I'm going to have a husband."

As the medical school lecturer said to his class "Today we're going to discuss the ancient practice of making house calls."

As the boss told the incompetent employee "You'll go far in this company, Benson. I'm sending you to our branch in Venezuela."

As the lawyer said to his client "If you want laymen's terms, go to a layman."

As the alien said to the petrol pump "Take your finger out of your ear and listen to me."

25

As the fat girl said "I'm crazy about George Clooney. I can't think. I can't sleep. I can't work. Thank God, I can still eat."

As the fat woman said sadly "My mother warned me about men. She should have warned me about chocolate éclairs."

As the wife said to her money-conscious husband "The government is short of money too, but that doesn't stop IT spending."

As the henpecked husband said to his wife "You weren't actually in my dream, but you did do the voice-over."

As the father said on the phone to the young man "I'm afraid my daughter's not in at the moment, but do leave your name, make, model and age of your car."

As the cop at the Missing Persons desk said to the spinster "Sorry, lady, we can't help you find a missing husband unless you've lost one first."

As the customer said to the travel agent "I'd like to get away from everything but my money."

As the school kid said to the doctor "I've passed on my measles to seven others in my class. Don't I get some commission?"

As the vicar said to his congregation "On the other hand there ARE some things money can buy. The church needs a new roof."

As the doctor said to his fussy patient "I can well understand how your gall bladder is irritating you, Madam. It's beginning to irritate me."

As the girl said to her lover "My mother warned me about men like you and gosh, I thought I was never going to meet one."

As the lady diner said to the waiter "Yes, you CAN bring me something from the bar – my husband."

As the young kid said to his father at bedtime "Try a different story tonight, Dad. That one always puts me to sleep."

As the private doctor said to his receptionist about a new patient "His X-ray looks O.K. but his credit rating has me worried."

As the whale said to the submarine "I think I love you."

As the actress said when collecting her G String from the Wardrobe Department "Oh, this is a costume movie?"

As the hypnotist said to the compulsive woman shopper "Now I want you to cast your mind back to the first time you said "Charge it."

As the Apollo theatre manager said when the roof fell in "Is there a doctor in the house...and a damned good lawyer?"

As the Hollywood child actor said to his Dad "Sure I want to settle down, Dad but I want to get married a few times first."

As the Eskimo photographer said to the posing family "Say freeze."

As the criminal being rejected by his girlfriend said "The police want me, Interpol wants me, and the Fraud Squad wants me...how come you don't want me?

As the alcoholic said "There are worse things than drinking. For instance – not drinking."

AUTOMOBILES

The rise in petrol prices has brought my wife and me closer together. We've bought a smaller car. They're making them really small now. I saw one so tiny the cigarette lighter doubles as the heater. The number plate was in shorthand. I got hit from behind by one. Took the doctors four days to remove it. It's the complete opposite to the Limousine an Arab Sheikh's just bought. It's so big it seats eight people. And that's just in the glove compartment. Well he can afford it. He's rich; instead of just water he fills the radiator with Perrier. He doesn't bother washing it. Once a week he has it dry cleaned.

We all know that figures don't lie, but unfortunately some used car dealers do. I saw one wearing a dunce's cap. He said it gives the customers a false sense of security. This guy boasted he stands behind every car he sells. I said "I'd rather you stood in front, so I can see if the brakes work." I never trust the mileage on the clock. Some of them have been turned back so far they're in Roman numerals. The salesmen always say they're letting it go for a song. Trouble is, by the time you get it home it's already out of tune.

When I worked for the BBC I always went that extra mile. It was the nearest I could find a parking space. What most motorists pray for when they go to church is a nearby parking space. In fact, the only exercise most motorists get these days is the long walk back to their cars. Statistics show that in England this weekend 33,000 motorists drove at least 200 miles. And that was just looking for a parking space. The traffic situation is so bad, I reckon by 2015, if every car in Britain was laid end to end, none of us would be surprised. Suddenly caravans have become very popular. They give the drivers somewhere to live while they're looking for a place to park. Actually I've got a great way to clear our roads of so much traffic. Just deport all foreign cars. I'm still rankled by the fact that the Japanese lost the war, but won the car market. I think all those Japanese cars are the reason so many people drive like they're Kamikazes. The two greatest dangers on the road are drivers under 25 going over 70 and drivers over 70 going 25. Never mind the seat belts, some drivers ought to be constrained with strait jackets. In America I saw a sign that said "Thirty days hath September, April, June and November…and anyone caught exceeding the 55 mile per hour speed limit. My wife complains that I drive too fast. She shouts her head off if I go over sixty. That's ridiculous. Jenson Button goes faster than that during a pit stop.

I really do feel they should abolish the 70 mph speed limit on motorways. What annoys me most is that I occasionally get stuck behind someone who obeys it. They should raise the speed limit to 80. That way, drivers who now do 90 will speed up to 100. They'll get home faster and leave the roads safer for the rest of us. Alternatively, they could lower it to 20. With everyone driving at that speed, they'd be a lot easier to pass.

My wife got stopped for speeding. She must have been going fast because the policeman asked for her pilot's licence. First he read her her rights and then he read her her wrongs. Last week my wife skidded the car into a brick wall, but she refuses to have the front bumper repaired. She says it looks better with a dimple. If my wife ever gave up driving at least three repair garages would go out of business. It was because she took up driving I had to buy a second vehicle. A tow truck. You can tell how little my wife knows about cars. One morning the car wouldn't start. She called the AA who told her that her battery was flat. She said "Well, what shape should it be?

I have a wife who's always rearranging the furniture. I don't mind that, but this week she rearranged the car. She went out shopping and came back with the two front wheels out of alignment. One was in Piccadilly and the other in the Edgware Road. When my wife's at the wheel they put up a special road sign. It's a pair of crossed fingers. In all the years she's been driving she's kept both the AA and RAC on their toes. Believe it or not my wife once got a safe driving award. It was for not driving for a year.

Last month the engine was making a noise so she took the car in for repair. The mechanic said "Your cylinder's missing." My wife said "it can't be. We lock the garage door every night."

It was only a week after my wife passed her driving test that she crashed into another woman driver. They were supposed to exchange names and addresses. Instead my wife wrote down the name of the woman's hairdresser, dressmaker and where she gets her nails manicured. Her parting words were "I'm so glad we bumped into each other, we must do it again sometime."

I always fear an intake of breath, especially when it's the garage mechanic doing an M.O.T. on my car. When I took it in for its last M.O.T. the mechanic shook his head. He said "If it was human, I'd be calling a priest by now." When he got to work he not only jacked up the car, he jacked up the price as well. When he finished he said "The bill will be two hundred and fifty quid. And that includes the £75 I quoted as the estimate." He even overcharged my battery. What he'd done was correct the brakes, the steering, the engine timing and his own cash flow problem all at the same time. His bill was so big I thought he'd added in the date. It looked like he was selling me the garage. All I wanted was a tune-up and I was being charged for a whole concert.

Sorry I'm late. I was behind a used car salesman at confession. British summer time's ending soon and we'll all have to turn back the clock. Mind you, my brother's been doing that for years. He's a used car salesman. Did you hear about the used car salesman's job applicant who was turned down because his CV said he was honest?

I always try to drive behind women. At least you know they're going to keep looking in their mirror. This American thought I must be a great driver because he saw my licence had been endorsed by three separate judges. Saudi Arabia has the worst driving record in the world. And somehow I don't think they can blame that on women drivers. My wife flunked her first driving test. She said the examiner made her nervous. He kept trying to jump out of the car.

Since my wife passed her driving test she's met a whole new class of people. Policemen, lawyers, judges.... My wife thinks I'm a lousy driver. After a few miles I always turn to her and say "Look dear, let's swap roles. From now on YOU drive and I'LL nag." The main reason women drive more carefully than men is because, if they're involved in a crash, the newspapers print their age. A reckless driver admitted to the judge "Yes, I was at the wheel, but my wife was driving."

A fellow phoned the police station and said "I've just crashed into three parked cars, a street lamp, a bus shelter and knocked over a telephone kiosk." The policeman said "I see, sir. And where are you now?" The man said "Wouldn't you like to know."

The vicar told the car mechanic "Your estimate runneth over." There was a powerful earthquake in Kent yesterday. It made everything move but the traffic on the M25. I saw a car wash advertised for just £1. For that money all they did was drive it through a puddle.

I've just been offered the cheapest possible car insurance. It's called a Bikini policy. It hardly covers anything. Did you hear about the new car being made especially for people who go on cruises? If you have a crash the air cushion comes out with a little chocolate on it. The car was able to cruise at 100 miles an hour. Fast enough to get from London to Leeds in just two hours and four speeding tickets. I arrived here late today because I had fan belt trouble. I met one of my fans and he belted me.

The motorist at Marble Arch asked a policeman the quickest way to Shepherd's Bush. "Are you walking or driving?" asked the policeman. "I'm driving." "The policeman said "Yes, that's the quickest way."

A cousin of mine earned a fortune in the motor industry. He made toupees for bald tyres. Isn't it terrible how expensive things are now? They did away with bucket seats in cars when the manufacturers realised not everyone has the same size bucket.

Show me a man who laughs when things go wrong and I'll show you a motor mechanic. The best safety device in a car is a rear view mirror with a police car showing in it. In England, the best way to kill an hour is to drive one mile on the M25. "Of course I'm honest" said the used car dealer. "I have to be. It's a condition of my parole." The salesman said "Another good feature is, if you have a drought, all you have to do is wash this car and the rain comes.

My wife's been driving since we got married. Mind you, only recently from the front seat. She considers herself to be a safe driver because she blows the horn when she goes through a red light. An unmarked car is one my wife hasn't driven yet. She once got a ticket for speeding. She said it wasn't her fault, she thought the sign "MAX 50" only applied to people named Max. I complained to my wife "That's the third rear view mirror I've had to replace this month." She said "Don't blame me. I never use it."

My new car's giving me a lot of problems. Especially keeping up the payments. They say new cars are being made with economy in mind. Unfortunately that doesn't include the price. Car prices are now so high the only deposits being made on them are by pigeons. Dealers now not only need a showroom, but once you've seen the price, a recovery room too. I hope one day to buy a car in which the warranty lasts as long as the payments.

Nowadays buying a £30,000 car is easy. You just buy a £20,000 car on time payments. Actually, the cost of buying a car is nothing compared with the repair bills. The repair garage is offering a special deal this week. They're not going to charge more than the original estimate. My car mechanic's got a degree in estimates. Last time I took my car in, he said "You're lucky; I only had to replace one part...the engine. I paid so much for the repair; I guess you can call me a screwed-driver. The smallest figure on his bill was the telephone number

With this current icy weather the roads are now more slippery than an insurance company when it comes to paying out time. With all those lazy policemen driving here in London is like being on a roller coaster. London's a dangerous enough place to drive in anyway. I put my arm out the window to signal a lane change and someone stole my watch.

I'd be happy if my car mechanic realised that just because something badly needs fixing, it doesn't need fixing badly. He calls himself a motor

31

mechanic. The only thing he knows about engines is you have to have one.

London's traffic always seems to be gridlocked. If a driver wants to hit a pedestrian he has to get out the car to do it. Yesterday I sat in a taxi for thirty five minutes and the only thing that moved was the meter.

It's not true, men don't cry. They do, especially when their wife crashes the car. I'm not saying my wife's a bad driver, but if she was an Arab she'd come home with a dented camel. She averages 15 miles to a bumper. She insists she's a careful driver because she always looks both ways before hitting someone.

The industry forecast is that in future cars will be shorter and lower. What they don't say is the payments will be higher and longer. My wife wanted something that would last her a lifetime. So I bought her a car on time payments. Cars are so small now, when you cross the road you have to look left, right and down. You don't run over people any more. You run under them. The main accessory you get when you buy a car now is a shoe horn.

He said the car was almost new. Turned out the only thing almost new about it was the cigarette lighter because the previous owner didn't smoke. The car was advertised as a real steal. So he stole it.

I'm not saying my wife's a bad driver, but yesterday she backed our garage out of the driveway. The car crash let him with a bruised face and broken arm. The other driver did it.

Mechanic says "If this car was a frog it would have croaked by now." The car's so small the engine's in the glove compartment. There's one group lobbying for the speed limit to be increased. They're all undertakers. He's not only a good car mechanic, but he overcharges less than all the others.

The salesman offered me a car so small, when I told him what he could do with it, it was actually practical. Car mechanic's sign says "FAST – EFFICIENT – REASONABLY PRICED," He asks customer "Which one do you want?" Once a year the clock goes back....on every used car in his car showroom.

DRIVING

The only time everything came my way was when I drove down the M1 on the wrong side.

Women love to see men in uniform, except when they're driving and the man in uniform is a cop.

I never drink when I'm driving. Only when my wife drives.

My wife only started driving last week and today she gave me the fright of my life. She came home from shopping and said "Guess who I just bumped into?"

My wife just failed her tenth driving test, but she isn't quitting. Unlike all her ex-instructors.

It isn't that my wife's a reckless driver. She just doesn't want to waste the money we spend on insurance.

The thing my wife hates most about parking the car is the crashing noise.

Women not only drive as well as men, they can do it from the back seat.

Too many accidents occur when a man is driving under the influence…of his wife.

Always try to drive so your licence will expire before you do.

I thought I knew how to drive a car until this morning when a traffic cop stopped and told me.

From now on the only time I'll let my wife drive is when we're playing golf.

The only driving my wife is good at is me up the wall.

Thanks to my wife's driving our car has so many dents that after it's been washed I have it ironed.

PETROL PRICES

I've been taking a course in speed reading. I want to be able to read petrol prices before they go up again. Petrol's now about £1.35 per litre. My car now goes from 0 to full in just £75. If this continues we'll have to get smaller cars or bigger litres. I bought a second hand car that's a real gas guzzler. Normally you ask how many miles it does to the gallon. With this one it's how many gallons to the mile. They say a used car is fine as far as it goes. But with the cost of petrol it isn't going far anyway. With petrol prices what they are now, I'd be happy to sell the car for what it costs to fill it up. I still remember back when petrol was just 35p a gallon. Now all you can get for 35p is a sniff of the nozzle. I pulled up at one petrol station. They asked if I wanted premium or super. I said "Neither. I just came in for an estimate." Soon, instead of getting petrol through the pump, they'll be delivering it by Brinks Mat. No wonder the Arabs ride on camels. They can't afford their own petrol.

Petrol prices are rising faster than Superman changing in a freezing telephone booth. They've risen so much, you don't put your credit card in the slot anymore. They want the deeds to your house. There were five cars ahead of me at the petrol station today. All there just to get an estimate.

Car sickness is what you get when you have to pay the high price of petrol. If the price of petrol keeps rising it'll soon be £3 a squirt. Petrol prices are like babies, they keep being changed. I've always bought petrol on my credit card, but soon I won't be able to. It only has a hundred pounds limit. A petrol station is a place where you can fill up your car and empty your wallet at the same time.

My car has a fantastic burglar alarm. Every time I pay for petrol it goes off.

CAR PARKING

Nothing makes you realise how precious time is until you pay by the hour to park your car. The Borough of Westminster is threatening to increase its parking charges again. It'll soon get to the point where, instead of printing the tariff on the meters, it'll just say "Give what you can." You used to be able to hire a car for a whole week for what it now costs to park for a day. I've had so many parking fines they're thinking of giving me a season ticket. I think it's my parking fines that are keeping this country going. Last week my wife got a ticket for double parking. It was on top of another car.

In every traffic jam there's a cross section of people. Most of them very cross. There is no scientific evidence that a stalled car can be started by the driver in the car behind honking his horn. I blame TV for there being so many cars on the road. People keep winning them on game shows. Today I was present at a miracle. I found a parking space in London's West End.

I've gone to every Harrods, Selfridges and John Lewis summer sale and never once found what I was looking for....a parking space. They give you a fine for parking in London's West End. I think they should give you a medal for finding a space. I'm convinced car windscreen wipers were invented solely for traffic wardens to stick parking tickets under. To a motorist, happiness is discovering that piece of paper under the windscreen is just an advertisement.

The thing that keeps most of us motorists going is trying to find a parking space.

My brother earns his living writing. He's a traffic warden.

STATE OF THE CAR

I bought a used car at an auction. I realised I'd made a mistake right away. When the auctioneer banged his gavel the door fell off. It looked like something you'd hire from Rent-a-Wreck. Instead of a warranty it comes with an apology. The auctioneer said it had been a get-away car. I found out he wasn't lying. The previous owner couldn't wait to get away from it. That car drove so slowly it wouldn't pass anything. Especially an M.O.T.

The salesman said this car has everything. I didn't realise he meant faulty brakes, worn out spark plugs and a leaky radiator. It didn't even have an exhaust pipe Mind you, it didn't need it. The whole car was exhausted. It shook so much the only thing on the car that didn't make a noise was the horn. And the tyres were almost bald. I've seen more

35

rubber on the end of a pencil The only advantage that car had was that it was safe to leave out on the street at night. Vandals thought someone else had beaten them to it. I finally got rid of it at a toll booth. When the attendant said "Two pounds" I said "Done!" and left it there.

My car's got to the stage where it has stopped depreciating and started decomposing. I only use my car for show. When I'm in a hurry, I walk. Last time I drove that car I was stopped by a policeman. I said "Officer I was not speeding." He said "I know. But so many parts fell off I'm arresting you for littering."

We bought a car that was so old it was made in England. My wife's already started spring cleaning. She said "Let's clear out the junk in the garage." I said "No, I'm still driving it" Last year I deducted my car as a religious expense. Whenever I get in it I pray it will go. The car was in such a bad state, when I phoned the AA for a tow they sent a dustcart.

I called that car Flattery because it got me nowhere. I drove the car to a service station and said "I want a new tyre for this car." They said "That sounds like a fair exchange."

CAR REPAIRS

My car mechanic is good. If he wasn't, why would I go back to him every week? The mechanic even charged for the time it took to add up the bill. My wife had an accident in the car. We now have a Mercedes Bent. When my wife puts her arm out to make a turn she keeps her fingers crossed.

ADDITIONAL GAGS

- The car was in such a bad condition, I parked it out on the street and got a ticket for littering.
- The salesman swears the car had only one previous owner. He must have been a stock car racer.
- I won't say my car is slow, but the only other cars it's ever passed are those that were stopping for petrol.
- My car's so old the clock on the dashboard's a sun dial.

- My car drives so slowly you can sit in it and watch the world go by.
- You'll never know how hard it is to drive a bargain till you've bought a used car.
- The used car salesman said the car had power brakes. He should have said 'poor' brakes.
- The used car dealer said the car had very low mileage, because the little old lady who owned it couldn't afford the petrol.
- The used car salesman said the car only had one previous owner. He didn't say it was Hertz.
- I bought a new car off a toy manufacturer. It wouldn't start and I found out why. The battery wasn't included.
- My wife has just failed her tenth driving test, but she isn't quitting…like all her ex-instructors.
- Women not only drive as well as men, they can do it from the front and back seat.
- Too many accidents occur when men are driving under the influence of….their wives.
- The thing my wife hates most about parking the car is the crashing noise.
- The only time I let my wife drive is when we're playing a round of golf.
- The only driving my wife is good at is me up the wall.
- Thanks to my wife's driving our car has so many dents that after I have it washed, I have it ironed.
- My wife's such a lousy driver, she's the only one I know who can take out the car and the garage at the same time.
- Always try to drive so your licence will expire before you do.
- I thought I knew how to drive a car until this morning when a traffic cop stopped and told me.
- It isn't that my wife's a reckless driver; she just doesn't want to waste the money we spent on insurance.
- I never drink when I'm driving. Only when my wife drives.
- My such a lousy driver, she's the only one I know who can take out the car and the garage at the same time.
- The thing that keeps most of us motorists going is trying to find a place to park.
- If cars get any smaller, they might have to travel in packs.

- The advantage of these new small cars is that you can squeeze so many more into a traffic jam.
- I wanted to bring my family closer together so I bought one of those tiny German Smart cars.
- Those new foreign cars are so small, I put my hand out to make a turn and one drove right up my sleeve.
- The new foreign cars are so small that when one hits a pedestrian the pedestrian can hit back.
- My inventive cousin took the wheels from a Ford, the grill from a Cadillac and the engine from a Mercedes Benz, and do you know what he got? Eighteen months in prison.
- When my daughter borrowed the car something in the back seat overheated. It was her boyfriend.
- My brother finally learned how to stand on his own two feet. They repossessed his car.
- I bought a car made especially for Muslims. You have to put on your seatbelt and take off your shoes.
- I'm unlucky with automobiles. My cars won't start and my payments won't stop.
- My brother lost control of his car. The Finance company repossessed it.
- Nine out of ten cars stolen are foreign. We need a new advertising slogan "Show your patriotism. Steal British."
- I took a picture of the traffic on the M25. Turned out perfect. Nobody moved.
- One very keen motorist wrote the history of his car. It was his autobiography.
- I'm not saying the traffic is bad, but yesterday I was on the M25 and got a ticket for parking.
- The rush hour is when a motorist travels the shortest distance in the longest time.
- A petrol station is a place where you can fill your car and empty your wallet at the same time.
- Building extra lanes on highways only leads to one thing…..wider traffic jams.
- The young lady parked with a boyfriend in the back seat of his electric car had a shocking experience.

- Just a 100 years ago it was considered a miracle if you managed to drive your car more than 20 miles an hour. With today's congested traffic, it's still a miracle.
- None of us actually needs buy a car. There are plenty of people around who want to take us for a ride.
- My neighbour's had his car souped up so much it'll only run on chicken broth.
- They've got some wonderful gadgets on cars now. One button makes the windows come down. Another button makes the seat come down. And yet another button makes the top come down. If only we could push a button to make the price come down.
- The used car salesman said "This car's practically NEW. It belonged to a GP who refused to make house calls."
- I've got a two-tone car. Black and rust.
- There's so much traffic on the road, the YIELD signs have been replaced by GIVE UP.
- As one foreign tourist said to another "Are you sure this is England, I haven't seen one foreign car."
- Mechanic says "If this car was a frog it would have croaked by now."
- The car's so small the engine's in the glove compartment.
- There's one group lobbying for the speed limit to be increased. They're all undertakers.
- He's not only a good car mechanic, but he overcharges less than all the others.
- The salesman offered me a car so small, when I told him what he could do with it, it was actually practical.
- Car mechanic's sign says "FAST – EFFICIENT – REASONABLY PRICED," He asks customer "Which one do you want?"
- Once a year the clock goes back….on every used car in his car showroom.
- Wife says to traffic cop "Just give me the ticket. My husband will give me the sermon."
- As far as driving is concerned my wife took out group insurance in case she runs down a whole group.
- My wife came home with dents in the car. She claimed the car in front of her got too close.

- My wife told the driving school instructor "I already know how to drive. What I want you to teach me is how to miss things.
- My wife saw the petrol gauge pointing to E. She thought that meant enough.
- My wife was arrested for speeding. I told her to stick to the truth- plead insanity."

BOXING

There's a fad now for women's boxing, but it will never catch on, it's too expensive. Give a woman a pair of boxing gloves, and she'll want a hat, shoes and handbag to match. Most frightening boxer of all was definitely Mike Tyson. What a talker! He could chew your ear off. When Frank Bruno fought him the referee told them to shake hands. Bruno said "No need. My hands are already shaking." One fighter that got in the ring with Tyson was disqualified for having a lucky charm. They found a horseshoe inside his glove.

I watched one boxing match on TV that was so short; when the referee raised the winner's arm I thought it was a deodorant commercial. When I was a boxer I ran thirty miles before every fight. It didn't help. My opponent caught up with me anyway. I was such a lousy fighter, I even lost when shadow boxing.

ADDITIONAL GAGS

- He's a failed boxer. He can take it but he can't dish it out.
- A boxer was disqualified because of his footwork. He kept kicking his opponent.
- I could tell the boxer was a middleweight. All his weight was round his middle.
- I said I could beat him with my eyes closed. So he said "Prove it" and closed both my eyes.
- What a lousy boxer. He couldn't even lick the back of a postage stamp.
- The palmist told the woman boxer "You're going to beat a tall, dark stranger."

CHILDREN

My son wrote home from university last week. It was a short note that said "I'm worried that I haven't heard from you for a while. Please send a cheque so I know you're alright." To my kids I'm not so much a father as a cash register. People ask me what my son's taking at university. I tell them, everything I've got.

You never stop doling out money when you have kids. I have three. When they were young I spent so much on shoes you'd think my wife gave birth to centipedes.

When you're a Dad there are two things you have to save for a rainy day. Money and patience. My teenage daughter gives me most worries. Last Sunday I asked the reason that she came home at seven o'clock in the morning. She said "Breakfast." She's only fifteen and she thinks she's already grown up. I caught her looking in the mirror saying "I have to lose five pounds." I said "That's easy. Just take off your make-up." They can't wait, can they? She was wearing uplifts before she had anything to lift up. That girl's just like her mother. She didn't start talking till she was two...and hasn't stopped since. Mostly into her phone. I'm certain the first person to tear a telephone book in half was the father of a teenage girl.

There's a sad lack of communication between the generations. Kids today would rather talk to their mobiles than their parents. My youngest son's the untidiest person in the world. He wants us to move. He says it's easier than cleaning up his room. I wouldn't mind, but his bedroom's equipped with an IPod, computer, music centre, video phone and 32 inch plasma TV screen. If we want to punish him, we send him OUT of his room. And he's far too precocious for his age. He's twelve and I gave him a talk about the facts of life. Next day he was telling his friend "My Dad told me all about the birds and the bees. You'd be surprised how little he knows about sex."

You hear so much today about guns and knives in schools. I'm not against that. I think the teachers SHOULD have some way of defending themselves. People think they don't have prayers in schools any more. Not true. You should hear the teachers just before each class starts. It used to be that teachers just needed a degree in Maths or English, now they also need a black belt in karate. It's a sad fact that the number of school drop-outs continues to increase. Even sadder that most of them are teachers.

I've had my share of bringing up kids. Now, if my wife ever says she wants to hear the patter of tiny feet again, it had better be mice. I asked the babysitter if she'd mind changing the baby while we were out. When we got back it was a girl instead of a boy. The film producer introduced his children as spin-offs from his first marriage.

It's an old truism that when you're young you want to change the world. And when you're old you want to change the young. Lots of children run away from home, but in my case it was the opposite. I lived in a caravan and my home ran away from me. Two children were deciding what game to play. One said "Let's play doctors." The other said "Good idea. You operate and I'll sue." The kids wanted to hear a fairy story, so I told them about my cousin Bruce.

The divorce rate is definitely affecting kids. Just think, a hundred years ago parents thought nothing of having ten kids. Now kids think the same of having ten parents. I just read where a woman had a baby using her dead husband's frozen sperm. That poor kid! Its bad enough hearing you were adopted, but even worse that you were defrosted. The 1970's was when they discovered weapons of mass destruction. Mostly in children's TV games. In families with kids you'll frequently hear the word "Please". It's the parents begging. Money isn't everything. But it's a good way of keeping in touch with your kids. You know your kids are growing up when your daughter starts putting on lipstick and your son starts wiping it off.

My daughter's at that awkward age, between Toyland and boy land. The hardest thing about telling children the facts of life is finding something they don't already know.

Kids today are so lazy. When my son wants to get to sleep he counts sheep...with his pocket calculator. The only way I can get my son to exercise is by hiding the remote control. You can see how much TV is affecting kids today. After coming out of church last Sunday my kid said "The music was alright, but the commercial was far too long."

Kids cost a fortune these days. Take my son for instance. £22 for a pair of shoes. £10 for a shirt. £6 for a tie. And that's just for his Action

Man toy. And those modern toys can cost a fortune, but at least they're educational. They teach you how little you get for your money.

I told my kids to forget expensive toys and play doctors and nurses like we used to. And this morning they did. My son played the doctor and his friend played his lawyer handling the malpractice suits.

I've finally find one thing I have in common with today's teenagers. They listen to rock groups singing and I listen to economists talking. And none of us understands a word of it. My daughter's favourite record is Des O'Connor's Dicka Dum Dum, because every time she plays it I give her £1 to shut it off. I sometimes think the generation gap just isn't wide enough.

Kids today are so lazy. When I was their age I wore out the soles of my shoes, not the seat of my pants. I told my young son to take a bath. He wanted to know what he was being punished for. I'm a very proud Dad. I even recorded my baby's first burp. One couple had a hard time thinking up names for all their nine kids. So after the last one they called it Quits. I was going to name our new baby Tarquin, but my wife objected. She said every Tom, Dick and Harry's named Tarquin.

Kids used to stay away from school because of colds or flu. Now it's more likely to be morning sickness. I gave my son a sex talk. Now he tells all his mates that babies are born when a woman sleeps with a stork.

My nephew's a slow learner. He was at school five years before he learned to roll a joint. But he was keen on learning English so it could help him in later life, writing ransom notes. When he was fourteen he was asked by the teacher "Do you know what happens to little boys who tell lies?" He said "Yes. They travel half fare." The teacher punished him, but he got his own back. Next day he brought her an apple and then reported her for receiving stolen goods.

When I was a kid my mother caught me smoking. She was furious. They were her fags. I didn't have a happy childhood. As a kid I was made to walk the plank. We couldn't afford a dog. My parents never liked me. One day I threatened to run away from home and they made me put it in writing. During my teenage years my parents moved a lot. But it was a waste of time, I always found them.

The trouble with parents today is they give their unruly kids a free hand, but not in the right place. The only way I can get my kids to obey me is by telling them to do as they please. This year I'm thinking of trying something new. Send my dog to summer camp and my son to obedience school. I have a built-in obstacle course in my house. It's my son's bedroom. It's the only room without carpets. They're not needed. The floor's covered with his clothes. He spends all his time watching TV. He's a slouch potato. I told him that children who watch TV all the time will go down in history. I was right. He went down in science, maths and geography too. The only thing I can say in his favour is that every Father's Day he serves me breakfast in bed. Mind you, I'd appreciate it more if he used a plate.

ADDITIONAL GAGS

- Today the only guarantee you get with children's toys is that sooner or later they will break.
- I bought my son an unbreakable toy. He used it to break his other toys.
- Kids toys aren't built to last these days, and that's just as well. We just bought our son a drum.
- They say most modern kids don't know the value of a £1. But then, these days nobody does.
- My son's very clever. He can do something I've never been able to do. Read his handwriting.
- The only thing children will take from their parents these days is money.
- The difference between my children and computers is computers do what you tell them to
- Father's Day is when millions of kids say something that brings tears to the eyes of their Dads "I thought it was NEXT Sunday."
- One woman I heard of had sixteen kids. I think she was trying to stop the human race from being extinct.
- All I have to do to make my kids thirsty is turn out their bedroom light.
- My kids are very good. They always help me with their homework.
- Insanity is hereditary. You get it from your children.

- Two children were talking about the chores they had to do at home. "Did your mother promise you something for doing those chores?" asked one. "No", replied the other. "Only if I didn't."
- Children today can be so violent. Now if a kid plays truant the teacher sends him a note saying "Thank you."
- Sooner or later every naughty child gets what's coming to him. He becomes a parent too.
- I come from a broken home. My kids have broken almost everything in it.
- Children will always brighten up a home, especially when they forget to turn the lights off.
- Kids really grow up fast. You no sooner finish sitting up with them than you anxiously sitting up for them.
- I remember when my daughter said her first word. Now I wait by the phone for hours waiting for her to say her last word.
- My teenage daughter never hangs up her hat, coat or the phone.
- I look at it this way, I'm not so much losing a daughter as gaining a telephone.
- I've taught my son everything I know and he's still an ignoramus.
- They say kids should be seen and not heard. But the way some of them dress now I don't want to see them either.
- I had to buy my kids new T-shirts. All the slogans were out of date.
- My son's idea of keeping his room tidy is when he can find the phone after only three rings.
- As one young kid said to another "I draw a ring round the tub with a black crayon so my Mum thinks I've taken a bath."
- The young boy complained that his mother always makes him go to sleep when he's wide away and always wakes him up when he's sleepy.
- A kid slipped in the playground and grazed his knee. The teacher tried to console him with "Big boys don't cry." He said "That's alright; I'm not going to cry. I'm going to sue."
- In Victorian times parents had lots of kids. Today with the divorce rate, kids have lots of parents.
- One school kid got into trouble when his teacher finally realised his transistor radio wasn't a hearing aid after all.

- When I was a kid we were often late to school. Nowadays they daren't be late or they won't get a parking space.
- Children on the back seat can cause accidents. And accidents on the back seat can cause children.
- The couple named their latest baby "Encore" because he wasn't on the programme.
- Any person who says they sleep like a baby, hasn't got one.
- When I sold my house I threw in the carpets, curtains and two of my kids.
- Did you hear about the grandmother who went on the pill because she didn't want any more grandchildren?
- He was so advanced for his age he reached his mid-life crisis when he was only twelve.
- I know my kid son will never achieve his ambition to be a surgeon. He hates washing his hands.
- The young boy was relieved to find his Mum's new baby is an add-on, not a replacement for him.

CHRISTMAS

Christmas is a time when turkeys wish the whole world was vegetarian. Last year we were so poor we couldn't afford a turkey. So we bought a budgie and gave it chest expanders. Actually we paid the same price for our turkey as we did last year. Except last year it was for a whole turkey. This year, just a drumstick.

We saw the worst effect of the economic crisis last Christmas. It was so bad some people were putting I.O.U.'s in their Christmas puddings. Instead of stockings, kids were hanging up ankle socks. But Christmas is a really wonderful time when everybody sings jingle bells, which is really appropriate, because after Christmas that's all we've got left to jingle. Even Santa had a bad time last Christmas. I didn't realise how bad till I asked him how Rudolph was and he said "Delicious!"

I was surprised at the high price of Christmas trees. For £15 all I could get was a decorated toothpick. I paid £25 for a Christmas tree and carried it home in my car. Not in the boot - the glove compartment. Even at that price it was so small I wasn't sure whether to put it up in the living room or wear it on my lapel. I suppose we could do without a Christmas tree, but we buy it for our dog. He sees it as indoor plumbing.

I always think of Christmas in the present tense, because if I don't give my wife a present she gets very tense. Last year I bought her clothes that excited her so much she couldn't wait to exchange them at the store. What my wife got me for Christmas made my eyes pop out. A shirt with a size 12 collar. Generally speaking, Christmas presents can be divided into two categories. Those you don't want and those you don't get.

Every Christmas we take the kids to see Santa at Selfridges. The queues are so long, by the time the kids get to the front, they're too old. Santa really should have two lines. One would be for kids wanting ten toys or less. I told the Selfridges Santa I don't envy him having to sit all those youngsters on his lap. The poor fellow said he has water on the knee...at least six times a day.

After 25 December Santa has to join the long dole queue. He says it's no fun being given the old heave Ho! Ho! Ho! As youngsters, my siblings and I always wrote to Santa. We had the same philosophy about getting toys. If you don't succeed the first time, cry, cry, and cry again. It's fantastic how Santa manages to deliver to the whole country in one night. We should get him to replace Royal Mail.

Yes, Christmas is the time when we have to consider the cost of giving. My wife and I have a Christmas arrangement. She signs the cards and I sign the cheques. We have to tip the dustman, postman and paper boy. It's known as Open Palm Sunday.... or Christmas greasing. Have you noticed how the dustmen leave less mess in your driveway when it's getting near to Christmas?

Yes, Christmas is that magic time when the year runs out, the relatives run in, the batteries run down and the bills run up. Heaven knows Christmas cards are expensive enough, but since the stamps have gone up to 63p, it's crippling. Now I not only stick my tongue out when I lick them, but when I buy them too. If you wanted a turkey last Christmas you bought a Toyota car.

We only buy a tree because of my grandchildren. Coming round to hook silver balls and hook tinsel on it is their greatest joy. We call them the happy hookers. When Dad became too poor to buy clothes for my sister's doll, he told her that Barbie had decided to be a nudist.

They had a Christmas service in Hollywood. The vicar sang "Come all ye Faithful" and only two men turned up. Someone tried to sell me a pair of Christmas stockings. I said "How do you know they're CHRISTMAS stockings?" He said "They're Carol's."

I've finally discovered the true meaning of Christmas. Greed and profit. I'd love to have an old fashioned Christmas, as long as it included the old fashioned prices. My brother tried to save money by making his own Christmas cards. But he got into trouble for making his own postage stamps too.

It's only October and already my wife is doing her Christmas hinting. My son enquired how Father Christmas knows who's been good and who's been bad. "Has he been phone tapping?" It takes kids to brighten up the home. Especially mine. They never turn off the lights.

ADDITIONAL GAGS

- As the department store Santa said to the doctor "It only hurts when I go Ho! Ho! Ho!"
- For their Christmas bonus the stingy boss gave every one of his employees a turkey…sandwich.
- Last Christmas was a lousy day for me. Even our tree gave me the needle.
- Lots of kids got Christmas toys with batteries not included. We were so poor I got a battery with no toy included.
- I enjoy Christmas bells. It's those Christmas bills that bother me.
- Christmas used to come just once a year. But with the time payments it now comes once a week.
- At Christmas we have a lot to be thankful for. For one thing, that we're not turkeys.
- No wonder Santa Claus goes Ho! Ho! Ho! He only works one day a year.
- Santa Claus is the only man I know who shows interest in an empty stocking.
- At Christmas a living room without a tree is a place not fit for a dog.
- The good thing about Christmas shopping is it toughens you up for the January sales.

- Dolly Parton never hangs up her stocking at Christmas. Instead she hangs up her bra, because you can get more in it.
- As the American kid asked his Mum "If Santa is a man, how come his name's Barbara?"
- Santa Claus rides with the royal hunt. He's the one that shouts "Tally Ho-Ho!"
- Santa's Christmas bag is so heavy. It's all heave ho ho ho!
- It's like saying to Santa Claus "We'd like to book you to do a talk. Are you busy on Christmas Eve?"
- Have you ever stopped to think that no one ever buys Santa a present back?
- A man has got to believe in himself. Especially Santa Claus.

CLOTHES

The radio he had on was too loud. And the shirt he had on was even louder.

This girl is so dumb she walks around in a soaking wet dress, because the label on it says "Wash and Wear."

The antique dealer selling a suit of armour said "It's in perfect condition. It belonged to a coward."

Women in gown shop complains to salesgirl "This dress is much too short. Wrap it up, I'll take it."

COMPUTERS

All I know about computers is that when things go wrong, I'm the curser. I'm useless with computers. The only thing I can do properly online is hang out the washing. Those technical terms drive me mad. I get my URL's mixed up with my PDF's and CD.ROMS to the point where I'm F.E.D. Up. We're living in a fast changing world. Last week's computer model is this week's antique. Seems everything's done online now. I think it's fantastic the way people in offices spend eight hours every day in front of their computers and then relax at night watching their TV screens. Everyone uses computers now. Even spiders have their own websites. It's got to the point where we need computers to assess the impact computers are having on our society.

This week I bought myself a new laptop. The salesman said a kid of five could work it. The following day I phoned and asked who the kid was and how much he charged. To me computers are like air conditioners. They work fine until you start opening windows. The new state of the art computers practically encourage illegal downloads of record albums. It's turning us into the pillage people.

The trouble with computers is they're always being attacked by new viruses. Mine was attacked by two. First was the Adam & Eve virus. It took a couple of bytes out of my apple. Then came the Star Trek virus. It invaded the system in places no other virus had gone before. For repairs they're now recommending cryonics. They freeze the computer till someone comes up with a cure for the virus. I spend so much money on repairs I now list the repair man as my main dependent.

No one in our family can work the laptop. Ours is a house of ill compute. Almost all the emails I receive are either spam or scam. They're repeated daily. I'm convinced the two hardest things to do in life are squeezing toothpaste back in the tube and getting off someone's mailing list.

They say to err is human. But to really mess things up you need a computer. The unions are trying to run everything. Even my computer. It's now refusing to work unless it gets two circuit breaks a day. My grandson had to take a week off from school because he had a virus…which he says he caught off the school computer. Last week the school computer broke down and the teacher asked the pupils "Does anyone here remember how to add and subtract?" Let's not forget it was a laptop that got a well-known sportsman in trouble this week. His wife caught him with a girl on top of his lap. We're living in a computer age when a baby's first word's no longer Dada, but Data.

My brother the computer expert has a permanent cold. It's his own fault for opening all those windows. There are still people working on computers without a net. I'm very fortunate. I have a wife and a computer and they're both working. Everyone uses computers these days. Even bank robbers are sending their hold-up notes by email. When my lazy brother went to buy a computer, the salesman said it would do half his work for him. So he bought two. I must confess I'm not computer literate. I don't understand the technical terms. I'm as confused as a cow grazing on Astroturf.

My computer goes down more often than Jonathan Ross's rating. Every office is now equipped with computers, word processors and digital telephones. Secretaries who used to say "I'm only human" now say "I'm THE only human."

ADDITIONAL GAGS

- We can't live without our computers these days. Last time I went on holiday I packed my hardware and my software. What I forgot to pack was my underwear.
- Computers can do so many things now. Yesterday I pressed the wrong button and accidentally did my laundry.
- The woman who's been breaking into other people's emails has been dubbed "The Happy Hacker."
- The prospective computer purchaser asked the shopkeeper "If you're really selling all your computers at half price, how can you stay in business?" "That's no problem" he said "We make a fortune on the repairs."
- The spinster in our office said "I know computers are supposed to do the work of ten men, but I'd rather have the ten men."
- Computers do more work than humans. That's because they never have to stop to answer the phone.
- The difference between computers and my kids is computers do what you tell them.
- I don't waste time talking to people at the bank now. I ask to be put straight through to their computer.
- The computer's a great invention. There are just as many mistakes as before, but they are no one's fault.
- I took a girl out on a computer date and she told me right from the start that she didn't want to be bent, folded or spindled.
- I had a terrible day yesterday. Both my computer and car crashed.
- I pressed the DELETE button and the whole computer disappeared.

- Before automation if you fired an employee you had to give them a pink slip. Now all you have to do is pull the plug out.

COOKING

We used to say grace before meals. Now we just say "ditto" because it's usually left-overs from the day before. My wife injured her hand preparing the supper. She got frostbite.

My wife gets annoyed when I complain about her cooking. Well, who else serves porridge in slices? Her Hungarian goulash tastes like it was made from real Hungarians. She made an upside down cake the other day. Not deliberately. She had the recipe the wrong way up. Her speciality is sponge cakes. We call them sponge cakes because she sponges all the ingredients off the neighbours. When we were first married she used to burn the steak. I didn't mind that so much, but she'd put ointment on it.

Now, before dinner my wife always asks me how I want my steak – raw or burnt. She's the only one I know who uses the smoke alarm as a timer. My wife cooked something for dinner last night that was so bad I gave it straight to the dog, and he licked his behind to get the taste out of his mouth. It was destined to happen one day. Stephen King bought one of my wife's recipes to use in his next horror film.

My wife's great at saving electricity. She doesn't iron, she doesn't cook, she doesn't use the vacuum cleaner.....And she's no great shakes as a cook either. She's the only one I know who serves coffee in slices. Who else can burn water? I'll never forget the first meal my wife cooked for me. I'm still being treated for it. The difference between my wife's cooking and inflation is, you can keep down inflation. She's such a bad cook, the last time we went on a picnic, thousands of ants picketed her food. She's wasteful too. She's well known for putting all her eggs in one biscuit.

ADDITIONAL GAGS

- My wife's very considerate. She not only chooses my favourite dish, she picks out the restaurant that serves it.

- My wife has cooked so many TV dinners she tells everyone she's in Show Business.
- I don't mind my wife serving me TV dinners, but most of them are re-runs.
- My wife's motto when cooking is "If all else fails, read the instructions."
- Where there's smoke there's my wife's cooking.
- The coffee my wife makes isn't just weak, it's helpless.
- My wife dresses to kill. Unfortunately she cooks the same way.
- Some wives can't even boil water. My wife can. She calls it soup.
- My wife's such a lousy cook, when she makes Ladyfingers they turn out all thumbs.
- No man should believe a woman's place is in the kitchen till he's at least tasted her cooking.
- When my wife cooks a meal it warms the heart. Or, to put it another way, it gives me heartburn.
- When my wife cooks the food starts out frozen and ends up burnt.
- I bought my wife a microwave oven. Now she ruins the meals in half the time.
- They say a woman's work's never done. Well, my wife's cooking proves that.
- You can tell how bad a cook my wife is. The mice in our house all eat out.
- I won't say my wife's a bad cook, but have you ever tried eating a slice of porridge?
- I broke two teeth on the food my wife cooked. And that was just the coffee.
- My wife feeds me like a God. Every meal's a burnt offering.
- My wife was furious when she came home from shopping and found the pan had boiled over. She said "I thought I told you to watch when the pan boiled over." I said "I did. It was twenty past twelve."
- I said to my wife after supper last night, "That was delicious. What happened?"
- My wife studied home cooking. She's got a diploma in defrosting.
- My wife really looks after me. If she's going out for the evening she always leaves me something on the table........like a note. Last night's was a bit dry, but it didn't taste too bad. Better than the last

one. She should have kept it a bit longer in the oven, the ink wasn't dry.
- All the cooking these days is done electronically. In the old days you gave a bride a cook book. Now it's a fuse box.
- My wife's so lazy she even hires a hit man to beat up the eggs.
- My wife makes Swiss cheesecake. It has holes in it.
- My wife makes the best coffee I've ever bitten into.
- His wife was annoyed when he remarked on her cooking. She thought he said "swill" instead of swell.
- Wife says to grumpy husband "Want to complain about your day now or do you want to wait till after dinner so you can include that too?
- I knew we had a salad for supper. I couldn't smell anything burning.
- My wife doesn't make ice cubes anymore. She lost the recipe.
- If this is Caesar salad, it's no wonder Brutus killed him.

COURTING

I've had no luck with girls. I gave up my girlfriend because she kept using that nasty four letter word "Stop!" I thought my second girlfriend was from the now generation, but she kept saying "Not now." That girl made a really big impression on me. Took six weeks to heal. I once proposed to a female magazine editor. She sent me a rejection slip. It said our astrological charts don't match. I'm Aquarius and you're obnoxious. I guess I just never met the right girl. I once did date a girl who I thought had everything. Unfortunately one of the things she had was a husband. For a while I fancied the two single girls in my office, but it didn't work out, they fancied each other.

ADDITIONAL GAGS

- Girl to boy she's ditching "It's over, Frank. I'm writing you out of my autobiography."
- When the young suitor asked for his girlfriend's hand, the prospective father-in-law said "Why not take her mother as well and make it a set?"

- I was just smoking a cigarette and blowing smoke rings when she put her finger through one of the rings and said "I accept your proposal."
- When I courted the sexy girl it was a case of a loaf of bread, a jug of wine and WOW!
- The caller at the door was so old I couldn't tell if he was my daughter's date or my mother's.
- We had a marvellous relationship. We got on so well till she said she was bored with me. But that was a fantastic afternoon.
- He promised her the world, but she turned him down. She said with the state it's currently in, she doesn't want it.
- The Dating Agency sent me a girl weighing eighteen stone. They asked what I thought. I said "Well, in the first place there's too much of her. And in the second place as well."
- I don't think her father liked me. The moment she took me to meet her parents he said "Can I get you anything. A drink, a snack, a cab?"
- I used to just sit at home contemplating my navel. Then I started courting a belly dancer and contemplated hers.
- The couple met by chance on a window ledge when their respective lovers' spouses returned home unexpectedly.
- He got the girls by promising to get them into pictures. Turned out he was a radiologist who does x-rays at the local hospital.
- He asked if she'd do him the honour of becoming his first wife.
- The girl told her parents "I think he's getting serious. He's trying to find me a job."
- It's alright for a fussy woman to keep rejecting marriage proposals thinking there's plenty more fish in the sea. But sooner or later she's going to lose her bait.
- She says "I know the shop sign says 'Say it with Flowers' but with the money you spent it is practically inaudible."
- After she accepted his proposal he said "You'll be a wife I'll be proud to swap."
- She tells everyone that dozens of handsome men ask her for dates. What she doesn't say is that she's a salesgirl in the fruit department.

CRICKET

Our English cricket team's not doing too well. They were better off when the Reverend David Shepherd was in the team. If they were losing he led the prayers for rain. When England played in the Ashes against Australia, the Aussies were said to be ahead by a nose. Judging by the size of their score, the nose must have been Pinocchio's. The way they're playing, I think the English cricket team would do better giving up Lords and moving to Lourdes.

CRIME

The best way to improve prisons is to send a better class of people there. The government wants to cut prison budgets. Apparently it costs £35,000 a year to keep a prisoner locked up. I heard of one persistent felon who told the judge "I want to save the country money, so why don't we just split it. Give me £17,500 and I'll stay at home." Our prisons are so overcrowded criminals have to take a number and queue up to get in. And when they get in they're released after just a quarter of their sentence. But there's one prison in America where a convict never got out at all. Hannibal Lector chose him as his last meal. There are very few prison break-outs nowadays. One convict explained why. He said "To escape you need friends on the outside. Trouble is, all my friends are now inside with me." He's the one who got into trouble trying to sell tickets to the prison governor's ball. Turned out it wasn't a dance. It was a raffle.

Crime is changing in this electronic age. Bank robbers no longer say "Hand over the money!" Now they tell the cashiers to transfer it electronically to their Swiss bank account. And they're using their ill-gotten gains sending their sons to university so that, with education they can live a better life, committing white collar crime. White collar crime's definitely on the increase. Last year alone, fifty thousand white collars were stolen.

Now that doctors have refused to do it, the only ones making house calls are burglars. Burglary is rife in my district. In fact a strange thing happened last night. I came home and actually found someone in my house that I knew. My wife talked me into buying a watch dog. And he was good. Trouble is, while he was watching the house, someone stole his kennel. My next door neighbour got a note saying "Unless you hand over £500 by midnight you may never see your wife and kids again." It wasn't a ransom note. It was from the electricity company about to cut his lights off.

London is very popular with tourists. They come from all over the world to shoplift here. The only place you can go to make sure you don't have your pockets picked is a nudist camp. I was in Oxford Street yesterday and tried to put my hand in my pocket, but had to wait my turn.

Tour brochures advise "Bring your camera when you visit London, as you'll see things you're never likely to see again. Especially your camera. I got mugged in the January sales. And I was just buying online. I was once mugged right outside my own house and my whole life flashed before me. Unfortunately not the part where I'd had karate lessons. It's a pity we can't go back to the days when mugging just meant swotting for an exam.

Crime is still on the increase amongst youngsters. I shouldn't be surprised if soon school uniforms don't include a gun holster. There's an awful lot of gang warfare among our youngsters. It's got so bad there's a "Back to School" sign in our local gun shop. The police are desperately trying to break up all the gangs that are about now. One school in Enfield has no less than three well-armed gangs. The Skulls, The Bloods and The Cobras. And they're just the teachers.

Criminals always have an excuse for their crimes. Like the wife murderer who told the jury it wasn't his fault. "She complained the bath water was too cold, so I threw in an electric heater." Or the strangler who pleaded mitigating circumstances because he'd just given up smoking and needed something to do with his hands. One guy was actually acquitted because he told the jury he shot his wife by accident. He said he meant to shoot himself, but missed.

The art world was amazed by the cat burglar who stole that famous painting from a gallery in Paris and escaped on foot. It was a case of take the Monet and run. The German police are thinking of replacing their Alsatian dogs with Daschunds because they want them to keep a low profile.

The police refuse to tell the Press what houses they are raiding. We used to just have invasion of privacy. Now we also have privacy of invasion. People are now getting arrested for all sorts of minor things. Like my cousin got arrested for turning the other cheek. He was mooning. His brother got arrested just for talking behind people's back. He said "Stick 'em up!" There is a bright side to robberies. At least we know our money is still worth stealing.

After sentencing two robbers, the judge ordered the bailiff to "Take those knickers down." One bank robber's hold-up note said he only wanted to borrow the money till he won the lottery. You can't trust anyone these days. They even arrested my local choirmaster. He was caught with one of his singers having choral sex. The public aren't helping the police as much as they used to. Yesterday six witnesses saw a bank robber drive off in a getaway car, but none of them called the police. They were too busy fighting over his parking space.

Modern films are like a training ground for immature degenerates and are full of violence, swearing and sex. Now when a film has an "X" certificate it means a kid of ten can see it. Kids today are growing up too fast. They're reaching the age of consent, dissent and resent all at the same time. One young offender was accused of stealing an armchair from a doctor's waiting room. He said a notice on the wall said "Take a seat" so he did.

To visit a high crime area now all you have to do is sit in front of your TV set. There'll soon be as much crime on the street as there is on TV. I think it's fantastic the way TV Inspectors Morse and Frost can solve two murders in an hour while it normally takes the police two years to solve one. One night Inspector Morse overran and solved two murders on Crimewatch UK. The trouble with crime shows on TV is they're not realistic. The criminals always lose. Well, let's face it, not all our police are brilliant. I know one who's so dumb he thinks arms control is some sort of deodorant. Our police admitted they weren't fully prepared for those recent London riots where they had bricks, iron bars and manhole covers thrown at them. But they took swift action. They arrested 200 culprits as litterbugs. One rioter was a comedian who managed to get the judge laughing which he wasn't too pleased about. He was laughing at his alibi. One man who wasn't actually involved in the riots boasted it made him a millionaire. He's a glazier. I wasn't surprised the riots took place, because our legal system can't cope. With today's lenient sentences juries are being locked up longer than the criminals. A forger who made bogus £50 notes got a lighter sentence because he used recycled paper. And one convicted thief said to the judge "I can't afford to pay the fine just now. Is it alright if I pay it out of my next robbery?" Today there are so many recidivists they now, when they meet on the street they ask "How long are you out for?"

One company told the lady at the Job Centre they were looking for an accountant. She said "But you hired one just last week." They said "Yes. That's the one we're looking for." The description they gave the police was that he was five foot nine tall and £50,000 short. Paris Hilton hated her time in prison. She didn't so much mind the food and lodging, but she objected to being with 500 other women wearing the same outfit as her.

Department stores are no longer prosecuting shoplifters. They're just so pleased to get ANYONE into their stores. A man found guilty of stealing cigarettes was ordered by the judge to stop smoking. I wonder what would have happened if he'd been stealing condoms. Today if a man is said to be living the life of Riley it's probably a case of identity theft. There have been so many documentaries on the subjects of drug taking, street-corner dealers are now saying "As seen on TV."

Did you hear about the businessman who was arrested for handling his Girl Friday on a Tuesday? Today's crime figures are shocking. I still remember when, before I went on holiday, I checked to make sure I didn't leave the light on. Now I check to make sure I did.

Alcoholics go to The Priory to take the cure. Pickpockets go to a nudist colony. A pickpocket that went to a nudist colony admitted he didn't make any money, but got a lot of job satisfaction.

Getting advice from my lawyer is a grand and glorious feeling. You give him a grand and he feels glorious. They're called criminal lawyers, which isn't fair. Some of them aren't criminals at all. The judge pronounced a criminal guilty and asked "Have you anything to offer the court before I pass sentence?" "No" said the man, "The lawyer took my last penny."

There's so much crime in London they no longer confer the key to the city. They just send someone over to help pick the lock. Crime here is so bad my bank now keeps its money in another bank. Yesterday a crook robbed my local bank and got away with a stack of I.O.U.'s.

I used to run to keep my figure. Now it's to keep my wallet. To me, mad money is what you keep in your pocket when you walk through the streets of London. I was actually robbed by an ex-bus driver, but he didn't take my money because I didn't have the exact change. Last week I put a Neighbourhood Watch sign in my window. Now my neighbours keep knocking on my door asking the time. Soho's even worse. Nobody asks the time there, they just steal your watch. Some crooks will steal anything. One asked a policeman the way to Battersea. The cop said "Take the Westminster Bridge." So he did.

ADDITIONAL GAGS

- When the restaurant waiter asked the masked man what he wanted, he said "All the money in your till…. to take out."
- Even as a kid I knew my nephew had criminal tendencies. He used to steal his granddad's false teeth to put under his pillow to get money out of the Tooth Fairy.
- West End stores are bending over backwards to get people through their doors. They're even gift-wrapping items for shoplifters.
- A mugger is a man who takes your money without having to be elected.
- A foreign tourist said about London "You Londoners are so stand-offish, if it wasn't for your muggers I'd have had no contact with the natives at all.
- The best thing about being a kleptomaniac is you can always take something for it.
- I dined in a Soho restaurant where the receptionist took my coat, the waiter took my order and the man just leaving took my wallet.
- Crime in this country must be on the increase. I was burgled and dialled 999. They told me there was a two year waiting list.
- He's had women chasing him for years. He steals handbags,
- Criminals are getting richer all the time. I saw one bank robber who's doing so well he has a Rolls Royce as his getaway car.

- I keep getting mugged. My hands are up in the air so much people think I'm practicing to be a goalkeeper.
- The world's worst train robbery is what they charge for lunch in their restaurant cars.
- At Christmas the stores were so crowded pickpockets were working by appointment only.
- I love watching crime on TV. Nowadays it's the only place where the bad guys lose.
- The perfect crime is when, after the court case, the criminal can sell the book, TV and film rights.
- Thieves got away with £2,000 from a toll booth. That's what you'd call highway robbery.
- The bank robber had an identity crisis. He left his fingerprints on the safe.
- The bank robber rushed into the travel agents and said "I'd like to get away from it all – fast!"
- The bank robber started out opening child proof caps on medicine bottles. After that opening bank vaults was a doddle.
- I was conned when I bought a half share in a horse. It turned out to be one of those on a fairground merry-go-round.
- I think people who falsely claim whiplash are a pain in the neck.
- It was one of those nightclubs where you knew there would be trouble. The car park had a space reserved for an ambulance.
- When a kid raises his hand in school you never know whether he wants to go to the toilet or has a gun in his back.
- I was dancing in a Soho disco when this fellow tried to cut in. I wouldn't have minded, but he had a chain saw.
- The police have a theory about the serial killer who stabbed all his victims with a knitting needle. They think he's working to a pattern.
- When the ugly woman was raped the police dropped the case. They couldn't find a motive.
- Before my cousin wound up in prison he was making big money. About half a centimetre too big. Among the criminal fraternity he's highly suspected.
- My brother got into trouble just for following a good example. He's a forger.
- A counterfeiter makes money in order to make money.

- The counterfeiter told the judge he was doing it for patriotic reasons to ease this country's money shortage.
- If the number of crooks keeps increasing I don't know where we'll put them. Our prisons and parliament are full.
- Do you know what the father said when his son was sent to jail? "Hello, son."
- The convict has four different numbers on his uniform. Three of them are aliases.
- The convict learnt a skill in prison that will serve him well when he gets out. Picking pockets.
- The Death Row convict was about to be gassed. They asked him what he wanted for his last wish. He said "A gas mask."
- As one convict said to his cell mate. "That's a co-incidence. The number they've given me is the same as the amount I embezzled."
- My neighbour's very security conscious, he's got six locks on his door. It's ridiculous because he hasn't any money to steal. He spent it all on the locks.
- As the wimp said to the potential mugger "Put that knife away or I'll bleed all over you."
- Latest statistics show that less criminals are being caught and more are being elected.
- It wasn't the young criminal's fault. He was just following in his father's fingerprints.
- A con man's brain is a scheme engine.
- They say crime doesn't pay. Well neither does my brother-in-law.
- I went to school with some Italian kids who had a Godfather. I felt so inadequate. All I had was a second cousin.
- A kid from a rough neighbourhood asked his schoolteacher "If an apple a day keeps the doctor away, what do you take for the cops?"
- If it takes a thief to catch a thief, why do we employ honest policemen?
- The government's doing its best to solve the traffic problem in London. Its encouraging car theft.
- Everyone knew my brother would go far, especially with the police chasing him.
- They tell us crime is down in the UK. Probably because they've run out of victims.

- Did you hear about the stupid mugger who tried to rob people on the way BACK from Las Vegas?
- It's strange that so many people take to crime when there are so many legal ways to be dishonest.
- My brother's with Scotland Yard's Flying Squad. They finally caught up with him.
- The one thing guaranteed never to be stolen is the office clock. Too many people are watching.
- The police witness told the judge "While I was reading him his rights he committed two more wrongs."
- To keep down car crime all car wash places should be banned. That way cars will look so bad no one would want to steal them.
- So many crooks are now writing books or confession articles for the papers that, now when a cop arrests you he has to read you your syndication rights.
- A woman was arrested in a knitting circle because someone tipped of the police she shared needles.
- Some criminals know that crime doesn't pay. But they do it as a labour of love.
- This serial killer stabbed all his victims with a knitting needle. The police suspect there's a pattern to it.
- The rapist told the judge it's all because he gave up smoking. He didn't know what to do with his hands.
- I'm so scared of burglars now that I sleep with one eye open. This one. So if my other eye falls asleep while I'm here onstage, you'll realise it's through lack of sleep.
- The only good thing about the wages of sin is that they're not taxed.
- Crime DOES pay. How else can you get all that free board and lodging?
- How can they say crime doesn't pay? I know lawyers and judges who earn over £100,000 a year.
- I used to contribute to a local needy charity, till I found out it was run by a Mr. Needy.
- He steals other people's jokes. His two writers are Cut and Paste.
- I fitted a fool proof lock on my door which just proved what a fool I was.
- I fitted a fool proof lock, but the burglar proved he was no fool.

63

- Criminals are now getting ridiculously light sentences. Next thing you know, the judge will just them write out "I Must Not Commit Another Murder" one hundred times.
- I spent my youth in a broken home. A remand home and I was the one that broke it.
- The murderer got the very utmost in punishment. Not only did they give him the electric chair, but they put a drawing pin on it.
- The prison governor wanted to celebrate the tenth anniversary of being in his job, so he asked the convicts what kind of a party they'd like to suggest. They thought about it for a while and then said "How about Open House?"
- Rolf Harris got five years in prison. Two and a half for hanky and two and a half for panky.
- Yesterday the police arrested 4,000 store Santa's who were known to have little kids on their laps.
- The murderer said he did it because his wife always insisted on having the last word. And this time she got it. The judge asked "And what were her last words?" He said "Please, don't shoot."
- The middle aged spinster shouted to the cop "Officer, catch that man. He tried to kiss me." The cop said "Calm down, lady. There'll be another one along in a minute."
- The man at the door was from the Neighbourhood Watch. He's been all over the neighbourhood trying to sell a watch.
- The convict complained "There are 63.7 million people in this country and they jail me just because twelve people said I'm guilty."
- The escapologist criminal pleaded insanity because he thought he'd find it easier escaping from an asylum than a prison.
- He got arrested when he joined the Moonies and was caught mooning.
- Three bank robbers were arrested outside the bank because someone stole their get-away car.

CRUISING

I was invited back on the same cruise as last year. I just found out why. They're hoping I'll bring the towels back. Cruising has brought my wife and I closer together. We always get such a small cabin. I love cruises, but the service charges are getting out of hand. You have to tip the cabin steward, the wine waiter, the food waiter, the assistant food waiter and the Maitre d'. I even had to tip the staff member who added up all the people I had to give tips to. On my last cruise they had a Gay Nineties Night. The men were all gay and the women were all ninety. The cruise was full of geriatrics. I didn't realise how old the passengers were till I put my glass down at the bar and someone put their teeth in it.

I know a couple that led such independent lives, that when they went on a cruise they asked for separate decks.

ADDITIONAL GAGS

- On the cruise it was all tipping. I even had to tip the cabin steward fort accepting my tip.
- My wife said "We have to go back to Malaga. None of our snapshots come out."
- I had a cruise on the MS Insolvent.
- On my last cruise the cabin they gave me was so small I couldn't brush my teeth sideways.
- Those cabin stewards on cruises keep the place absolutely spotless. Complete change from my home where the only dusting ever done was for fingerprints.
- These days I never order wine on a cruise. I find I either can't afford it, or can't pronounce it.
- On a cruise ship going to Egypt a lady passenger asked a crew member "Where is the nearest toilet?" He said "Port Side" She said "Oh no. I don't think I can wait that long."

DARTS

In darts my idol was the late Jocky Wilson, the man they called "Mr. One Hundred And Eighty". Nothing to do with his score. That was his waist size. Once, when Jocky decided to go on a diet, the doctor put him on a weighing machine and he immediately sucked in his tummy. The doctor said "That won't help you." Jocky said "Yes, it will. Now I can see the numbers" He was so fat that in all those years of playing, Jocky never once saw the oche. In his first darts tournament they told him he had to start with a double. So he went and had a double and by the time he got back it was all over.

The commentator says "Bristow is leading with two lagers, a Guinness and a pint of stout. But Wilson has countered with a Johnnie Walker, a Dubonnet and a quart of Pils.

DENTIST

I've got a very expensive dentist. Every time I go there he makes me stick my tongue out and say "Owe." The costly dental treatment didn't improve my smile. But when I paid the dentist it certainly improved his. The dentist not only pulled my teeth, when I got the bill I thought he was pulling my leg as well. My dentist charges a fortune. Last week he put in a crown. It cost so much I think it must have belonged to the Royal Family.

I knew I was in for pain when the dentist put those little wads of cotton in his ears instead of my mouth. The only time it really hurts the dentist more than it hurts you is when you don't pay your bill. Last year the dentist sold me an electric toothbrush which he said meant I wouldn't have to see him so often. He was right. Now I see an electrician instead.

My wife went for treatment yesterday and was asked to take off all her clothes. She says she'll never go to that dentist again. I needed a dentist but couldn't find one on the NHS, so I went private. All the man kept saying was "You need to open up wider. Wider still. Even wider than that." It wasn't my mouth he was talking about. It was my wallet. I try to keep clear of dentists and their exorbitant fees. With them it's a case of putting lots of your money where your mouth is.

When my dentist promised me teeth like a star I didn't realise he meant they'd be coming out at night. One man went into the dentist with buck teeth and came out with bunk teeth. One upper and one lower. You can tell if a golfer is a dentist. He gets the hole to open wide.

DIET

I tried three diets at the same time. Well, one wasn't giving me enough to eat. Toughest was undoubtedly the Chinese diet where you are allowed to eat what you like, but only with one chopstick. My wife even dressed my salads with glue in the hope I'd stick to the diet. After six months of strict dieting I felt successful because I'd only gained 3lbs. It got to the point where I even gained weight swallowing my pride. So I let my wife talk me into seeing a diet specialist. "After all" she said, "you've got a lot to lose and nothing to gain."

My doctor said he'd put me on a simple diet that, to a man like me would be a piece of cake. Sounded great till I realised there was no cake involved. I had to keep away from anything sugary. Can't even look at the words on a Valentine's Day card. No puddings. I had to desert desserts.

The toughest part of being on a diet is not watching what you're eating. It's watching what other people are eating. My wife tells everyone she's dieting religiously. What she means is she eats what she likes and prays it won't make her fat. She's on an appetite depressant which she likes so much she keeps taking seconds. She's put on weight in many places. Mostly the dining room.

I've discovered that ice cream is only fattening if you put something into it. Like a spoon. The biggest advantage of rising prices is it helps with my diet. Now I only eat what I can afford. I'm overweight although I do try to watch what I eat. I guess my eyes just aren't quick enough. In less than two months I've gone from fabulous to flabulous. I'm so overweight they've nicknamed me The Man from La Muncha.

You need to go on a diet if the light of your life is the bulb in the fridge. Always remember, the first rule of dieting is "We are what we cheat." My wife's eyes used to be bigger than her stomach, but now her stomach's caught up. She's so fat that when she went on jury duty the other eleven had to wait outside. She's now into weightlifting. She lifts 15 stone every time she stands up. This morning she asked me if the dress she was wearing made her look fat. I said "No. It's the ten years of eating cakes and chocolate that made you look fat."

On Sundays I go off my diet, just so I've enough strength to stay on it for the rest of the week. I was on a diet for six weeks and all I lost was my sense of humour. The only really sound advice on dieting is, if it tastes good – spit it out.

Don't delay your diet. Never put off till tomorrow what you can take off today. If you're really serious about dieting the first thing you must do is give up seconds. And the second thing you must do is give up firsts. Be convinced the best way to lose weight is by skipping. Skip breakfast, lunch and dinner. If you indulge you'll bulge. You won't lose it by wishful shrinking. It's no use just talking about losing weight; you have to keep your mouth shut. Remember, adding sugar and starch to a meal can be expansive. The golden rule is, if you're slim count your blessings, but if you're fat count your calories.

ADDITIONAL GAGS

- With ever-rising food prices my budget is doing more for my figure than my diet.
- They've come up with a simple device to make you eat less. It's called a food bill.
- You know it's time to diet when you get a big electric bill just for the light that comes on when you open and close the fridge.
- I knew it was time to go on diet when I got in the bath and there was no room for the water.
- I still remember the good old days when I used to count my blessings instead of my calories.
- With food prices rising as they are, my budget is doing more for my figure than my diet.
- My diet doctor says I can eat as much Chinese food as I like…as long as only use one chopstick.
- As the doctor said to the fat priest "Your belly runneth over. For the next few weeks skip the part about the daily bread."
- The doctor said I can cut out meals altogether, as I'm eating enough between them.
- They now have what's called The Drinking Man's Diet. You don't have to cut out food. You just drink enough to forget that you're fat.

- I diet religiously. I just eat what I like and pray it won't make me fat.
- My brother tried smoking to help with his diet. Now he has so much tar in him, when he dies he's going to donate his lungs to Macadam.
- People go on a diet to mend their weighs. If you don't stick to your diet you're just wishful shrinking, Indulge and you'll bulge.
- Don't delay your diet. Why put off till tomorrow what you can take off today?
- The reason there are so many obese people is because most of them gave up their diet instead of food.
- The doctor said I only need to give up two things. Liquids and solids.
- The quickest way to lose your will power is to go on diet.
- My wife's diets are never successful. She's what you'd call a poor loser.
- My wife's always on a diet. I've loved her through thick and thin.
- She loves those weightwatchers meals. In fact, she likes them so much she has three at a time.
- Her diet wasn't working, so she changed her name to Violet to help with her shrinking.
- She went on a seven day diet which she completed in three days.
- Most people give up their diets because they find it's easier to change their mind than their body.
- My wife went on a diet once. She claims it was the most miserable afternoon she ever spent.
- I'm all in favour of diets. I just wish I could talk my babysitter into going on one.
- The only thing a diet does for most people is make them a bore.
- They say you can add years to your life by cutting out smoking, drinking and eating fat foods. But if it doesn't actually add years, it will at least seem longer.
- Old soldiers are supposed to fade away. My ex-soldier brother's 20 stone. He did the opposite.
- Adding starch and sugar to your meals can be expansive.
- I lost weight after a triple bypass. I bypassed restaurants, bars and bakers shops.
- A good way to lose weight is skipping. Skipping breakfast, skipping lunch, skipping dinner.

- He's so fat; yesterday he was standing next to his car and got a ticket for double parking.
- Sandwich spread is what you get from eating between meals.
- Most diets only have a slim chance.
- You can't lose weight by just talking about it. You have to keep your mouth shut.
- Dawn French claims she never eats between meals because, for her, there IS no between meals.
- When some people go on a diet all they lose is their sense of humour.
- Dieting is the penalty for exceeding the feed limit.
- Some people are just no good at counting calories and have the figures to prove it.
- Destiny may shape our ends, but a diet is supposed to do it more quickly.
- Now that I've got to the point where prices don't matter, calories do.
- The diet clinic's a waste of time. Even the Violets aren't shrinking.
- Did you hear about the fat cannibal who went on diet and only ate pygmies?
- The doctor says I can eat all the carbohydrates I like…as long as they're not in food.
- The diet doctor says I can eat anything I like. I just mustn't swallow.
- She's keeping me to my diet. She's put a "visiting hours' notice on the fridge.

DIVORCE

One husband divorced his wife because she liked sex in the morning. Right after he'd left for work. Another woman divorced her husband claiming he'd deceived her. He said he'd be out of town and came home unexpectedly. One woman said her husband tricked her into marriage. He told her she was pregnant. A woman divorced her husband because she didn't like him using four letter words, like wash, iron and cook. Her grounds for divorce were housemaid's knee. She caught her husband with his hand on it.

It's often a lack of communication that causes divorce. Counsellors advise you to ask your partner what they want. I asked my wife what she wanted and she said "Someone else."

One divorce was applied for because the wife was said to be seen out regularly with her husband's best friend. Turned out to be his dog. The husband claimed their divorce was caused by the wife's boob job. It drove a wedge between them.

You never know how long a marriage will last. I mean, Paul McCartney's marriage to Heather Mills only lasted 47 cheques. Zsa Zsa Gabor was a good housekeeper. After each divorce she kept the house. She was so angry at her ex-husband she gave him the ring back. But she kept the stone. She wasn't THAT angry. Zsa Zsa made a fortune out of her divorces. You could say she got richer by decrees.

John Cleese was stung for over £12,000,000 by his third wife in their divorce settlement. He's had three wives. All American. When asked what state he married them in, he said "Temporary insanity." They asked how his wife took it when he said he was divorcing her. He said "In cash!"

Joan Collins always insisted on a pre-nuptial agreement. It's now in its sixth printing. The deal is if Joan and her husband get divorced, they share the house. She gets the inside and he gets the outside. Both of them have their divorce lawyers on a permanent retainer.

Divorce settlements are seldom fair. I heard of a case where the wife got custody of the kids and the husband just got to see the dog every other weekend. Now when a divorcing couple split their finances down the middle it means her lawyer gets half and his lawyer gets the other half. Divorces can be expensive. I heard of one case where the wife got the furniture, the husband got the kids and the lawyer got the house. A diamond is the hardest substance known to man. Especially when he's trying to get it back. Divorce occurs when the better half becomes the bitter half. Because of the divorce rate even children are demanding more realistic bedtime stories. Now they have to end with "And the couple lived separately ever after." Every week we hear of another Show Biz couple splitting up. Paul McCartney and Heather Mills, Madonna and Guy Richie, Mel Gibson and his wife. The only couple I know that is still together is Keith Harris and Orville.

Paul McCartney and Heather Mills had a special cake made to celebrate their divorce. It had icing all over it to reflect their feelings for each other. She said that she wanted a divorce because she couldn't take any more from him. But her lawyer found that she could, it's a divorce lawyer's job to handle separations. They separate the ex-husband from his money. In Heather Mills' case she told the judge she wanted everything but her husband. Paul's now joined a group called Divorce Anonymous. If he ever gets the urge for another divorce they send over an accountant to talk him out of it.

The phrase "Out with the old and in with the new" used to apply just to Spring. Now it's anytime Mickey Rooney and Joan Collins feel like changing their spouses. One divorced woman told her friend "George and I had a fight over the children's custody, but I won. I only have to have them till Christmas.

The breakdown of a show business marriage is as predictable as a crystal gazer telling an astronaut "You're going on a long journey." Sinatra blamed himself for his divorce from Ava Gardner. He said for their anniversary he took her to a plush restaurant and said she could have anything she wanted. She chose the waiter. Sometimes it's the men that do the cheating, like the actor who suddenly started bringing his wife flowers every week. She found out he was sleeping with the florist. In another case the wife was granted a divorce because of her husband's knee trouble. She caught him with his secretary sitting on it.

To a man divorce means he's going through a change of wife. Some marriages end so quickly they put the wedding announcement in the obituary column. There's hardly time between "I do" and "adieu."

Statistics show that half the marriages in America end in divorce. That's probably why they call it the land of the free. Divorce is sometimes referred to as the forget-me-knot

There are lots of reasons why couples start out as lovebirds but soon find the TRILL has gone. Most divorced couples will tell you that their happiness was multiplied by division.

They've just published a book for divorced people. It's called THE JOY OF EX. I wouldn't trade my wife for anything in the world. Anyone interested can have her for nothing.

Hollywood, famous for its adults and adulteresses, has just passed a new law allowing husbands into the Delivery Room....along with the child's father. Divorce has never crossed my mind. However, taxidermy has once or twice.

A successful divorce case is where the ex-wife gets almost as much money as the lawyer.

The most common reason for divorce is a couple realising they're not fit to be tied. Their marriage went from a duet to a duel. They usually blame the minister who mispronounced them man and wife.

Liz Taylor's lawyer drew up a great pre-marital agreement which had them sharing everything. If her husband got double pneumonia she's get half of it. Her marriage to Eddie Fisher was dissolved on the grounds of insanity. The judge said she was mad to have married him in the first place. Liz was a creature of habit. Every year she went to New York for business, Miami for sunshine and Reno for divorce. Zsa Zsa Gabor got all her divorces on religious grounds. She worshipped money and her husbands lost theirs.

There are all sorts of reasons for a marriage break-up, like the nudist couple who got fed up seeing too much of each other. Or the husband who discovered his wife was leading a double life. Hers and his. Or the woman who divorced her husband because of all the housework. She didn't like the way he was doing it. Or the woman who dumped her sea Captain husband when she found out he had a second mate. Another just got divorced for the alimony. She wanted an ex-husband she could bank on.

ADDITIONAL GAGS

- They're updating the opera to make it more modern. Last night I saw "The Divorce of Figaro."
- The judge refused the wife's petition for divorce because she found blonde hairs on her husband's collar. He said it was quite reasonable seeing as he's a barber.
- We divorced because my wife said she couldn't take any more from me. But her lawyer found she could.

- The woman divorced her husband when she found out the woman at the door calling wasn't Avon, it was his girlfriend Yvonne.
- Liz Taylor and Richard Burton decided to re-marry when they realised the magic had gone out of their divorce.
- After his wife made him give up drinking, smoking and gambling, he divorced her. He realised that with all those vices gone, he could get someone better.
- Even though they had a pre-nuptial agreement she divorced him after their wedding night.
- She found out the print on the agreement wasn't the only thing that was small.
- When the wealthy couple divorced, the custody of the children went to the nanny.
- It's difficult to decide who brings the couple more happiness. The preacher that marries them or the judge that grants the divorce.
- The best way to save a marriage is to find out what a divorce lawyer costs.
- It's a proven fact that divorce lawyers can be hazardous to your wealth.
- The United Nations was founded to create peace. The same as divorce.
- She went to the RSPCA for her divorce because she reckoned she'd married an animal.
- Italian wives don't bother with divorce. They just hire a hit man.
- Common sense would prevent a great many divorces. On the other hand it would also prevent a great many marriages.
- With the current number of marriage break-ups it seems more parents are running away from home than children.
- The only good thing about our divorce is my wife gets custody of her mother.
- I had to divorce my wife. I couldn't afford to support her AND the government.
- The judge ruled that the divorcing couple split the house. The husband got the outside.
- A woman asked the judge for a divorce because after a year of marriage she was still a virgin. The judge asked the husband what

the problem was. He said "I'm sorry Judge, I didn't know she was in such a hurry."
- A gold digging wife told her lawyer she wanted a separation from her husband, but not his money.
- A woman wanted a divorce after complaining about her husband's appearance. Apparently he hadn't appeared at home for two whole years.
- Judging by the high divorce rate, a lot of people who said "I do" didn't.
- To get someone to smile you say "Cheese" Or if it's a lawyer, "Fees."
- She divorced her husband when she discovered she was allergic to nuts.
- The couple hated each other so much anyone who could stop them fighting would qualify for the Nobel Peace Prize.
- After the divorce their son had to be brought up by his lawyer, because neither party could afford to keep him.
- Paul McCartney's ex boasts she has everything, except Paul McCartney.
- The best way to reconcile a rowing couple is to tell them the divorce lawyer's fee.
- They had a quiet wedding and a noisy divorce.
- I know my faults and I'm prepared to live with them. Unfortunately my wife wasn't.
- I've adjusted well to the divorce. It was the marriage I couldn't adjust to.
- Even though the couple are no longer married, they remain good friends. Every year they send each other a divorce anniversary card.
- Modern stories now end up with "So they got divorced and lived happily ever after."
- It used to be if a woman wanted to get rid of a pain in the neck she went to a chiropractor. Now she goes to a divorce court.
- In a divorce court the judge said to the husband "Your wife claims that you beat here every single day of the week. What do you have to say to that?" The man answered "You can't believe a word she says, She's punch drunk."

- I wish I had half John Cleese's money. So does he, but he gave it away in alimony.
- On our first anniversary she said "I love you and you love me. So let's get divorced now before we start hating each other.It's a fact that divorce often turns a short matrimony into a long alimony. Alimony, which some men describe as a splitting headache, is the arrangement by which two people make a mistake and just one pays for it.
- It's also been described as the fee a wife charges for name-dropping.
- I married a cowboy. He remembers the Alamo, but keeps forgetting the alimony.
- A divorced husband no longer has to bring money home to his wife. He mails it.
- They don't call it alimony anymore. It's now called "severance pay."
- My wife made me give up smoking, drinking and gambling, which is great, because it's allowed me to save up enough money to divorce her.
- We split up because of religious differences. She worshipped money and I didn't have any.

EDUCATION

Kids used to go to university hoping to be lawyers or doctors. Now they're happy if they can just be solvent. Teachers hate giving sex lessons at school. Especially when the students keep correcting them. Before sex education schools had a lot of drop-outs. Now they have a lot of drop-ins. One teacher was actually arrested for teaching a pupil about sex. It was in the back of his car.

Sex education in schools has made kids so precocious. I drove by a school and saw two pupils openly kissing and cuddling in the playground. And it was an all boy's school. Schools are preparing our kids for the future by teaching them all about the birds and the bees. In today's dodgy share market they'd do better learning about the bulls and the bears. They're being taught how babies are made. It would be better if they taught them how babies are NOT made. One teacher asked her class if they knew what to do if they didn't want babies. A boy in the front row said "I know, Miss. You practice contradiction." In my day sex was never taught in schools. Till I was 12 I thought babies came from sleeping with storks. Sex books that used to be banned are now recommended reading. My son was very disappointed when he took a sex education exam at school and it turned out to be written. Personally, I think they're teaching them too young. My granddaughter's only eight and she's already learnt how to fake a headache. I'm not against our kids having sex lessons at school. It's the homework that bothers me.

The government's right in wanting to change our education system. I heard of one local school where the only tests the girls were passing were for pregnancy. With all those sex lessons at school, it seems the three R's now stand for Readin', Riotin' and Reproduction.

The government's ensuring there will be a lot less university places available. They don't want the future generation to be bright enough to see through their promises. I hear the Minister for Education gave a lecture on absenteeism and no one turned up. I left school at fourteen. I had to. I played truant so much the headmaster made me take early retirement.

Kids used to rub out the blackboard. Now they're more likely to rub out the teacher. I went to a school run by the Mafia. They bumped off the cleverest boy in the class because he knew too much. A teacher today won the 100 metres dash at the school's athletic meeting. Actually it was no surprise. Most teachers make a dash when they hear a gun go off. Some people think they don't have prayers at school anymore. That's not true. You should hear the teachers just before they open the doors.

My wife and I are doing pretty well financially. We are lucky none of our kids are smart enough to go to university. I can never understand why students have to pay £9,000 a year just to learn how to survive on £6,000 unemployment benefit.

Everything's going up. The term "Higher Education" now refers to the cost. It's ridiculous that university students have to pay £9,000 a year with no definite prospect of a job. But I heard of one student who, the day after leaving Oxford, got a job in advertising. I saw him down Regent Street with a sandwich board. His sister graduated with a tassel on her hat. Now she wears two, one on each nipple. She got a job as a stripper. My son made a big mistake in dropping out of university. He was on the third floor at the time. I thought he'd wasted his time at university because he ended up not even being able to tell the shortest distance between two points. But even that was useful. He became a taxi driver.

The steep increase in university fees has made a big difference. Used to be if a kid got a place at university he could be proud. Now if he DOESN'T get a place, he could be solvent. My son's been away at university for three years and this year gave me a special treat for Father's Day. He didn't write home for money. It's thanks to him I have stretch marks on my wallet. I really don't mind giving my son an allowance. But now he's demanding pension rights as well.

The government's already closed down lots of hospitals. Now its thinking of closing down schools so we can have a classless society. What we're short of are good teachers. It's not easy. To qualify you need a degree in English, a degree is Maths and a black belt in Karate. There's so much violence in schools today it's the teachers that are playing truant. So many kids from my old school wound up in jail, now the school photo comes in a pair. Full face and profile.

Education standards are still dropping. A ten year old schoolboy was asked to explain the tenses. He said "That's easy. If I bought a watch yesterday, that would be in the past. But if it was gift wrapped, it would be the present." Our kids were brought up with groups like The Beatles, The Byrds and The Monkees, so it's no wonder they can't spell. A recent report shows that most eight-year-olds are fluent with their ABC. It's the other 23 letters they're having trouble with. Mind you, today's kids can count higher than I did at their age. They have to. There are more TV channels. When I was young everyone wore a cap. In my case a dunce's one. I was never a clever student. My school report had more D's than in Dolly Parton's bra size. I flunked every exam. My teacher said I'd even have trouble passing wind.

Oxford and Cambridge are renowned for turning out politicians and comedians. Unfortunately too many of the former act like the latter. Statistics show that only 50% of university students are taking up useful subjects. The rest are just taking up space. Education's become so specialised now. One graduate being trained for a career in journalism has already achieved a degree in phone hacking. Whilst another with two first class honours degrees, now works for a big City firm as its Head of Purchasing. He's sent out lunchtimes to get the sandwiches. I've got a nephew who can't afford university, so he's learning to be a doctor by correspondence course. For the first lesson they sent him a book with instructions to take out its appendix.

I always wanted to be a writer. When I was thirteen I wrote my first book. I sent it to a publisher who said it needed cuts. So he put it through their shredder. The second publisher I sent my book to agreed to print it. He didn't give me an actual date. He just said "When hell freezes over."

They're planning to scrap prayers in school and my grandson is dead against it. With his English and maths he needs all the help he can get. School kids used to bring teachers apples. Now they drive them bananas. The government's said to be working with the BBC on a new series about primary education. It's called Strictly Come Duncing. The present education system in schools is cockeyed. Teachers ask such questions as "If it takes Jack an hour to chop down three trees. Fred, three quarters of an hour and Bill half an hour...how many trees will they all have chopped down in a day?" It's stupid. Why don't they just let Bill do it, he's the quickest."

The education system can be improved. I saw my grandson buying a Get Well Soon card for his parents. I asked "Why? Are they sick?" He said "Not yet. But they will be when they see my school report." My biggest expense is our son at university. When he left home I was devastated. He's the only one who knew how to work the VCR. Statistics show that one out of four adults in this country has no understanding of simple maths. Unfortunately most of them work in the tax office.

Universities are going broke. I have an uncle who lectures at Oxford and every week writes home to his kids for money. Every time I watch TV there's a war going on in some corner of the world. I'm starting to think that war is a way of teaching us geography.

None of our kids want to be tradesmen anymore. They're all at university chasing degrees. My son's at Cambridge learning to be a writer. For practice, he writes home every week for money. Thanks to my pocket calculator I now know how many pockets I have. A kid showed his dad his school report and said "Who says history doesn't repeat itself? This is the fourth year I've got a "D" in the subject.

I well remember my own schooldays. They say nice guys finish last. I reminded my Dad of that when I showed him my school report. I kept my school reports, so if the Tax People ever question my returns I can prove I was lousy at arithmetic. I was also rotten at poetry. I was thrown out of Poetry Class because I wrote something that rhymed. I was that unruly the headmaster wasn't satisfied with having me expelled. He wanted me deported. I'm now paying £9,000 a year to send my son to university so he can booze, snort drugs and flirt with girls. I don't regret the £9,000. I'm just sorry I didn't go myself.

The young attractive schoolteacher was concerned about one of her eleven-year-old pupils. She took him aside after class and asked "Billy, what's your problem? Why has your schoolwork been so poor lately?" The boy replied "I can't concentrate. I'm afraid I've fallen in love." The teacher said "Is that so- and with whom?" The boy answered "With you. I want us to get married." The teacher smiled. "But Billy, don't you see how silly this is? It's true I'd like a husband of my own one day, but I don't want a child." "Don't worry," said Billy. "I'll be very careful."

ADDITIONAL GAGS

- The teacher told my parents I show a lot of originality. Especially in my spelling.
- The mother reading her son's school report said "Don't worry about flunking sex. Your father does too."
- My school report was so bad I could have sued the school for deformation of character.
- When I read my son's school report, I said "There must be a good reason you got such lousy marks." He said "There is. It's called heredity."
- One university student said to his mate "The only way I can get my Dad to send money is by threatening to come home."
- Some kids' toys today are really educational. They teach you that you've wasted your money.
- He worked hard to get to university and his parents had to work even harder afford to keep him there.
- I told my university student son the facts of life. That I'm not made of money.
- Sending my kids to university has resulted in my getting poorer by degrees.

- Why is it that the worst behaved kids in the class always have the best attendance record?
- The latest statistics in Britain's primary schools show that 20% of students fail English, 30% fail maths and the other 50% fail to show up at all.
- This training school teaches salesman how to make house calls and doctors how not to.
- The teacher told her class that five thousand cats are used every year to make violin strings. One small kid was amazed. He said "Isn't it fantastic what they can teach animals to do these things?"
- The geography teacher asked the student "Where would you find Florence, Victoria and Virginia?" He said "Let them find me. I don't believe in chasing girls."
- If my son was getting half as much out of university as the university is getting out of me, I'd be happy.
- My young son says he's bottom of his class, but it makes no difference, they teach the same at both ends.
- My son says he's fine with arithmetic. It's just numbers that confuse him.
- This morning my son said to me "Dad, why did you ask me to pass the salt, you weren't eating anything?" I said "I know. But I just read your school report and I wanted to see if you could pass ANYTHING."
- I heard of one kid who went to school exhausted because the battery was dead on his toothbrush.
- During the Religious Education lesson the teacher told her class "We are here to help others." One little boy put his hand up and asked "Then what are the others here for?"
- I just read The Daily Mail to keep myself misinformed.
- If children didn't ask questions they'd never realise how little adults know.
- A little knowledge is a dangerous thing if a prospective employer realises that's all you have.
- The school kid refused to attend sex education classes because, he said when he grew up he was going to be a priest.
- My son was caught smoking at school. They expelled the kid that set him alight.

- The teacher told her very young pupils that if any of them badly needed to go to the toilet they should hold up their hand. One little boy turned to the teacher and said "How will that help?"
- The girls school came top this year with less pregnancies than the rest.
- Father tells his son "Ask your mother about girls, she used to be one."
- The female university student who keeps phoning home for money…each time she needs an abortion.
- The current school system's getting out of hand. Pupils carry knives guns and knuckledusters and it's the teachers who get into trouble for just spanking them.
- He did his bit to lower the illiteracy rate in the U.K. He moved abroad.
- Schooldays are the happiest days of your life. Especially if your kids are old enough to go.
- I asked for a student loan, so they loaned me a student.
- My daughter at university's made a lot of money out of writing. She writes home for money.
- I got a note from my son's schoolteacher saying "You did such a good job with your son's homework I'd like you to help me with my income tax."
- I'm not saying he's a slow learner, but he was the first one to reach retirement age while still in infant school.

EXERCISE

If you think the Lord works in mysterious ways, you should see my wife's yoga class. Till recently I did yoga for gentle stretching. Now the only stretching I do is out on the sofa watching TV. I'm getting lethargic. I used to conserve energy. Now I hoard it. The only exercise I get is when I can't find the remote control.

I'm always being advised to exercise. People tell me to take a running jump. I'm pushing eighty. That's about the only exercise I get these days. I don't touch my toes anymore. I figure if God meant us to touch our toes he's have put them higher up on our body.

ADDITIONAL GAGS

- He's so lazy he bought an exercise bike that only goes downhill.
- If his muscles were as hard as his arteries he'd be in good shape.
- They were charging £5 for ten minutes on the trampoline. I thought that was a bit steep till I realised it was next door to a nudist camp.
- He calls himself a weightlifter. He can't even pick up the bill in a restaurant.
- One day I jogged backwards and put on 8lbs.
- I get my exercise from magazines. Bending down to pick up all those leaflets that fall out.
- I get tired just thinking about exercise.
- I told my wife she needs more exercise so now a she spends my money faster.
- I've stopped going to the beach. I can no longer hold my stomach in that long.
- The only exercise I get these days is bending to my wife's will.
- With exercise I manage to work off the fat from my stomach. It's all behind me now.
- The only reason my wife took up jogging was so she could hear heavy breathing again.
- The only exercise some politicians get is side-stepping issues.
- The nearest he ever got to exercise was when he had athlete's foot.
- The trouble with jogging is, by the time you realise you're in no condition for it, you've got a long way to walk back.
- What I can't understand is why some men take up golf to get exercise and then go from hole to hole in one of those golf mobiles.
- He says he keeps in shape. Heaven knows why. If I had his shape I wouldn't want to keep it.
- Since I started walking for my health I've been bitten by a dog, mugged and knocked down by a bicycle.
- I get enough exercise just pushing my luck.
- I was at the gym today. I went all out, now I'm all in.
- He's so unfit the doctor didn't know whether to give him an examination or an autopsy.

- Jogging every day's made me two inches taller. I'm standing on my blisters.
- The time and motion study showed that at no time was he ever in motion.

FASHION

My wife bought one of those hats that never go out of style. They look just as ridiculous every year. She hardly ever wears it. She just brings it out occasionally to cure my hiccups. She paid £75 for the hat, but that's understandable. Laughs like that don't come cheap.

My wife's always writing away for clothes catalogues. We've got hundreds of them. This year what she gave the postman for Christmas was a hernia. She goes to the clothing stores and drives the sales staff mad. In her case, if the shoe fits, it's bound to be the wrong colour. She was overheard in Selfridges asking the sales girl "If my husband likes this dress, can I bring it back?" I was shocked to find my wife's actually got six different evening handbags. I asked her what she could possibly want with six handbags. She said gloves and shoes to match.

If, as Shakespeare said, brevity is the soul of wit, then modern women's fashion has never been funnier. It seems modern women's fashion aims to show a lot of style and a heck of a lot of the woman wearing it. Some dresses are so skimpy it's hard to tell whether the wearer is out to catch a man or a cold. These women are determined to conceal nothing but their age. I saw one with a neckline so low I'm surprised she didn't trip over it. Her skirt was that short it could have doubled as a belt. Even worse was the Hollywood starlet who wanted to be noticed, so she turned up in a two-piece outfit…slippers.

They say clothes make a man, but what they don't say is his wife's clothes can break him. I once had to stop my wife buying a new dress for £600. She said she'd only wear it on special occasions. I said "Like what, my bankruptcy." It's funny how the lower the neckline the higher the price. The main thing a woman should look for when she buys the latest fashion is a husband who can afford it. We men have to face the fact that women will always be slaves to fashion. They're what I call Kelvin

Clones. They can't help wearing those same cut trousers. It's in their jeans.

I no longer complain when my wife brings home an expensive gown. Instead I use a cunning technique of pretending to be enthusiastic and say "Darling that is a lovely dress. It's really beautiful. You don't even have to put it on, I already know what it'll look like because my Boss's secretary's got one and the cleaning woman at the office has got one…"

When it comes to buying clothes my wife will have her mind set on a certain item, right up till the moment she enters the shop. Then it's anyone's guess what she'll wind up with. I keep telling her that though changing her mind is a woman's privilege, it isn't compulsory. I asked my wife why she's always buying new clothes. She says she wants to dress like a lady. I said that's fine, only make it Lady Godiva.

Singer Cher admitted splashing out this week on an expensive dress, but she claims it ISN'T extravagance because she'll only be wearing half this year and half next year.

Fashion is about designers who live off the fad of the land, putting the neckline where the waistline used to be. We are now in the middle of summer. I can tell because my post is full of catalogues for winter clothes. I got worried this week when I read the headline "Paris has gone bust" till I realised they were referring to the low neckline in women's fashion. Tight tops look great on Dolly Parton, but the only thing those sweaters do for my wife is make her itch. Top fashion journalists always have two trays on their desk. One for "What's in" and the other for "What's Out."

I stopped my wife buying that new dress. I had to. It clashed with my salary. It's funny how my wife says she's got nothing to wear, but she needs two wardrobes to keep it in. My wife's suddenly become very fashion conscious. She's a born again Christian Dior. Fashion is what a her does to a hem to catch a him. I'm always cheered by the arrival of summer, when the days get longer and the skirts get shorter. Since we've been married my Valerie wears her skirts longer. About three years longer.

The woman brought the bra back to the shop and complained "When I bought this bra you said it breathes. Trouble is, when I wear it, I can't."

My brother's a bra manufacturer. He knows the bra business from A to D. There's no doubt a well fashioned bras brings out a woman's best points.

Sometimes you can't judge a woman by her clothes because there isn't enough evidence. Often the only thing holding up a woman's dress is the law. Women wear tight sweaters to accentuate the positive and corsets to eliminate the negative.

My husband belongs to a women's support group. They manufacture bras.

ADDITIONAL GAGS

- Do you realise that without elastic women would take up 25% more space?
- I've just seen the latest thing in women's clothes. Eddie Izzard.
- The British clothing industry is no more. My wife bought a tailored suit this week and the label said "Made in Britain." It turned out that the label WAS made in Britain, but the suit was made in Pakistan.
- The sexy girl tourist guide in Spain was wearing a neckline so low she could get arrested for hiccupping.
- Women live longer than men because they have so many dresses they wouldn't be caught dead in.
- Did you hear about the wife who refused to accompany her husband to the nudist camp because she said she hadn't a decent thing to take off.
- I had great difficulty trying to look fashionable by tying the sleeves of my jumper around my waist. Perhaps I should have taken my arms out of them first.
- Some women have a run in their stockings. Hers was more like a stampede.
- High heels were invented by a woman who was always being kissed on the forehead.
- One woman I know has worn the same dress for so long it's been in and out of fashion five times.
- If you have one hole in your jeans that's a sign of poverty. If you have more than one hole, that's fashion.

- This fellow's so cautious he wears both belt and braces……on his underpants.
- I think it's strange the way some nightclubs make you wear a collar and tie to watch a topless dancer.
- This young starlet bought two things in the summer sales. A diamond ring that is the real McCoy and a padded bra that's the real decoy.
- My wife has a dress for every day of the year. Actually she's wearing it now.
- I saw this girl on the beach with a bikini so small it only had three polka dots.
- My wife told the salesgirl "This dress is very nice, but it's less than I wanted my husband to spend.
- The best thing about women's fashions is they don't last long.
- Hot pants are a breech of promise.
- The mother of a newborn baby sent a letter to Mothercare cancelling her order for a maternity dress. She said "My delivery was quicker than yours."
- Her husband was shocked when his wife bought a very thin lace dress. He said people could see right through it. She said "Not when I'm wearing it."
- I don't mind my wife wearing skirts above the knee, but I don't like it when they're above my budget.
- When she wears a mini-skirt men turn to look….the other way.
- The thing some women conceal best in slacks is their better judgement.
- Some women who dress to please themselves are too easily pleased.
- Today's women get a lot out of a dress. And they leave it out too. My wife would never wear a bikini. She hasn't the figure or the nerve.
- If you wonder why they call women's clothes high fashion, just take a look at the price tags.
- My wife bought two dresses that are absolutely stunning. When I saw the price I was absolutely stunned.
- Bikinis were designed to keep women cool and men hot under the collar.
- Often the last word in strapless gowns is "Oops!"

- My wife bought one of those hats that give the impression there were no mirrors in the shop.
- My wife quickly stopped me laughing at her new hat. She told me the price.
- She was wearing one of those bikinis where the only thing concealed was the maker's label.
- A corset is a device that holds a woman in when she's going out.
- Fashion is a strange thing. A designer makes a mistake and millions of women rush out to buy it.
- The only thing I ever do behind my wife's back is zip up her dress.
- The reason women's fashions keep changing is because designers don't make the same mistake twice.
- Some women show a lot of style and some styles show a lot of women.
- When it comes to wearing sweaters some women choose a tight size as the right size.
- I was going to buy my girlfriend a wired bra, but I don't know whether she's A.C. or D.C.
- The only ability that actress has is filling out a sweater.
- They're making a new film about Imelda Marcos. It's called Guys and Dolcis.
- Modern girls are now wearing their skirts shorter than their hair.
- A wife tells her friend "I bought this expensive Givenchy gown as a conversation piece. My husband hasn't stopped talking about it.
- My wife tried on 20 hats in the shop. I liked them all. Everyone was a barrel of laughs.
- She stuffs Kleenex down her bra, but it's too obvious. She ought to take them out of the box first.
- She has so much rubber in her bra it's erased her breasts.
- She said her dress wasn't a perfect fit, but her husband's was when he saw the bill.

FILMS

Seventy five per cent of all movies made in Hollywood last year were horror films. Mind you, the producers didn't intend them to be. Film producers have defended the explicit sex scenes by saying they had a legitimate reason to be there. To take your mind off the terrible scripts. Film companies are looking for any excuse for their female stars to go topless. That's why I avoid them. If I want to see two big boobs I'll watch Cameron and Miliband. Did you know that Gandhi won the Oscar in 1982 because it was the only film that year featuring a sheet with only one person under it?

As one film producer said "We had no trouble passing the censor. Now we've got to make the public think the film's dirty." In just five generations films have gone from silent to unspeakable. Modern films are so full of sex you can't even read the reviews unless you're accompanied by an adult.

They're remaking so many old films now. I hear they're even making a new version of Madame Butterfly. In the original they said "Yankee go home!" In this version the Japanese girl's holding a baby and says "Yankee come back!" British films can now only be made with foreign funding. In fact, there's an Arab one being made right now. It's called "The Man in the Iron Mosque." Most modern films follow the same old story. Boy meets girl, boy gets girl, boy goes broke, boy loses girl.

There are so many weepie films out now. Cinemas are making a fortune selling ice cream, popcorn and handkerchiefs. Films today are full of violence and debauchery. I daren't take my wife to the cinema. Just the thought of sex gives her a headache. I think the film industry ought to be more discerning. I say they should get rid of their projectionists and replace them with rejectionists. On TV now when a film's rated X, it probably means it's to be shown at Xmas. Most of the films I've seen recently should have been rated NG. No good. One was so bad, the audience asked the projectionist to switch to another channel.

ADDITIONAL GAGS

- John Wayne said when he first played a cowboy outlaw he was so bad they featured his face on posters saying "NOT WANTED"
- As self-appointed censor Mary Whitehouse might have said "That film was awful. I get more disgusted each time I watch it."

- In the new film the lead part is a real pirate. He wears a patch over both eyes.
- I've just seen a film that ran for three and a half hours. That's twice as long as two of its star's marriages.
- He had two parts in the film "The Good, The Bad & The Ugly" He played the latter two roles.
- They're doing a follow-up to "Jaws" It's another film about sharks. It's called "Gone with the Finned."
- They're making a sequel to "Jaws" It's called "It Happened One Bite."
- The sex film started with the female star wearing just a two-piece outfit. A pair of slippers.
- More and more we're learning you can't judge a book by its movie.
- Many of today's films are mysteries. The mystery is how they got made in the first place.
- I think a movie hero is anyone who can sit through a modern action film.
- You used to be able to sit in the cinema for three hours and see two full length feature films. Now in that time all you can see is the first half of one.
- I was in the cinema and watched a torrid love scene for half an hour before I realised I was facing the wrong way.
- Today a film has to be a sin to be appreciated.
- I can't go to the cinema anymore, it's too noisy. Especially from all that popcorn.
- I know an actress who plays a hooker in all her films. She speaks five different languages, but isn't allowed to say 'no' in any of them.
- Movie morals have certainly changed. I still remember when a film was considered obscene if the horse wasn't wearing a saddle.
- Hollywood's just made a film so bad they had to re-shoot it before they put it on the shelf.
- The impoverished actress didn't want to undress for the part, but in the end she had to grin and bare it
- The director of his last film made an extra cut. His wrists.
- A long-married couple were watching an intense love scene in a film. The wife turned to her husband and said "How come you never

make love to me like that?" He said "Do you know how much they have to pay that actor for doing it?"
- The film was adapted for television audiences. They cut out the clean parts.
- I'm not saying the film was pornographic, but prostitutes use it for training.

FLYING

I travelled on a no-frills airline that was so cheap there was no film onboard. Just slides. Just before we took off the captain asked us all to fasten our scotch tape. Other airlines have their logo on the tail of the plane. All this one had was the captain's "L" plate. I asked the stewardess for a double whisky. She said they'd run out. The pilot just finished the bottle. It was such a rough flight the stewardess cut out the middleman and put the food straight in the sick bags. The flight was listed as non-schedule, which meant we were stacked so long over Heathrow Airport, by the time we landed the plane was obsolete. Last I heard of that plane, it had vanished without trace, like Andrew Lloyd Webber's latest musical.

Those pretty Airline Hostesses ask you what you want. Then they strap you down so you don't get it. One male passenger got a nose bleed at 30,000 feet He tried to kiss the stewardess and his wife thumped him.

I love flying. I just wish I'd been to as many places as my luggage. I've got one suitcase that's travelled 10,000 miles more than I have. I wondered what happened to my luggage till I went to the Lost Property department and found the clerk there wearing my clothes. Funny thing is, they suited her more than they did me. On my last flight they lost two of my cases. I didn't mind that so much, but what did they do with my wife who was carrying them? The airline's baggage-handlers were going on strike, but cancelled at the last minute. Someone stole their picket signs.

I used to travel by Concorde which flew faster than sound. Only problem was the films had no sound till two hours after you'd landed. Now that Concorde no longer exists, the only thing travelling faster than sound is gossip when my wife has a hand in it.

British Airways' financial troubles are easy to see at Heathrow. Their windsocks have holes in them. They've just announced they're merging with a foreign airline. It'll give them more cities to lose your luggage in. I only wish I could afford to go to some of the places my luggage has been. I heard a man at Heathrow ask for "A ticket to wherever you're sending my luggage." I've just discovered I have property in Spain. Apparently that's where my Terminal Five luggage wound up. We flew from Stansted and I was amused by the sign on the concourse with an arrow which said "YOU ARE HERE. HEAVEN KNOWS WHERE YOUR LUGGAGE IS." Once, within ten minutes of landing I saw my suitcase coming round on the carousel. But it was the one they lost last year. A friend of mine took a nudist holiday this year. He didn't intend to, but the airline lost his luggage. Some airlines are only keeping afloat because of their in-flight sales. Passengers are buying luggage to replace the cases they know will be lost. When FLYME went broke it was a unique achievement. Other airlines just lose luggage. They lost a whole airline.

The way things are going; household expenses are getting to be as hard to keep down as airline food. On my last flight the Air Stewardess asked "Would you like dinner?" I said "What are the choices?" She said "Yes or No." I've had complaints concerning my jokes about airline food. The airlines say they are as good as any top class restaurant. That may be, but I've yet to see a top class restaurant that gives you a sick bag just in case.

They're even allowing roulette tables on planes now. Saves time. People will be arriving in Las Vegas already broke. I personally would never gamble on a plane. If I had money to waste I'd save time by putting it in my luggage and let the airline lose it for me.

All of us onboard commended the pilot for personally getting out of the cockpit and chipping ice off the wings. That was until we found out he wanted it to put in his whiskey. We were on a bumpy flight and the man in the seat next to me said to the Air Stewardess "I'll have whatever the pilot's having" It's no joke when the stewardess says "I'm sorry, sir, we're out of whisky. We only carry one bottle and the Captain's just had that." I heard they are now refusing to serve champagne on flights. Every time the captain hears a cork pop, he dives for cover. Airlines are dissuading some show biz passengers and who can blame them. I mean, would you want to board a plane that Jedward just got off of? One English actor actually did get arrested on a plane flying to Hollywood. He was overheard saying he was going there to shoot a pilot.

They've tightened up airport security. Next thing you know they'll insist on examining the bags under your eyes. A couple this week got married at Heathrow Airport to save money. It cut the cost of a photographer. They used the security film from the CCTV cameras. The airlines are even more stringent now. They used to march passengers off planes in handcuffs for hijacking. Now it's just for smoking.

Recently so many airlines have gone bust, there'll soon be only two airlines left. The one you're flying on and the one your luggage went on by mistake. Most airlines are still fighting to survive the recession. Some are now even offering Frequent Flier Yards. Whenever I take a flight now, I only book a one way single. That's because I can never be sure they'll still be in business when I return. I met one air stewardess who didn't mind being made redundant. She got a job immediately as a Stripogram Girl. They wanted someone with experience of taking off.

I travelled on one of those cheap no-frill airlines. For about half the normal price you not only get the flight but a cup of tea, a biscuit and a shoe horn to get into your seat. To attract more customers airlines are offering ridiculously low fares. So low, some people are taking planes just to see the onboard movie. You get a cheap fare but they make you pay heavily for anything else. I flew on one where it cost a fortune to spend a penny. I travelled on one airline that was really frugal. All they gave the passengers was one cheese sandwich and by the time it got to me there was only the chewed up crust left. They couldn't even afford to show a film, so they just had the stewardess pass round her holiday snaps. The cutbacks on staff have got to the stage of being ridiculous. On a recent flight they only had one stewardess, and she was so busy serving coffee she didn't have time to land the plane.

Return air fares are now cheaper. The only snag is, on the way back you have to eat the left-over's from the way out. Airline cost cutting means less maintenance staff. I was on a flight where the toilets were out of order all the time. Now I know what they mean by a holding pattern. There's a new air carrier especially for old age pensioners. It's called Incontinental Airlines. It seems some airlines are turning a blind eye to sex on planes. It came to light when a passenger took exception to being told to put his girlfriend back in an upright position.

The airlines are still losing millions. Not pounds, luggage. I took so many air journeys British Airways made me a member of its frequent lost luggage club. Always be sure to put your destination address clearly on your luggage. It gives the airline something to read while they're sending it someplace else. I now know the derivation of the word "luggage." LUG is what you do when you want to take it onboard. And AGE is what you do while you're waiting for it to come round on the carousel. I certainly miss flying to New York on Concorde. It was so fast; when you got there you had an extra couple of hours to look for your luggage.

The Air Stewardess said "There may be fifty ways to leave your lover, but there's only one way to leave this plane." The airlines are really cutting back. Now, if you have to jump out, instead of a parachute they give you an open umbrella. But I think the most dangerous thing about flying is the airline food.

ADDITIONAL GAGS

- Film stars love aeroplanes. It's the only place people can't walk out on their movies.
- I travelled on one airline that treated me badly, but I got my revenge. I booked a return ticket to Malaga and didn't come back.
- I got worried when I noticed the other people on my plane were buying accident insurance. Especially as one of them was our pilot.
- As the pilot said when we were approaching Heathrow "We are about to land in England. It's time to tighten your belts."
- One thing always puzzles me. How can a plane that travels at six hundred miles an hour be four hours late?
- You could tell it was a cheapskate airline. During the movie they came round selling popcorn.
- The airline issued me with a standby ticket which entitled me to stand by and watch the plane take off.
- At Heathrow Sir Galahad was ahead of me at the check-in desk. He was booking a knight flight.

- Some people go to Las Vegas to gamble. I gambled before that, at Heathrow when I handed in my luggage.
- I didn't mind my luggage going to the wrong place, but I think it had a better holiday than I did.
- I was really worried on my last flight when a voice came over the tannoy saying "Would any passenger with 20-20 eyesight please make their way to the cockpit. The Captain needs help to find his contact lens."
- The airline issued me with a standby ticket which entitles you to stand by and watch while the plane takes off.
- Talk about no-frill airlines. Just before we took off the captain asked us all to fasten our Scotch Tape.
- I've got suitcases that have travelled 30,000 miles more than I have.
- I wondered what happened to my lost luggage till I went to the airport check-in counter and found the man there wearing my clothes.
- I don't understand airport security. Before I boarded the plane they confiscated my nail clipper. But when we were in the air they dished out steak knives.
- I didn't mind my luggage going to the wrong place, but I think it had a better holiday than I did.
- We were stacked so long over Heathrow Airport, by the time we landed the plane was obsolete.
- Notices on airport board announces arrivals, departures and mergers.
- Air traffic is so busy I hear a tiger moth just landed at Heathrow it's been stacked up for that long.
- Talk about no-frill airlines. Just before we took off the captain asked us all to fasten our Scotch Tape.
- I don't understand airport security. Before I boarded the plane they confiscated my nail clipper. But when we were in the air they dished out steak.

FOOD

I was in a fast food restaurant when the man at the next table asked the waiter "Where's the toilet? Your food is faster than I thought." I ate a hamburger at one of those fast food restaurants. The meat was so thin I

95

could have eaten three and still be a vegetarian. And those pizza places are now making the crusts so thin they can fax them to you.

Fu Tongs in the High Street has started selling frogs legs. From now on they'll be known as the Chinese Hop-a-way. If you eat Chinese food an hour later you're hungry. If you eat Mexican food, an hour later you'll wish you ate Chinese food instead. I went to a restaurant in China where, if you ask for a doggy bag, they give you a bag with a doggy in it. In Britain we love our dogs and put them on a pedestal. In China they put them on a plate.

Even the Chinese are having bad times. I heard of one restaurant in Beijing that's now selling mis-fortune cookies. But it's true what they say about Chinese restaurants. You eat at one and two hours later you need another bank loan. They now have a combined Chinese and Italian restaurant where you are expected to eat spaghetti with chopsticks. I tried it. I didn't get much inside me, but during the hour I was there I knitted three sweaters.

The restaurant service was so slow I couldn't pay my bill. By the time I got the meal my credit card had expired. I'd already reported the waiter to the police as missing person. As the cannibal said to the explorer "Guess who's coming to be dinner?" One cannibal wife cooked a German because her husband wanted a Frankfurter.

More than half the chocolate eaters with allergies have switched to a new brand called Eunuch. It's guaranteed to have no nuts. I went to one of those topless restaurants where the waitresses are covered by little more than insurance. You realise why these places have topless waitresses as soon as you taste their food. I still remember the days before topless restaurants when you only had to worry about the waitress getting her thumb in the soup.

I don't mind my wife serving left-overs, but not from last year. Her food is so bad; when I get home from work I always ask "What's the slop-of-the day?" Since she bought a microwave I get heartburn in half the time. But nobody's fussier when we eat in restaurants than her. Yesterday she sent her steak back saying it was too medium. Actually I complained too. I told the waiter my steak was so tough I couldn't eat it. I demanded he call the manager. He said "What's the point? He won't be able to eat it either!" The man at the next table was saying a prayer. I thought he was religious till I found out he'd eaten there before. I also found out why the main dish was called "Chef's Surprise." Apparently the chef was surprised anyone would eat it.

I've eaten in lots of international restaurants. I dined in a Paris restaurant that was so posh the frogs legs were served pedicured....An Italian restaurant where the coffee is so strong, a week later you're sleepy again. A kosher restaurant where the portions were small because they didn't want you to make a pig of yourself...and a Russian Deli which they aptly called The Hammer & Pickle. One restaurant I ate at was so strict about the no-smoking rule, if you ordered smoked salmon you had to eat it outside.

ADDITIONAL GAGS

- The waiter said it was the dish of the day. I said "Which day? Was it this year?"
- As the restaurant waiter said "We don't have a menu. If you can't smell it, we don't have it."
- The restaurant serves coffee that's half and half. Half in the cup and half in the saucer.
- They call Camembert a two handed cheese because you have to eat it with one hand while holding your nose with the other.
- I was in an usual restaurant. I ordered hot chocolate and the waiter brought me a Cadbury's bar and a match.
- Almost everything you eat is purported to be bad for you. Looks like the only way to stay healthy is to starve to death.
- The day I went the service was so slow I had to change my order from "To go" to "Today."
- The restaurant's new cook kept burning the food. He couldn't help it. He used to work in a crematorium and couldn't break the habit.
- The restaurant serves two kinds of steak. Lukewarm or cold.
- Talk about bad restaurant service! I think the vegetable-of-the-day was the waiter.
- I asked the waiter why he had his thumb on my steak. He said he didn't want it to fall on the floor again.

- My wife knows exactly what she wants when she buys food. For instance, she'll only buy a breast of chicken if it's a 38D.
- The restaurant chef said "Of course I can cook a meal at half the price, but it will only taste half as good."
- Our oceans are 50% more polluted than ten years ago. Half the fish being caught now are so full of mercury they could take their own temperature.
- There's a new branch of Alcoholics Anonymous that lets you drink as much as you like. But you wear a mask so you remain anonymous. The waiter at The Ivy restaurant approached the new customer reading the prices in the menu and said "Are you ready to order now, or are you still in shock?"
- Jewish people eat more Italian food than the Italians. And they eat more Chinese food than the Chinese. Just think, if Jews stopped eating they'd close down two countries.
- Never waste household scraps. Open the windows and let the neighbours enjoy them.
- I know a family so poor all they have for dinner is a scrambled egg. Mother puts the egg on the table and they all scramble for it.
- Yesterday instead of saying grace before the meal we said "Ditto" because the food was leftovers from the day before.
- She's an experimental cook that's got her through 43 recipes and six husbands so far.
- The recipe for cheesecake's been in my wife's family for years. It's been passed down from one lousy cook to the next.
- The grocer said my coupons were out of date, but that was alright because so was his food.
- I went to a topless restaurant and got soaked to my skin. The place had no roof.
- Diner asks waiter "What the official name of this dish? They may want to know at the hospital"
- The waiter asked how I want my steak – medium or well burnt?
- I like to have a drink with my meal, but what wine goes with leftovers?
- The complaining customer shouted at the waiter "Why is it, whenever I come to this restaurant I never get what I ask for?" "Perhaps, sir" the waiter said "It's because we're too polite."

- Cannibal looking up at dropping parachutists says "For what we are about to receive....."
- I have a pour-and-serve breakfast, a shake and bake lunch and a thaw and heat dinner.
- As the restaurant waiter said "We don't have a menu. If you can't smell it, we don't have it."

FOOTBALL

There are too many boozers connected with football. Gazza and George Best were prime examples. They were great at passing a ball, but hopeless at passing a bar. There's also too much violence. My nephew's a Millwall fan. He's just forked out half his spending money for their supporters' kit. Two knuckle dusters and a bicycle chain. These days if a star footballer plays a friendly game it's probably with his mistress. Professional footballers are vastly overpaid. David Beckham recently had to miss a match because his foot was broken. He dropped his wallet on it. Worse would be if he broke his fingers, he wouldn't be able to count all his money. Not all the famous ones are worth the money. Right now I can think of one halfback who's more of a drawback. Footballers are told they have to cut down on sex before a match. One player refuses to sleep with his wife at all, because she wanted too many instant replays.

I used to think that Premier League footballer's numbers on their shirts were their team places. They are not. They are the number of millions the players were bought for. The top footballers now have an extra training session. It's to learn how to negotiate a contract. I heard of a Premier League football team that got so desperate it started using English players. I watched one football match on TV that was so boring, the only replay worth showing was the tossing of the coin.

Football teams are the same. Next time they get a throw-in, it should be the towel. They badly need a new manager. Trouble is, the one thing the England managers can't keep, is their jobs. They need to recruit the help of Heather Mills or John Cleese's ex-wife, because they know how to get the most out of their men. My wife's a great football fan. When the England manager said he was going to play a new striker, she couldn't wait to get to the match. She thought he said streaker.

Some football managers deliberately hire fat players. It's so when their team mates foul, they hide the referee's view. Luton were over the moon when they clocked up seven against Southampton. Next week they hope to increase the crowd number to eight.

ADDITIONAL GAGS

- I'm not expecting England to do all that well in the next World Cup. In fact, I'll be happy if they win the coin toss. The England football team manager was jealous when he heard that British Rail had 12,000 determined strikers. He said he'd be happy with just two.
- The manager of Fulham Football Club said "This year we'll be the team to beat" And he was right. Everybody beat them.
- After the England Football team won the toss they should have had the sense to quit while they were ahead.
- As the husband said to his wife "What do you mean you're being neglected? You know I always talk to you at half time."
- The Italian football team have Roman numerals on their shirts.

GAMBLING

They don't allow gambling on planes. They figure eating airline food is a big enough gamble. Friends of mine have flown to Las Vegas three years running and lost every penny they took with them. This year they're not bothering to go. They're sending a cheque instead. When I was in Las Vegas I tried to pay the pharmacist for some Aspirin. He said "I'll toss you double or nothing." I wound up with two headaches.

I go to Las Vegas every six months to visit my money. And I usually leave a little interest.

Las Vegas is a place where the climate and scenery can't be beaten. Nor can the slot machines.

The only people who bring money back from Las Vegas are pickpockets.

The gambling casinos in Las Vegas are very strict about attire. They insist you wear a tie to lose your shirt.

I told a friend I was taking my wife to Las Vegas. He said "Won't the climate disagree with her?" I said "It wouldn't dare."

Las Vegas has doubled its population in the last ten years. That's because so many people that gambled there can't afford to leave.

I've just come back from Las Vegas where they have fabulous hotel service. My wife phoned down for room service and they sent up a table and a dealer. My wife doesn't gamble so she sent the table back. Just before I left the room I sent the dealer back. I don't gamble either.

Anyone who believes you get out of something what you put into it, has never played the slot machines in Las Vegas.

I've got property in Las Vegas. The hotel confiscated my luggage.

The only sure way to beat the horses is to become a jockey with a whip.

GOLD DIGGERS

I asked her to feel my biceps. She said she'd rather feel my wallet. She soon turned my fat wallet into a flat one. She turned down my marriage proposal. She said she didn't want to live as cheaply as one. Girls there claim to marry for love, but they divorce for money. A typical Hollywood marriage is where he marries for beauty and she for booty

As Bernie Ecclestone's wife said of her hubby "He's not that short when he stands on his wallet." Some modern wives confine their reading to just their husband's chequebook. She married the art collector for his Monet.

GOLF

When Tiger Woods lost the Open he was completely demoralised. Mind you, he didn't have that many morals to begin with. It was alleged that when Tiger Woods' wife caught him philandering, she refused to let him see their kids. So he got his own back by making some more. After Tiger was caught playing around with more than his golf clubs, his wife's lawyer drew up divorce papers ensuring the only thing he'd be allowed to keep was his name.

They televised a women's golf match and one player told her caddie "We're on TV. Give me a number three iron, my lipstick and a comb." I'm into playing golf now and after only two weeks I can almost hit the ball as far as I can throw the clubs. The golfer's wife was angry when she saw his bar bill. She said "If that's what it costs for drinks, from now on you can forget about getting another hole in one. I took up golf and after only one session with the club's professional, he gave me a list of the things I'd need. A driver, a putter and a compass. Golf clubs are now making drastic cutbacks. They used to supply golf carts to go around in. Now its pogo sticks. I tried playing golf. My first game was with Ronnie Corbett. Miniature golf of course.

My doctor told me to give up playing golf. He said at my age it's too dangerous being near an open hole. To be honest, I was never much good at golf. In fact, I was so bad; when I entered the course they lowered the flag to half-mast. With every stroke I dug up so much turf they made me an honorary archaeologist. Mind you, after a few games I developed a backswing that got me a big following. Mostly sailors. Every ball I struck landed in the sand. Even to this day I can't bear to look at an egg timer. I spent so much time in the bunker I was getting mail addressed to Hitler. Perhaps it's not surprising I don't get invited to tee any more.

I did try to improve my golf. I took lessons from a well-known professional. I'd mention his name, but he's paid me not to. His main advice was "If you keep your head down, it'll pay off." It did. I found a lot of lost golf balls. I once played a round with Ronnie Corbett. He had special dispensation because of his height. When he hit the ball he only had to shout "Three and a half!" He came onto the links wearing multi-coloured trousers. I thought they were multi-coloured trousers. Turned out he had varicose veins. His wife was playing too. She had nothing on but her underwear. She said Ronnie told her she had to go round in as little as possible.

When I play golf I always wear very cheap socks, in the hope I'll get a hole in one. Nowadays I'm happy if I hit the ball in one. I know one lady golfer who claims her average score is exactly the same as her age. So nobody knows what it is.

After their wedding the groom confessed he was golf mad. He said "You won't see me at weekends and most other days during the big golf tournaments." She said "I have a confession to make too. I'm a hooker." He thought for a moment, and then said "That's no problem. Just keep your head down and your left arm straight."

ADDITIONAL GAGS

- In golf what matters is not whether you win or lose, it's who's keeping the score.
- The new golfer complained when he got a hole in one. He said "Damn it, just when I needed the putting practice."
- He had a really lousy day. He didn't score well on the golf course and he scored even worse in the bedroom.
- London's roads would be great for golf. They're full of potholes.
- I find playing golf great exercise. Especially getting in and out of the golf cart.
- He cried off a game of golf because of a pressing engagement. His wife wanted him to stay home and do the ironing.
- Golf used to be a rich man's game. Now there are thousands of poor players.
- A golfer is a person who yells "Fore!" shoots six and marks down five.
- Lots of golfers lie about their score. I heard of one fellow who got a hole in one and put it down as a zero.
- My golf game is improving. Yesterday I hit the ball in one.
- My golf instructor keeps telling me to keep my head down and today I found out why. He doesn't want me to see him laughing.
- He doesn't want me to see him laughing. I was out on the links this morning and just missed getting a hole-in-one...by a mere five strokes.
- Life is like a game of golf. As soon as you get out of one hole you head straight for another.
- As one golfer said to another "If it was cricket, that score would have made you a hero."
- I bought the golf ball Tiger Woods got his first birdie with. Look, it's still got the feathers.

103

- The golfer bought a bottle of champagne to celebrate because he hit the ball in one.

HOLLYWOOD

Hollywood is the place where most films have a happy ending and most marriages don't. I've just heard of a Hollywood actor who's telling everyone he's been married five years. He's so proud. Well, it's his personal best. Another Hollywood actor promised he'd always be faithful to his wife, and the next one and the one after that. Before Liza Minnelli married ugly David Gest she had to have a blood test. She should have had an eye test. It was a fairy tale wedding. Beauty and the Beast. Their very short marriage was known as the other Six Day War.

Hollywood looked upon Tarzan as the first real swinger. At one time they considered Twiggy for the part of a pirate. Well, she already had a sunken chest. When the Hollywood actor got a starlet pregnant he promised to do the right thing. He sued the contraceptive company. Did you hear about the Hollywood star that came home and found his wife was taking drugs? He was furious. They were HIS drugs. It's the new fashion in Hollywood to have long engagements. It makes the marriage seem shorter. One Hollywood actress claims to have had ten husbands. Twelve if you count her own.

Hollywood's the place where girls look for husbands and husbands look for girls. Usually when a Hollywood couple break-up, she goes back to her mother and he goes back to his wife. Some ageing Hollywood actors are marrying girls so young, instead of a marriage licence they take out adoption papers. The wedding cake often outlasts the wedding. Hollywood marriages have been described as much "I do" about nothing. It's a fact that most Hollywood actresses don't bother to change their name when they get married. They find it easier to change their husbands.

One Hollywood starlet said of lecherous Alfred Hitchcock "It was always easy getting in to see him. The hard part was getting out again." They asked, if a Hollywood producer made a pass at her, what she would do. She said "Star in all of his pictures." Hitchcock always claimed to have been an overnight success, especially with the girls he was overnight with.

Some Hollywood actors are so egotistic they have a phone, an alarm clock and a doorbell which never ring. They just applaud. They never take a hot shower, because it clogs up the mirror. If they break a limb they insist the x-rays are directed by Steven Spielberg. They deny they're getting old. If they're over fifty they say they are just in their youth-part two.

The two greatest things to come out of Hollywood belong to Dolly Parton. When Dolly Parton took off her bra it was such a let-down. Almost to the ground.

ADDITIONAL GAGS

- The actor left it in his will that he was to be cremated and ten per cent of his ashes thrown in his agent's face.
- I heard of one famous Hollywood couple who took six whole weeks ironing out their divorce settlement. And now they've got that out of the way, they're getting married.
- The Hollywood star said being a celebrity you have to sacrifice your privacy. He said people follow you everywhere. "Even when I go to the lavatory they expect me to sign the toilet paper."
- Hollywood's the only place I know where they have wedding rings to rent.
- Where they settle the divorce arrangements before the wedding ceremony.
- The Hollywood actor trying to woo a young starlet, said "Come closer my dear. I want you to melt in my arms." She said "No thank you. I'm not that soft and you're not that hot."
- There's room for lots more men in Hollywood. Joan Collins hasn't married everyone yet.
- The aged Hollywood actor told his young wife he was sacking their chauffeur because "he nearly killed me twice." She said "Give him another chance."
- The Hollywood actor hated being single. He had no one to cheat on.
- Hollywood stars want their names in the gossip columns but not in the phone book.

- Because of heavy traffic in Hollywood I turned up late for a wedding and arrived just in time for the divorce.
- The famous Hollywood actor claimed he never forgets his humble beginnings. Once a year he goes back to the slums to visit him wife and kids.
- I met a Hollywood actress who could actually remember her first kiss, but not her last husband.
- In Hollywood a marriage is considered a good way to spend a weekend.
- It's the place where actors and actresses don't live happily forever after. They get married forever after.
- Hollywood actors have become so canny now; they even make their offspring sign a pre-natal agreement.
- The starlet told the lecherous Casting Director "When you said you were going to enter me I thought it was a part in a film.
- The producer told the aspiring young actress "Don't think of it as a casting couch. Think of it more as a launching pad.
- The starlet with loose morals. Known as the slipping beauty.
- The film producer made the young girl a star overnight. And all she had to do for it was stay overnight.
- Mickey Rooney had eight wives. He wasn't just divorcing, he was being recycled.

HOMOSEXUALITY

Graham Norton's going into pantomime in Snow White and the Seven Dwarfs. He'll be playing Sweetie. Norton says every woman he's ever been intimate with during his adult years has been....disappointed.

Every night I read my kids a fairy tale. Julian Clary's biography. All that glitters is not...necessarily what Julian Clary wears onstage. Openly gay characters are nothing new to TV. Why, way back in the 1960's we had a series where three men in high heels were living together. It was called Bonanza. I was watching Eddie Izzard. It was a case of seeing a T.V. on TV.

You can tell which Julian Clarey's dog is. It's the one that barks with a lisp. We're an eclectic group. Leroy here is our token Negro.

106

Moishe is our token Jew. Jock is our token Scotsman. And Julian and Sandy are here too.

HUSBANDS

The wife told the Marriage Counsellor "My husband's always lying. He even tells people he's the father of our kids. While his wife was in hospital the house felt empty, except for the sink which was full of dirty dishes.

INCOME TAX

There's a lot to be said for those Inland Revenue do-it-yourself tax forms. The same as I said when I hit my thumb with a hammer. I just paid my tax for last year. I didn't need to sign the tax form; the inspector knew it was mine. He recognised the tear stains. I have absolutely no objection to paying my taxes. In fact, I'm proud to pay my taxes. Mind you, I could be just as proud paying half the amount. Considering what the government's done with the money I gave it last year. I think paying that tax was my worst investment. Actually I've been lying on my tax return for years. I put myself down as head of the household.

I've got a neighbour who pays an absolute fortune in taxes He pays tax on his Rolls Royce, his yacht and his mansion in Spain. Mind you, it's his own fault for choosing to be a plumber in the first place. Now that Broadband has speeded up, it's made a huge difference to the Inland Revenue people. They can make the same mistakes in half the time. I went to my accountant and returned with a frown - my taxes are up and my earnings are down. I just read about the prostitute who owes a lot of back taxes. They're called back taxes because that's how she earned the money – on her back. My son asked me what to wear to a fancy dress party. I told him to put on rags and go as a tax payer'

You have to hand it to the Tax People, they'll get it anyway. I think it's a privilege paying taxes. Mind you, if they get any higher I might have to forgo the privilege. We should all be willing and happy to pay taxes to decrease the national debt, as long as it doesn't increase our own.

Making out your tax return is like do-it-yourself mugging. I used to do my tax return on line in the hope that if it's wrong they would blame the computer. The first year the Tax Man phoned to say there were only two things on my tax return he was willing to accept. My name and the date. He said he laughed harder at my return than he ever did at my jokes. He said I'd obviously taken a course in creative writing, but like Sherlock Holmes my deductions were elementary. So now I use an accountant who works for me like a stripper. He takes off just as much as the law allows.

ADDITIONAL GAGS

- My son became a successful accountant because I helped him with his homework. It proved useful because he now helps me with my tax evasion.
- As the Tax Inspector said to Sherlock Holmes "That's a brilliant deduction."
- Some big companies avoid paying income tax because they have their financial base abroad. All they keep in this country are their rich, fat executives.
- When the Tax Man came knocking at my door, I told him I gave at the office.
- The difference between taxes and taxis is with taxis you at least get a run for your money.
- A tax payer is a person who doesn't have to pass a Civil Service exam to work for the government.
- If you don't think it pays to be British, just wait till you see your income tax bill.
- They made April 5th Income Tax Day. That's four days after April Fool's Day proving a fool and his money are soon parted.
- We should all consider paying income tax as a good thing. It keeps us out of prison.
- As far as income tax is concerned I'm quite willing to pay as I go, if only I could catch up on where I've been.
- There are very few tax refunds in Britain today. The government only believes in giving money away to people in foreign countries.

- I know a man who keeps three different account ledgers. One for the tax people, one for himself and a different one for his partner.
- The Tax Inspector spent six months in hospital for heart surgery. Five months were spent looking for it.
- The tax people are so thorough. They even taxed the £1 I got from the Tooth Fairy when I was ten.
- As the chancer said to the Tax Inspector "That's for me to know and you to find out."
- As far as paying your tax is concerned, honesty is the best poverty.
- The tax inspector said to the client whose accounts he was investigating "Shall we go over this nice try by nice try?"
- The difference between an accountant and a Tax Inspector is that one does all he can for you and the Tax Inspector does all he can TO you.
- My bank account is where I keep the Treasury's money until income tax time.
- It's hard when your friends don't believe you make as much as you say and the Tax Man doesn't believe you make so little.
- His last tax return was so good it almost made the Booker Prize.
- I tried to take advantage of the Tax Inspector's good nature, but I found out he didn't have one.
- The Tax Inspector said to the client "You missed out one thing on your tax return. It should have started with 'Once upon a time…'"
- In this life just two things are certain. Death and tax increases.
- The prostitute owes £10,000 back taxes. Heaven knows what she owes on her front.
- The Tax Inspector thought my income tax return was nice. Or as he put it "Nice try."
- My Income Tax rebate came today. I used it in a parking meter.
- Income Tax inspector to worried client "Call; me a nostalgia nut if you like, Mr. Benson, but I'm going back over the last ten years."

INSULTS

He's so thin the hair on his chest makes him look like a discarded toothbrush.

He's so lazy he won't even exercise his discretion. He believes there's nothing wrong with a little hard work, as long as someone else does it. He was so ugly; it's the first wedding I've been to where the groom wore a veil. He always uses his head because he knows it's the little things that count. He isn't very popular. In fact, if it wasn't for his probation officer he'd have no visitors at all. But I'll say one thing for him, he has an even disposition. Miserable all the time.

Meeting this man proves you don't have to break a mirror to get bad luck. He doesn't have a job because of back trouble. He tries them for one day and doesn't go back. I won't say he's an egotist, but yesterday he went through the tunnel of love alone. He's not interested in literature. In fact, the longest thing he ever read was the inscription on a T-shirt. Most of his friends are wise. He's otherwise.

There are a lot of people who believe this man is a genius. They're the same people who believe in the Tooth Fairy and Santa Claus. I'm not saying he's unpopular, but his Dad spent the last ten years trying to scratch his name off his birth certificate. He went through his whole life without once begging or borrowing. If he wanted something he just stole it. He's so lazy he even has an electric nose picker.

He's so stupid that he recently went out of his mind and nobody noticed. He spent his last £5 note buying a wallet to keep it in. When they asked if he had a pen name he said "Yes. Papermate." People call him Bungalow because he has nothing upstairs. He thinks assets are little donkeys. If you gave him a penny for his thoughts you'd be entitled to change. He gets lost going up an escalator. If you gave him the key to the city he'd lock himself out. You've heard of the Great Wall. Well, he's the great wally.

He's such a bore that as guests go, I wish he would. When I phone him I pray I'll get the answering machine. The plants in his house all wear earplugs. His nickname is Piles because he's a pain in the bum. He's had a personality bypass. I think that chicken crossed the road just to avoid him.

He's so lazy, even when he plays miniature golf he uses a caddy. He only goes through a door if someone else pushes. When he leaves his house he finds out which way the wind is blowing and goes in that direction. He bought an exercise bike that only goes downhill.

He's such an egotist he signs autographs to himself. He joined the navy so the world could see him.

ADDITIONAL GAGS

- The only time I've seen my mother-in-law with a broom is when she's been for a ride on it.
- She has a horrible speech impediment. A big mouth!
- He's as insincere as someone sending a get well card to a hypochondriac.
- He's a great limbo dancer. Got lots of practice sliding under pay toilet doors.
- He's found his place in life. It's on a barstool in a pub.
- He thinks he's God's gift to women. But he's the kind of gift that always gets returned.
- He used to have a negative personality, but that's all changed. Now he has no personality at all.
- He's a lousy gardener. Other people talk to their plants. He apologises.
- She's footloose. And the rest of her can do with some tightening up too.
- She's such a sourpuss, when she puts cream on her face it curdles.
- He fulfilled his potential and reached a new peak in mediocrity.
- She advertised for a husband with a sense of humour. The way she looks, he's going to need one.
- I didn't mind discovering she had grey hairs. But on her chest?!!
- As a typist she's a fast learner. Within a week she was up to twenty five mistakes a minute.
- She's so miserable she starts every day with a smile, just to get it over with.
- Even when things go wrong he keeps a smile on his face, because he knows he can always find someone else to blame.
- I believe him when he says he's never taken orders from anyone. He's a travelling salesman.
- He often goes to Paris to look at the Mona Lisa. She's the only woman who still smiles at him.

- One time he was so short of money he was forced to take some out of his wallet.
- Even when he donated to the blood bank, it bounced.
- He has an unfortunate drinking habit. He never buys.
- She's had her face lifted so many times, they now take the easy route. They lower her body.
- He's completely lost his attention span. Now he can't even read the inscription on T-shirts.
- He's never taken a thing that didn't belong to him. At least, not while people were watching.
- He's a man of the world. Unfortunately not this world.
- He's got no personality at all. In fact, if it wasn't for his varicose veins he'd be completely colourless.
- She's got such a big mouth her teeth don't fit anymore…in the glass.
- The girl asked her blind date "Did anyone ever tell you you're attractive to women?" He said "No." So she asked where he got the idea from.
- A woman came up to me in the street and said "I hope you won't feel insulted, but are you Brad Ashton?"
- There are two things about him I can't stand. His face.
- He's the kind of fellow most people take an instant dislike to. It saves time.
- I love going to his performances. I wake up so refreshed.
- He always says if a thing's worth doing it's worth doing well. That's why he never does it.
- She's so dumb she lit a match to see if she'd put out the candle.
- He's so big headed his barber charges him double.
- As an author I think he's a writer worth watching. Certainly not reading.
- He says he's a self-made man. I can't help wondering who interrupted him.
- She has a winning smile. Unfortunately she has a losing face.
- He drinks to forget, and he'll keep drinking till he remembers what he's trying to forget.
- He only drinks to pass the time. Right now he's just passed 2025.

- He's the kind of man everyone wants to help out……as soon as he comes in.
- She's no slave to fashion. I've seen scarecrows better dressed.
- She was due to have a face lift, but when she heard the price, she let the whole thing drop.
- He's so stupid he once asked Gorbachev how long he'd had that birthmark.
- She takes after her father. They both have the same moustache.
- As a debutante she was so coarse she never came out. She was thrown out.
- He's not well educated. The only thing he's read in the last 20 years is am optician's eye chart.
- His crew-cut looks like it was done by a wrecking crew.
- She has a hairdo that should have been a hairdon't.
- She never stops talking. She wore out two pairs of lips before she was twenty.
- She says she's just turned forty, but it must have been a U-turn.
- The author said "I could not have written this book without the help of my wife, who went to live with her mother till it was finished.
- She's so narrow minded, her ears touch.
- He's really lazy. The good thing about him is he'll never wear out. He has no moving parts.
- She was born so ugly when they asked the doctor if it was a boy or a girl, he said "No!"
- She's so flat chested she has to staple her bra on.
- Other people have a welcome mat in front of their street door. She has hers in front of her bed.
- His motto is "Never put off till tomorrow what you can avoid altogether.
- He's a perfectionist. He not only takes pains, he gives them to everyone else.
- His mind used to wander. Now it's gone completely.
- He got lost in thought. To him that's unfamiliar territory.
- She's the kind of girl to whom an unnatural act seems natural.
- I won't say what she does for a living, but she's worn out four beds this year.

- He's such a lousy worker, when he went into hospital his Boss sent him a "Stay Sick" card.
- He doesn't trust anyone. He even makes his shadow walk in front of him.
- You should see him dance. He does a terrific tango, no matter what the band is playing.
- I'm now calling her names, but in India she's be considered sacred.
- He's such a failure. He went to the sperm bank and his sperm bounced.
- She's a real slut. Been on her back more than Michelangelo.
- He's one of the minority groups like Druids, Mexicans and Jonathan Ross fans.
- He's so gullible he even paid for a hot tip on the Grand National. They said the jockey knew a short cut.
- Her face has been lifted more times than Joan Collins' nightie
- I don't want to make a joke of his face. The plastic surgeon already did that. (Barry Manilow).
- He was so lazy he'd been dead for five days before his wife even noticed.
- He's so lazy he gets up at the crack of noon.
- He's such a wimp. They asked him what he's been doing since he got married. He said "What I'm told." She was at home pressing his shorts while he was out picketing. It was a case of ironing while the strike is hot.
- He's such a snob he'd never admit to having a common cold.
- She's so dumb I asked what the capital of England was and she said "E".
- He's so vain he won't even join a police line-up till he's had a big introduction.
- Other women have dishpan hands. She has a dishpan face.

LAW

One thing you can be sure of, where there's a will there's a lawyer making money. I hired a lawyer to make out my will. By the time I'd paid his fee all I had left was regret. I heard a criminal lawyer say to his client "I hope you DID rob that bank, otherwise you'd never be able to afford my fee." Who else but a lawyer would write 30-page documents and call them briefs?

The defence lawyer grabbed the woman from the stand and danced with her. The judge told him off for leading the witness. The man charged with putting his hand inside a woman's blouse claimed it wasn't his fault. He said he used to be a ventriloquist and couldn't break the habit. The barrister told his client "I'll point out to the jury you've been married four times. It'll help with your plea of insanity." The witness thought it wasn't perjury if she crossed her fingers.

I have to ask what's the point of the government making new laws when it can't even enforce the old ones. People are saying the law in Britain doesn't have teeth anymore. I agreed with them till a police dog bit me.

ADDITIONAL GAGS

- People think a wife can't testify against her husband, but that's not true. When my neighbour was charged with bigamy, three of his wives gave testimony.
- Did you hear about the alcoholic law student who failed to graduate because he couldn't pass the bar?
- Lawyers never prepare briefs that are.
- The wife accused of murder told the police "It was suicide. He criticised my cooking."
- To a lawyer the best things in life are fee.
- Lawyers charge so much I'm now convinced honesty is not only the best policy, it's a lot cheaper too.
- The rapist told the judge it's all because he gave up smoking. He didn't know what to do with his hands.
- One accused was asked how he pleaded. He said "Innocent till proven guilty your honour."
- As the Court Reporter said to the judge "Your Honour, I can't find the transcript. And that's the truth, the whole truth and nothing but the truth."
- Leniency amongst judges has gone too far. I heard of one man let off a conviction because he told the judge it would look bad on his CV.

- The motorist was told by the judge that he wouldn't be allowed to drive for two years because he was a danger to pedestrians. "But, your worship" said the motorist, "My living depends on it." "I know" said the judge, "So does theirs."
- As they say "It takes a thief to catch a thief" and a judge to let him off.
- With all these light sentences the quality of mercy is being strained too much.
- Old lawyers never die. They just lose their appeal.
- I signed one of those dodgy contracts where the first paragraph forbids you to read the rest of it.
- The witness said "I have sworn to tell the truth, the whole truth and nothing but the truth, but the court must understand that I am an estate agent."
- The defence lawyer complained to the judge that one of the jurors had fallen asleep. The judge said "Well you put him to sleep. You wake him up."
- The accused told the judge "The fact that the prosecution provided two witnesses saying they saw me take the car means nothing. I can provide a dozen witnesses who'll say they didn't see me take it."
- The judge asked the accused if he had a lawyer. He said "I don't need one, your honour. I'm going to tell the truth."
- The man managed to get off jury duty by claiming to be deaf in one ear. He said the law insists members of the jury hear both sides.
- As the receptionist said to her divorce lawyer boss "I told the couple your fee and that reconciled them."
- "Is it true," asked the judge "that while riding your motor bike over a period of just two weeks you knocked down six people?" "No, your honour" he replied. It was only five. I knocked one person down twice."
- The murderer's defence council said to the judge "My client pleads guilty and is willing to admit he made a boo-boo."
- The divorced husband died and in his will it said "to my ex-wife who hated my guts I leave my main intestine."
- The man in the dock said he didn't report his wife had her head in the gas oven because he thought she was just drying her hair.

- The widow said "I've had so much trouble settling my late husband's will, sometimes I wish he'd never died."

MARRIAGE

Jo Brand's husband had to give up working after their wedding. He did his back in carrying her over the threshold. Joan Collins was once quoted as saying that it's every woman's goal to get married. So far she's scored six goals. She's made a charm bracelet out of her old wedding rings.

Recycling is very popular in Show Business. Everyone marries someone that's been married before. Joan Collins walked down the aisle so many times she can now do it blindfolded. She's writing a book about her marriages. It goes Chap 1, Chap 2, and Chap 3, etc. She wanted a man for all seasons, so she married four men. Then she went on to marry another two because she couldn't break the habit. In the end, in her wedding ceremonies she stopped saying "I do" and changed it to "Don't I always?" She says her future weddings will be more environmentally friendly. She'll be using recycled confetti.

Mickey Rooney's been married nine times. He's a compulsive gambler. Zsa Zsa Gabor had eight husbands. She had a drip-dry wedding dress. To most women a wedding is an occasion. To her it was a hobby. Zsa Zsa's last husband serenaded her on their honeymoon singing "I can't give you anything but love." She found out it was true and dumped him the next day. Her vow has always been "For richer or forget it."

Paul McCartney who has £280,000,000 just married a woman with £200,000,000. It wasn't so much a marriage as a merger. The two witnesses at the ceremony were their accountants. Marriages are still breaking down at an alarming rate. It's mainly because girls who used to marry for money are now divorcing for it. It cost John Cleese £12,000,000 to divorce his third wife. A reporter asked him how "When you told your wife you were divorcing her, how did she take it?" He said "In cash!" All three of his marriages were in America. When asked what state he was in when he last got married, he said "Temporary insanity!" When gay comedian Michael Barrymore divorced his wife he consoled her with "Don't cry dear, you'll soon find another man. I did."

TV presenter Simon Cowell and his fiancée can't work out their wedding plans. Apparently she wants to get married and he doesn't. At Dawn French's marriage she was so fat it took three relatives to give her away. Nine times married Mickey Rooney says he treats each of his wives as a sequel. Hugh Heffner's announced he's marrying a woman half his age. At the ceremony she'll say "I do" and he'll say "I'll try."

Our marriage has lasted fifty years and we're not drifting apart. Falling apart, yes, but drifting, no. In March Valerie and I will have been married 53 years. She's told me not to buy her a card. She doesn't want to be reminded. I suppose I should buy her a present, but I've run out of ideas. What do you buy a woman who already has everything…and wants more? We didn't get married right away. We waited till we'd saved enough for a live-in cook. My wife and I have what's known as a Show Biz marriage. I produce and she directs. It seems the only magic left in our marriage is when she makes my money disappear.

When a banker got married this week, guests giving him cheques were asked to show two forms of identification. A female TV cook was recently jilted at the altar, but it wasn't a waste of time. She used the rice to make a pudding. A skinhead advertised for a new wife. He insisted she have the same name as his ex. He didn't want to waste his tattoos. Keeping a wife can be very expensive. That's why the wording in many marriage ceremonies is now changed to "Till debt us do part." There's a lot to be said about marriage, and I wish I had the nerve to say it. I shall never forget the day I got married. And God knows, I've tried.

Marriage, they say, is an institution that separates the men from the joys. When I married my wife she was a thing of beauty, but she's certainly not been a joy forever. They say it's a man's world and it probably was until Eve came along. In my house I'm the one who wears the trousers. Right under my apron.

We've been very happily married for ten years. Mind you, not all in a row. Till I got married I was a bachelor by choice. By choice of all the girls I proposed to. I see millionaire Bernie Ecclestone's daughter squandered a small fortune on her wedding. Seems the something borrowed was her Dad's credit card.

Did you hear about the lesbian looking for a third husband because her body rejected the first two? Did you hear about the much-married

Hollywood actress who buried ten husbands? And two of them were only napping. Did you hear about the Hollywood starlet who chose to marry a millionaire because she heard he was down to earth and owned so much of it? Did you hear about the Eskimo who backed out of his wedding because he got cold feet? Did you hear about the couple whose wedding cake had three figures on top, a bride, a groom and a judge. They had a trial marriage.

In San Francisco a Marriage Bureau was approached by a transsexual looking for a man just like the man she was before the operation. My neighbours are a perfectly matched couple. She's a zoologist and he's an animal. A frustrated wife was asked by the marriage counsellor "If as you say, your husband's always glued to the TV watching football, why don't you leave him?" She said "I did, twice, but he never even noticed." When the much-married actress was asked which man made her the happiest, she said "My lawyer."

Marriages are over so quickly these days. I know one man who gave his daughter away in the morning and had her back again by the afternoon. When the Agony Aunt was asked how long a couple should be engaged, she said "It depends what they're engaged in." Most women want to marry a man with spirit. It gives them something to break. The good thing about nude weddings is that you can easily see who the Best Man is.

It's true that many shaky marriages are held together by the children. Neither partner wants to end up with them. My spinster sister can be had for a song. The Wedding March. The main difference between an old fashioned wife and a modern one is the old fashioned one saves her wedding dress for sentimental reasons. The modern one saves hers for her next wedding. Newlyweds can always tell when the honeymoon is over. That's when he phones to say he'll be late for dinner and she's already left a note to say it's in the fridge.

A yawn is nature's way of allowing a married man to open his mouth. Lots of new wives think when they've swept down the aisle, that's the end of their sweeping. Anniversaries and birthdays complicate my life, because I'm an absent minded husband with a present-minded wife. Women used to cry to get things out of their system. Now it's to get things out of their husband.

My wife is so sure she'll get her own way, she writes her diary a week in advance. A wife can't make her husband do everything she wants him to. But she can certainly make him wish he had. In my local they won't even let you mention marriage during the Happy Hour. I learned today that they have trial marriages in Sweden. Mind you, I think all marriages are a trial. My wife ran out on me. I took her for a mate and she turned out to be a skipper. My wife used to be a raving beauty. She's no longer a beauty, but she's still raving.

My wife and I always do things together. Like argue and fight. I've never been able to get in the last word when we argue. I can't stay up that late. When we first argued she got hysterical. Now she gets historical. I still remember the first time we argued. I couldn't look at my wife for a week. After that, I could see a little out of one eye.

My dad used to tell me fairy stories which always ended with "They got married and lived happily ever after", which is why I knew they were fairy stories. It's no wonder the marriage licence is often referred to as a "noose-paper." I got married in 1961. It was the year I lost my good luck charm. When I bought her an engagement ring she wasn't happy about the diamond. She wanted one. We started off with a meaningful relationship. Now our relationship has no meaning at all. She promised to love, honour and obey. Right now I'd settle for any one of them. Our marriage is run like a business, with me as the silent partner. I quickly learned that the best way to avoid an argument with my wife is by saying two words, "Yes, dear."

There's only one thing that keeps me from being a happily married man....my wife. Mind you, she's a clever woman. When we have an argument she no longer says she's going home to mother. She says her mother's coming to us. She has that annoying habit of lowering her voice when she wants something and raising her voice when she doesn't get it. Some wives are always going on about their last husband. My wife goes on about her next. Statistics show that married men live longer. So if you're looking for a long life and a slow death, get married.

Since we bought a waterbed my wife and I have been drifting apart. I should have guessed our marriage was on the rocks when my wife suggested I move into another bedroom…in a different time zone. Originally my wife said she was marrying me for life. Now she wants to divorce me because I haven't any. I wanted to rekindle our flame of love, but she says it's too late; the pilot light's gone out. But for all that, I still think marriage is like being in the army. Everyone complains, but you'd be surprised at the number that re-enlist. So, if you're thinking of getting hitched, just remember that marriage isn't just a word, it's a sentence.

ADDITIONAL GAGS

- I was a witness at my cousin's wedding, but only at the ceremony. They told me they didn't want a witness for what they were doing afterwards.
- I heard one tall girl tell another about her new boyfriend "He's not too short for me when he stands on his wallet."
- When we got married I had a devil of a job putting the ring on. She wouldn't uncross her fingers.
- As the spinster said "Every time I find a man I think would make a good husband, he already is."
- Marriage is when Cupid attacks the man with an arrow then finishes him off with a battleaxe.
- In my house I never have to worry about bad breath. With my wife I never get the chance to open my mouth.
- I know it's a woman's privilege to change her mind, but she keeps trying to change mine.
- Some women take up law and become lawyers. Others lay down the law and become wives.
- I've got so much life insurance I can make my wife's day by just sneezing.
- I married my wife on an income of just £75 a week. Fortunately she earns more now.
- My wife's the really careful type. Since we've bought a water bed she sleeps in a life jacket.
- Some fellows marry poor girls to settle down. Others marry rich girls to settle up.
- I married my wife for her looks, but not the ones she gives me now.
- Very few things last as long as they used to. Marriages, for instance.
- A successful marriage is one where the wife's the treasurer and the husband the treasury.

- This woman stood up in court and said "I don't want alimony. I just want my husband to leave me as he found me. A widow."
- One couple I know now sleep in separate rooms, have dinner apart and go on holiday on their own. They're doing everything they can to keep their marriage together.
- I let my wife know who the boss right from the start is. Well, there was no use kidding myself.
- The recipe for a happy marriage is the husband being honest and telling his wife everything and the wife being generous and believing it.
- My wife wanted to go to Niagara Falls for our honeymoon, but we couldn't afford it. So we did the next best thing. I took her through a carwash with the top down.
- The trouble started when we both took up ski-ing. Our marriage has been going downhill ever since.
- The longer you're married the more you learn about your spouse. Till she decorated the lounge I didn't even know my wife was colour blind.
- The only thing my wife and I have in common is we were both married on the same day.
- It's not true that married men live longer than singles. It just seems longer.
- Home is where a married man can speak his mind. No one listens to him anyway.
- Bigamy is when you have one wife too many. Monogamy can be the same thing.
- Wives have an unfair advantage over husbands. If they can't get what they want by being smart, they get it by playing dumb.
- When a man steals your wife there's no better revenge than letting him keep her.
- Every person needs a spouse. You can't blame everything on the government.
- Marriage is like a cafeteria. You pick out something that looks good and pay for it down the line.
- Marriage gives a man the right to criticise his wife. But usually not the nerve.

- We have been married ten years and I can boast that sexually I've always satisfied my wife. Both times.
- The Marriage Guidance Counsellor solved my problem. He ran off with my wife.
- My obese neighbour has all the hallmarks of a married man. I mean, even his chin isn't single.
- You know you've made a bad marriage if you go in for wife swapping and have to throw in the maid.
- I remember our honeymoon well. That first night I was as nervous as a surgeon operating on a lawyer.
- Her father objected to paying for her wedding gown. He said he didn't mind giving her away, but he didn't see why she should be gift wrapped.
- I'm not saying who wears the trousers in our marriage, but my wife even gets cards from our kids of Father's Day.
- Too often the only people who listen to both sides of a domestic argument are the next door neighbours.
- For an anniversary present my wife left £5 in our joint account.
- Our 20th anniversary was china, so she bought me chop suey.
- My wife and I have a great bond between us, but she insisted we put it in her name.
- She said she married me because I had that certain something. Money.
- The only thing open about our marriage was my wife's big mouth.
- She gave me that come hither look. So I went hither and the rest is history.
- We always have a drink on our anniversary. She drinks to celebrate. I drink to forget.
- The only time my wife and I agreed on anything was when we both said "I do."
- She told me she had an insurance policy on her first husband. I said "What did you get out of it?" She said "My second husband."
- Some wives are more economical than others. I know of one wife who went without a honeymoon so her husband could save up for the alimony.
- For our anniversary my wife bought me a "do-it-yourself-and-then-get-someone-else-to-fix-it" kit.

123

- As the much-married Hollywood actress said to her new boyfriend "I like you and I want you to be my hobby."
- There's been a lot of talk about same sex marriages. All marriages are same sex. You get married and every night it's the same sex.
- She sent herself a sympathy card because her husband was retiring the next day.
- In America before a man gets married he has a blood test. It should be a sanity test.
- I told my fiancé about my rich uncle. Now she's my rich aunt.
- The wife caught her husband cheating for the fifth time this month, but he had a good excuse. He was trying to get into the Guinness Book of Records.
- This fellow went to the police station and said "I'd like to report my wife missing. Unfortunately, she isn't, but I'd certainly like to report it."
- They say opposites attract. That's why my wife and I get on so well. I write and she reads.
- A good marriage lasts forever. A bad marriage just seems to.
- Even at our wedding I knew I was in for trouble. When I said "I do," she said "Oh no, you don't!"
- My wife insisted on changing my marriage vows to make them more realistic. They included silence and poverty.
- I still remember the day I saw several flying saucers. It was when I forgot our wedding anniversary.
- Theirs was a marriage of convenience. He owned a car and she owned a parking space.
- In marriage, love means never having to say you're sorry. Unless, that is, you forgot to buy a card for your anniversary.
- A husband should never tell his wife he's not worthy of her. He should let it come as a surprise.
- Zsa Zsa Gabor never got married until she found Mr. Right-amount.
- Marriage is the most expensive way of discovering your faults.
- When we got married my wife asked if I wanted a large family. I said "Yes." So she sent for hers.
- Any man who thinks talk is cheap never said "I do."
- She sent her picture and details to a marriage bureau with a note saying "Please answer by return male."

- If you're looking for a woman to marry pick an Avon Lady. They're already trained to take orders.
- My wife and I had an open marriage, but right now it's closed for repairs.
- Marriage is like a violin. After the beautiful music has ended the strings are still attached.
- After paying for the wedding all the father had left to give away was the bride.
- He married his secretary. Now he's the one taking dictation.
- I didn't mind my wife's mother acting as matchmaker, but now she also wants to be referee.
- The couple got divorced even before the wedding pictures were developed. And they were Polaroids.
- Happiness is when a wife sees a double chin on her husband's old girlfriend.
- They told me I was to be Best Man at the wedding. Unfortunately they never gave me a chance to prove it.
- A man needs a wife because he has socks to mend, clothes to wash and buttons to sew on. And the wife knows where to get these things done.
- I belong to Bridegrooms Anonymous. Whenever I feel like getting married they send over a woman in a dirty, greasy apron and curlers in her hair, to burn the toast for me.
- For a woman to consider a man to be a good husband he has to keep his mouth shut and his chequebook open.
- The starlet decided she was certainly going to get married, as soon as Mr. Right-amount came along.
- Girls no longer want to marry go-getters. They want men that have already got.
- When we first got married we sat real close for love. Now it's so we can hear each other.
- As one gold-digger said to her friend "Yes, I know he's old enough to be my father, but he's still rich enough to be my husband."
- For the whole of our married life my wife never found out I had false teeth. It's her own fault; she never let me open my mouth.
- My wife and I have been successfully married for fifty years, because we have the same tastes. We both like to fight.

- Marriage is one of those few institutions that allow a man to do as his wife pleases.
- She refuses to re-marry her ex-husband because he was after his money.
- Marriage gives a man a new lease on life, at double the rent.
- A confirmed bachelor just wants one single thing in life. Himself.
- He married a rich girl because he wanted to give everything her money could buy.
- Only a woman without any sense marries a man without any money.
- Before we were married my wife said those three little words "I love you" After, the three words were "Let's eat out!"
- I'm a man of few words. I'm married.
- There were ten years in which I never spoke to my wife. I didn't want to interrupt.
- Nowadays there's a way of transferring money that's even faster than electronic banking, its called marriage.
- Any man she marries would have to have money, good looks and really bad eyesight.
- She goes on cruises on the GO NOW-PAY LATER plan, hoping she'll find a man who'll take care of the pay later part.
- Her figure is her fortune and she's invested it in all the right places.
- I married her because we got on so well. Then I realised we got on so well because we weren't married.
- I took her for better or for worse. I've yet to see the better part.
- She claims her husband's a bigamist because he's married to his job as well.
- At the ceremony the modern vicar said "I now pronounce you Man and Ms."
- My wife and I met through an internet dating programme. Yet another computer error.
- As the bride said to the groom at the wedding ceremony "I can't go through with it, but have a nice day."
- She married her husband for what he was....rich.
- Women used to save their wedding dress for their daughter, now it's for their next wedding.
- A bachelor is a man who'd rather not knot.

- When we were courting I was a go-getter. Now I'm sorry I got 'er.
- I went to a wedding where the bride was so ugly everyone kissed the groom.
- My sister's a bachelor girl. She's still looking for a bachelor.
- Marriage is choosing the right person with whom you can be incompatible.
- In marriage the biggest disappointment comes when the husband realises he's married a big spender and the wife realises she didn't.
- Helping with the dishes and housework makes for a happier marriage. Unfortunately my wife won't do it.
- If I married a girl like Dolly Parton the wedding vow would be "Love, honour and Oh Boy!"
- I know a married couple whose bathroom has two baths in it. That's so they can sing duets.
- Today an old fashioned couple isn't one that's stayed married. It's one that gets married.
- If a husband is foolish enough to put his wife on a pedestal he shouldn't be surprised if she looks down on him.
- My mother never cried at my wedding, but my father did. He paid the bill.
- I went on my honeymoon alone. My wife had already been to Spain.
- The Marriage Counsellor said he wanted to hear both sides of the story, so the wife told it to him.
- Before marriage we held hands. Now we hold arguments.
- Before we got married it was sweet nothings in the ear. Now it's sweet nothing in the bank.
- I'm against men attending childbirth. I had enough trauma being at my own.
- Isn't it funny how times change? In the old days men rode chargers. Now they marry them.
- Zsa Zsa Gabor was married nine times and gave all her husbands the same thing for their first anniversary. A set of luggage…packed.
- She's desperate to get married, but the only way she'll ever get rice in her hair is if a Chinaman throws up on her.
- They said marriage would be a pot of gold at the end of the rainbow, but it's turned out to be just a pile of bills at the end of the month.

- She married a man who had everything. Diabetes, asthma, hay fever, bronchitis.....
- The bridegroom turned up with his dog. He said I couldn't find a best man so I brought a best friendHe's very fussy about privacy. He even put a curtain around the birdbath.
- We had to queue up for four hours at Relate. The person ahead of us was a Sultan with six wives.It was easy to see what kind of a marriage they were going to have. At the ceremony she wore a wedding gown and he wore an apron.
- I borrowed the money to get married and the bank repossessed my wife.There are a lot of good things to be said about marriage, but I can't think of any.
- There's mutual love in our marriage. We'd both love to have a divorce.It's wasting time, like asking Joan Collins to have a wedding rehearsal.
- He hated his ex-wife so much he had a tattoo of her face on his backside.
- He promised her the moon and he kept his promise. During the wedding ceremony he mooned.
- He does all the housework. He's not so much a husband as an assistant wife.
- The three wise men were the ones that stayed single.
- He not only agreed to let her keep her job after they married, he insisted on it.
- I knew their marriage wasn't going to last when I saw the groom carrying the bride over the threshold OUT of the house.
- She married a TV actor and had to provide an autocue for him to say "I do."
- When I asked him how his marriage was, he said "I can't complain. My wife won't let me."
- If a man has more than one wife they call it bigamy. But if a woman has more than one husband that's called insanity.
- A man with two wives is called a bigamist. If he has three wives he's called a pigamist.
- She had a very quiet wedding. The groom didn't show up.
- He claims he was forced into marriage because he won a honeymoon for two on a TV quiz game.

- He says that since he got married he's never looked at another woman. He's completely discouraged.
- A girl tells her father "George has finally set the date. We're getting married the first Saturday after he wins the National Lottery."When he was single he slept with a gun under his pillow. Now he's married he sleeps with a battle-axe by his side.
- When we were married my wife and I had a lot of billing and cooing. Now we're divorced all I get from her is the billing.
- Love may be blind, but marriage is a real eye-opener.
- There's a local firm that employs travelling salesmen, but only if they're married. The Boss says it's because they're used to taking orders.
- There's only one thing I hope to get out of our marriage. Me!
- My wife and I made the same marriage vows. "Never again!"
- My wife refers to our marriage certificate as "proof of ownership."
- Marriage counselling usually comes too late. The marriage has already taken place.
- After I took her for a drive we had to get married. I ran out of petrol and she ran out of pills.
- We seldom agreed on anything because we both wanted different things. For instance, I wanted a new set of golf clubs and she wanted a divorce.
- People are now getting married older. They're waiting till they can afford the divorce."
- The Sultan was lonely. He had a row that morning and all his wives went back to their mothers.He took his wife to Relate. She complained it's the only place he's taken her in years.
- You can tell marriage is going out of style. So many bathrooms now have towels marked "His!" and "Ms."
- Our marriage is a power struggle. She has the power and I have to struggle.
- With the current economy situation, the only reason couples are getting married now is because they need the gifts.
- She says she wants to try a second honeymoon, but this time with someone else.
- A bachelor is a guy who's cheating some poor girl out of getting alimony.

- At our wedding when the toastmaster said "Now, a few words from the lucky man" the bride's father stood up to speak.
- We've been married fifteen years and not had a dull moment. Just fifteen dull years.
- Marriage is a case of give and take. For most of our marriage my wife's been giving me her lip and I've been taking it.
- My wife and I were happily married until she took some magazine test.

MEDICAL

I went to this private clinic and there was this terrible noise of moaning. And that was just in the cashier's office. I got fed up waiting for an NHS appointment for my hearing aid, so I went private. It cost me a fortune. I went in with only 40% of my hearing and came out with only 50% of my income.

My next door neighbour's great at spotting a bargain. Yesterday she came home from the maternity hospital with twins. They had one of those offers 'buy one and get one free'.

The private doctor charged me £1000 for three stitches. I'm glad he's not my tailor. He said being a doctor is a grand and glorious feeling. You give him a grand and he feels glorious. He's come up with a great idea for a stress test. He shows you the bill first. But he is exceedingly meticulous. Always washes his hands before touching your wallet. He doesn't make house calls. Except when he's playing Bingo. If you're sick for more than five days he sends you a Get Well Soon card. Seems the only ones making house calls now are burglars and Jehovah's Witnesses. But one GP did become famous for making house calls, Dr. Shipman. But most of his house calls were followed by Hearse calls.

To avoid a long wait I went private for my quadruple bypass. The surgeon said that after an operation like that, one ought to take a nice, relaxing holiday abroad. So after I paid, he took his wife for two weeks in Cyprus. But I must say that after that operation, I felt like I did when I was a kid. Penniless. Yes, in private medicine money still talks. It's what the doctor hears when he puts his stethoscope to your chest. My surgeon's a specialist in expensive sinus operations. He makes you pay through the nose. His Harley Street clinic has two recovery rooms. One for after the treatment and the other for after you've paid the bill. My advice it to watch out if the doctor admits you into his private clinic to drain something. It'll probably be your bank account.

I now use private medicine, or as they now call it – The National Wealth Service. When I didn't feel well I phoned the Harley Street doctor and told him my symptoms. I said "What can you make of that?" He said "£200 a visit." I once went to see him with chest pains. He phoned the next day to say he'd taken a second opinion and recommended an immediate operation. I asked "Who did you speak to, a heart specialist?" He said "No, my accountant." Doctors say they have to charge such a lot because of malpractice insurance. They get sued for all sorts of things. I heard of one doctor who got sued for sneezing during a vasectomy. When I think a doctor's overcharged me, I get my own back. I send an apple to all his patients.

Prescription charges are up again which means that every drop of medicine you take will definitely have a side effect. Poverty. It's now £7.40 for a prescription. That alone makes me feel ill. Last week I went to my doctor with an infection. He told me to take one pill whenever I could afford it.

The NHS is always in a financial crisis. Instead of first aid, what they need is fast aid. They say they're finding it difficult to meet expenses. I don't know why. I keep meeting them all the time. But there are big plans in the NHS to increase the capacity of our hospitals. They're building larger waiting rooms. I had a long wait in the hospital last week because the fellow ahead of me had been shot....in the Spanish civil war. The NHS is short of staff and it's no wonder. All the doctors and nurses are on TV.

There's too much form filling in the NHS. Before they can treat you they ask lots of questions like "When did you first notice you had amnesia?" "Are you taking anything for your kleptomania?" And "We're short of funds. Do you mind sharing a bedpan?"

50% of sex change patients are men. That is, till after the operation. Many men who have been castrated talk about it afterwards. But usually in a much higher voice.

I know why they say a woman's face is her fortune. It's because that's what it costs for all those facelifts. Hospital waiting lists are so long I was thinking of joining BUPA, but at my age the price alone will make me sick. To save my life they took my life's savings. From now on I'll avoid operations. I'll just settle for Get Well Soon cards.

The woman expected BUPA to pay for her divorce because she said her husband made her sick. Scientists say a man's lifespan is now to the age of 81, which is good news unless you happen to be 81 right now. I had a headache so I bought a bottle of aspirin with one of those complicated childproof lids. It worked well. By the time I got it open my headache had gone.

I know a man who's such a hypochondriac he even puts syrup on his pancakes. Cough syrup, that is. The doctor says I'm doing so well now he's taking me off tranquilisers and putting me on placebos. You can catch a cold just by kissing your girlfriend. Heaven knows what you have to do to get pneumonia.

The doctor told the fat golfer he was about four inches over par. A man I know became a brain surgeon. Took him ten years, He started as a chiropodist and worked his way up. My cousin's a big drinker. He's donated his body to science, but says he's preserving it in alcohol meanwhile. Doctors give you appointments weeks ahead and then ask "Why did you wait so long before coming to see me?"

A librarian was admitted to hospital for surgery. She got a Get Well Soon card from her associates which read "If they take anything out – make sure they sign for it." Medicine is so specialised these days. One patient I know had to switch doctors when his athlete's foot moved from his right foot to his left. If you have to go into hospital these days you can get MRSA, C.Diff or even swine flu. In fact, anything but a bed.

I find Cameron's speeches are like hospital food. Hard to swallow. I may be wrong, but I have a theory that hospital food is deliberately bad to make the medicine taste good. Figures don't lie, except where breast implants are involved. A lot of female stars admit to having the odd nip and tuck. Over the years Joan Rivers has had so much plastic surgery, no two parts of her body are the same age.

After staring at the optician's eye chart the woman patient told him "I don't know what it says, but your spelling's atrocious. Statistics show the most common cause of tooth loss among men is being caught in bed by her husband. If I ever need a heart transplant I hope I get the Chancellor's. It's hardly been used.

Doctors are so worried about being sued for malpractice that when my son was born and the doctor slapped him, he claimed it was in self defence. I remember when we had our first baby, my wife screamed so loud it woke half the street. And that was just during the conception. The NHS is still closing more and more hospital wards. Soon being an outpatient will mean you're left on a stretcher in the car park.

A patient this week had his operation delayed because he was such a baby. He wouldn't be put to sleep without his teddy bear. A woman recently knocked down by a car was approached by a man offering aid. She said "Are you a doctor going to help me recover?" He said "No, I'm a lawyer going to make you a fortune." Probably the same lawyer who said "Lying will get you into trouble, unless you do it properly."

My doctor says I look like a million dollars…after the tax has been deducted. I told the doctor I had a migraine. He said it's all in my head. The doctor said all my ailments are hereditary. So I told him to send his bill to my father. The doctor said I should get more fresh air. Trouble is he never told me where to find it. It's depressing how many reports there are of patients dying from C.Diff and M.R.S.A. I've managed to live this long because I have a hospital plan. I plan never to go near a hospital.

My doctor says I'm a bit overweight, I should stay away from anything sugary. I'm not allowed biscuits, cakes or reading the poems on Valentine's cards. Carrots are supposed to improve your eyesight. I had so many I couldn't sleep. I kept seeing through my eyelids. The doctor says even in my state of health I can still chase women, as long as I don't catch any.

Scientists have said that mobile phones CAN cause cancer. Their best advice is, if you have a mobile phone; don't waste money buying long life batteries. The couple were made for each other. He's a throat specialist and she's a pain in the neck. He didn't take any medicine. The label said "Keep this bottle tightly closed." So he did.

The hospital nurse told the patient "Yes, that IS a beautiful butterfly, Mr. Benson, but it's not the kind of specimen the doctor asked for."

ADDITIONAL GAGS

- A psychiatrist is one who stops you worrying about your problem and starts you worrying about his bill
- The psychiatrist dug up things I thought I'd never remember and then gave me a bill I don't think I'll never forget.
- The psychiatrist said I have a split personality. So I only paid half his fee and told him to get the rest from the other fellow.
- Old psychiatrists never die. They just shrink away.
- Psychiatrists are called shrinks because that's what they do to your bank account.
- One psychiatrist charged fat Jo Brand £250 for a session. £50 was for the treatment and the other £200 was for repairs to the couch.
- I told my psychiatrist I have suicidal tendencies. So he made me pay in advance.
- She told her psychiatrist she's been making long distance phone calls to herself. He said "Isn't that rather expensive?" She said "No. I always reverse the charges."
- It's easy to spy a psychiatrist at a nudist camp. He's the one listening instead of looking.
- The psychiatrist said "I'm going to help you wipe out the past." The patient said "Good. I hope that includes the money I owe you."
- Two old friends meet in the psychiatrist's waiting room. One asks the other "Are you coming or going?" He said "If I knew that, I wouldn't be here."
- He worked as a psychiatrist for British Telecom. He had to cure some nasty hang-ups.
- When his new client laid on the couch the psychiatrist asked "Now tell me, what's bothering you?" The man said "Your fee, for a start."
- You go to a psychiatrist if you're slightly cracked and finish when you're completely broke.
- The NHS is really cutting back. I asked for something for my dry hair. They gave me an umbrella with a hole in it.
- The people running the National Health Service urgently need donors. Brain donors for themselves.

- The National Health Service has come up with an idea to speed up operations. They're installing sewing machines in hospital theatres.
- If you have the NHS and your health you've got everything. But if you have private medicine, sooner or later the doctor gets everything.
- National Health doctors are behind with their work. They still have piles to deal with.
- The hospital visitor told the patient "We took up a collection at the office and used it down at the pub drinking to your health."
- When the driver crashed his car into a tree they immediately phoned for medical assistance. Within minutes the doctor turned up. He was a tree surgeon.
- When two elderly women doctors met they showed each other X-Rays of their grandchildren.
- An obstetrician makes his money on the stork market.
- I went to this private hospital and they were very generous. They gave me a free tranquilizer before handing me their bill. The private patient said to the doctor "I've just discovered you cured me with a placebo. So I'm paying you with Monopoly money.
- I don't mind paying the doctor £100 for a suppository, but I do object to him telling me where to stick it.
- I'm paying my son's fees for medical school. He says when he's a fully fledged doctor he'll pay me back the equivalent in free treatments. Gosh, I hope I never get that ill.
- I went to a private clinic and shed 60 pounds right away. And that was just the first payment.
- My wife complained to the Medical Council because she is a paid up member of BUPA but she still had to pay to see Dr. Doolittle. My son was a surgeon in a private clinic, but he had to give it up. He developed an allergy to money.
- It was a very delicate operation in which the surgeon separated me from my life savings.
- The doctor took my pulse and refused to give it back to me till I'd paid his bill.
- My doctor recommended a consultant. In other words he was calling in an accomplice.

- The average private patient goes to their doctor five times a year. And the average private doctor goes on a cruise six times a year.
- My doctor says if I don't pay his bill soon he's going to put my appendix back in.
- The doctor is quite happy to pump Botox into my face as long as I'm willing to pump money into his bank account.
- When I was born the first thing the doctor did was slap me to make me cry. Then he gave my father the bill and made him cry.
- My next door neighbour is a man who really enjoys bad health. He's a private doctor.
- The private clinic specialises in double open-heart surgery. They open your heart and wallet at the same time.
- It seems what four out of five doctors recommend these days is another doctor.
- One private doctor I know charges £100 a visit. More if you're ill.
- When I was a kid my father was a Harley Street doctor. The Headmaster never asked him to come to the school because he charged £100 a visit.
- I paid the Consultant £1,000 and all he gave me was an aspirin and a ticket to Lourdes.
- When the private doctor presented her with twins she thought she had to make a choice.
- My private doctor is a nose, throat and wallet man.
- If laughter really is the best medicine, you can be sure doctors would have found a way to charge for it.
- The surgeon at the private clinic told his patient "We'll release you when we think you're better and not a hundred and fifty pounds sooner.
- A private doctor is a man who acts like a humanitarian and charges like a plumber.
- The doctor refused to make a house call, but he did agree to send a Get Well card.
- My doctor hasn't made a house call in years. Even his wife is out looking for him.
- You know you have a drinking problem when you wake up in the morning and find your clothes on the floor, with you still in them.
- I learned to knit the hard way. I went skiing.

- The best thing you can do when you're run down is take the car's licence number. I told my doctor I had déjà vu. He asked if I've ever had it before.
- Anyone who's fit enough to jog doesn't really need to.
- You can tell how healthy a man is by what he takes two at a time. Stairs or pills.
- I went up in a chairlift and was terrified. Heights frighten me. I even get vertigo when I raise my eyebrows.
- I asked my doctor what I should do about the continual ringing in my ear. He said "Get an unlisted number."
- I told the doctor I wanted a second opinion. He said "Come back tomorrow and I'll give you one."
- The poor chap died of a broken leg, but it was entirely his wife's fault. The doctor she called was a Vet.
- The doctor told the patient the problem was all in his head. And it was right. Turned out to be a brain tumour.
- As one doctor was heard to say "Patients who claim to have whiplash are a pain in the neck. (Patients who claim to have piles are a pain in the arse.)
- The doctor cured my bad back. He told me to stop making love in the rear seat of my mini.
- I think my pacemaker needs some adjustment. Every time I sneeze my garage door flies open.
- The doctor told the sexy lady "I think you may be a nymphomaniac. I'll have to do some tests to make sure."
- The doctor suggested a mustard plaster, but it didn't work, even though I had a terrible job swallowing it.
- As the sexy girl patient said when she undressed for the doctor "I thought it was me that's supposed to say Ahhhh!"
- The doctor was embarrassed when he was seen making a house call. It was a house of ill repute.
- Hospitals are known for their accidents, many of which occur in the kitchen ovens.
- My GP knows people waiting to see him get impatient. So his waiting room's full of books to pass the time. I read through one yesterday. War and Peace.

- My flu got so bad the doctor called in Dynarod to unclog my sinuses.
- My flu was so bad the doctor had to stand on a chair to read my temperature.
- My nose ran so much I entered it for the London marathon.
- If my muscles were as hard as my arteries, I'd be in great shape.
- In today's polluted atmosphere, if a doctor tells you to take a deep breath, it can be fatal.
- When I came to, I knew I was in hospital because the clock on the wall had one hand in a sling.
- The Dental Association is holding an exhibition at Olympia tomorrow. At 9.30 the doors open wide.
- The most common reason people give for not going to work is an allergy. Usually they're allergic to working.
- I had so many painkilling injections it now hurts when I sit down.
- So many doctors, nurses and medicines are imported; I'm surprised you can still get a local anaesthetic.
- My brother spent seven years at medical school……being studied.
- They say exercise kills germs, but they don't tell you how you get the little buggers to exercise.
- My doctor says I should play eighteen holes a day. So I went out and bought a harmonica.
- I'm so unlucky. I'm the only man I know who's ever got a paper cut from a Get Well Soon card.
- As far as I'm concerned it's alright for a dentist to feel down in the mouth as long as it's not my mouth he's feeling down in.
- My sister goes to a very friendly psychiatrist. He gets on the couch with her.
- I know a doctor so poor he has his stethoscope on a party line.
- This week one doctor was struck off for having an affair with a patient. He was a vet.
- I told my doctor I was losing my memory and asked what to do. He said I should pay him in advance.
- I've just paid my dentist bill. Now there's a cavity in my bank account.
- I yelled at the dentist "You've pulled the wrong tooth. That wasn't the one!" He said "Don't worry. I'm getting around to it."

- What keeps my doctor away isn't an apple. It's all those cruises he can afford to go on.
- Dentists put your money where your mouth is.
- My dentist never works on Wednesdays because he has some cavities to fill on the golf course.
- The poor patient promised to pay the doctor's fee out of his malpractice award.
- The new private doctor said he was thankful for small fevers.
- They say an apple a day keeps the doctor away and an orange a day keeps the nurse away. Well I eat garlic and keep everyone away.
- My dentist said he charges £100 for a cavity. So I gave him £100 and he gave me a cavity.
- I told my doctor every bone in my body hurts. He said "Just be thankful you're not a herring."
- What four out of five doctors mostly recommend is another doctor.
- She went to her dentist about her wisdom tooth. She wanted one put in.
- Plastic surgery can do everything with a nose but keep it out of other people's business.
- With all the recent malpractice suits, now if you want to get the doctor's opinion on something you have to do it through his lawyer.
- Always check what car is parked right outside your doctor's surgery. If it's a Rolls Royce you can guess who's going to pay for it.
- An apple a day keeps the doctor away. So will not paying his bill.
- I'm worried. The prescription my doctor just gave me turned out to be for an airline ticket to Lourdes.
- When my dentist spotted the £50 note in my wallet he said "I'm afraid that'll have to come out."
- My publisher insists I have an MRI scan. He wants to see if I have another book inside me.
- My doctor's just bought himself a new Rolls Royce so he has something NOT to make house calls in.
- An obstetrician is a doctor who makes money on the stork market.
- The screaming in the dentist's surgery had nothing to do with the drilling. It was a patient reading his bill.
- The private doctor told his patient "I'm going to be honest with you. What you have you can't afford.

- A wonder drug is one you wonder if you can afford.
- I swallowed a ten pence coin and the doctor made me cough up twenty quid.
- My psychiatrist's into group therapy. Instead of a couch he has bunk beds.
- I'm doing so well my Psychiatrist lets me sit up on the couch.
- I've finally managed to quit smoking. Had to. I can no longer afford the petrol for my lighter.
- My pregnant sister works for Pizza Parlour. She's having her baby delivered by motor cycle.
- I told the dentist my teeth were yellow and asked what I should do. He said "Wear a brown suit so it'll match."
- The doctor examined me and then sent me for a second opinion....to an undertaker.
- When I was in hospital I used to wait all morning for the doctor to finish his round. He was out playing golf.
- Sitting Bull got haemorrhoids. Now he's Standing Bull.
- The doctor said my recovery was a miracle. So I sent his fee to the church instead.
- The doctor made every one say "Ah", except the priest who had to say "Ah-men."
- After his operation the patient complained to the Medical Council because he heard the surgeon use a four letter word "Oops!"
- As the surgeon said when he entered the operating theatre "May I cut in?"
- The hospital gave me a local anaesthetic. It was made right here in London.
- One thing you can't buy is good health. Especially if you've got no money.
- I went to the doctor with a bad cough. He gave me medicine. Now I have a good cough.
- The psychiatrist told the henpecked husband his wife's mind had completely gone. He said "I'm not surprised. She's been giving me a piece of it for years."
- My son went into the medical profession. He was determined to start at the bottom, so he became a proctologist.

- Twenty years ago I had double pneumonia. Today I couldn't even afford single pneumonia.
- When I was in hospital I waited four hours for the doctor to finish his round. He was out on the golf course.
- I hate to think what the Six Million Dollar Man would cost today.
- The doctor said my recovery was a miracle. So I sent his fee to the church instead of him.
- His transplant worked alright, but the insurance company rejected the bill.
- I finally got my head together and now my body's falling apart.
- One man went to see a psychiatrist because he thought he was a goat, and he'd been that way since he was a kid.
- As the doctor said to the patient "If I've told you once I've told you a thousand times I do not treat amnesia cases."
- I told the private doctor he charges more than our plumber. He said next time I get a sore throat I should go see the plumber.
- The private doctor said "Stick out your wallet and say 'Ah'.
- My son went into the medical profession. He was determined to start at the bottom, so he became a proctologist.
- The witch doctor was dressed up in a mask, feathers and shark's teeth. I think the only thing he could cure was hiccups.
- I went out on the slopes on skis and came back on crutches.
- I broke my arm and my leg and I think it's all because I first broke a chain letter.
- The boss told his new employee. "Here we have a sick leave policy. If you get sick, you leave."
- My neighbour's a tree surgeon. Lost five thousand patients in that last storm.
- His transplant worked alright, but the insurance company rejected the bill.
- The only people who should look down in the mouth are dentists.
- Doctor asks everyone to say "Ah" except the priest who has to say "Ah-men."
- After his operation the patient complained about the four letter word the surgeon used. The word was "Oops!"
- The doctor told me to relax, but it didn't worked. Relaxing just makes me tense.

- The hospital sent the patient home early because they needed his parking space.
- The patient heard the surgeon ask for "Glue". He never could thread a needle.
- I was in such a rundown state the doctor didn't know whether to conduct an examination or an autopsy.
- He's afraid of heights. He's the only one I know that goes to the psychiatrist and lays on the floor.
- As one cancer research scientist said to another "Do you realise that if we DO find a cure we'll be out of a job?"
- The doctor said he needed exercise and should try parallel bars. So each day he walked from one bar to another.
- I used to be a schizophrenic, but I'm happy to say we're OK now.
- The doctor recommended Prozac for my depression and a divorce for what's causing it.
- As the plumber said to the doctor "Sure, I'll be glad to look at your sink, Dr. Benson. Bring it in two weeks from Thursday at 2.45."
- The doctor told his male patient there was good and bad news. The bad news was that he sneezed while performing the vasectomy. The good news was he can now sing as a soprano.
- According to the doctors on Holby City what I have is sciatica, but now I'm going to watch Casualty for a second opinion.
- The only people who should look down in the mouth are dentists.
- He trained to be a tree surgeon, but had to give it up. He faints at the sight of sap.
- The doctor said it's all in my imagination. So I told him I'll imagine sending him a cheque.
- He's so terrified of dentists he has to have a valium just to make an appointment.
- The private doctor asked his patient "When's it most painful?" He said "When I open my wallet."
- She's such a hypochondriac she even complains of side effects after taking placebos.
- He claims to be in the medical profession, but all he does is send out Get Well Soon cards.

- The doctor said in my condition I need a bypass. He said I should bypass the fridge, then cake tin and the sweetshop. He said I should think more sweatshop than sweetshop.
- Man says to salesgirl in stationery shop "Do you have any Get Well cards I can send to the NHS?"
- The doctor wasn't sure of his tuberculosis diagnosis. TB or not TB.
- I gave the doctor a post-dated cheque and he gave me a post dated prescription.
- The doctor's receptionist said "Yes, the doctor will see you. Which year did you want the appointment for?"There's a sign outside the doctor's surgery "OPEN 24 HOURS". Beneath it in tiny print it says "PER WEEK."
- Husband queries medical diagnosis "How can she have legionnaire's disease, they don't accept women?"
- Man with bandaged head says "I told that barber the little off the top I wanted was hair, not skin."
- When I was in hospital I got a "Better Get Well Soon" card from the finance company.
- As one surgeon in the operating theatre said to another "Whose turn is it to open?"
- I paid my medical bill. Now my wallet has been declared legally dead.
- I couldn't afford to have my face lifted, so I had my body lowered instead. (Ronnie Corbett).
- As Doctor Jekyll said to Mr. Hyde "You must stop taking a bath in the hair restorer."
- This fellow went to a psychiatrist because; when his phone rang he was afraid to answer it. Now after six months of treatment he answers the phone whether it rings or not.
- The doctor's wife divorced him for making house calls. She found out they were to his mistress.
- He studied women's bust surgery. He went to the school of hard knockers.
- His wife's given him the will to live. She wants a divorce.
- The desperate patient said to the surgeon "Give it to me straight, Doc, How long have I got?" The surgeon looked at his watch and said. "Well, right now it's nine thirty….."

143

- I went to see my doctor this morning. He's given me six months. Not to live, to wait for an appointment.
- Psychiatrist says to empty couch "I assure you it's nothing to worry about. Lots of people talk to themselves."
- I hadn't realised how bad the cutbacks were in the NHS till the nurse times my pulse with an egg timer.
- I went to my doctor with a rash on my back. He gave me something for it. A backscratcher.
- As the private doctor said to the man "You're very, very sick. I like that in a patient."
- The cheap acupuncture clinic. For £10 they just make you sit on a hedgehog.
- The doctor told me I'd have to give up wine, women and song. At least till I've paid his bill.
- The doctor examined the woman patient and said "Either you've got a big bust or a bad case of mumps."
- The psychiatrist told the depressed convict he should try to develop some outside interests.
- I have to take a pill every four hours or as often as I can get the cap off.
- As the nurse said when she brought the drip machine over to the patient "Do you want your dessert now or later?"
- The way prescription charges are rising I don't know how much longer I can afford to be a hypochondriac.
- This woman took one of her triplets to the doctor. She said actually all three are ill, but she just brought one as a sample.
- It turns out I'm allergic to allergy tests.

MISCELLANEOUS

- What the opinion poll proved is that 75% of people are not interested in other people's opinions.
- It takes a big man to admit his mistakes. But it takes a stupid one to make them in the first place.
- When telling jokes always try your best. If that doesn't work, try someone else's best.

- It's so frustrating when you've very carefully wrapped a gift, and realise you forgot to take the price tag off.
- I can never understand why tube trains are fitted with unbreakable glass yet have a sign which says "In case of emergency break glass."
- My parents didn't want me to be spoiled. So they kept me in the fridge.
- We British are known for our apathy, but who cares.
- It's like an astronomer refusing to work nights. Or a priest refusing to work Sundays.
- Last night I lay in bed looking up at the stars, and I thought to myself "Where the heck's the ceiling gone?"
- I always wanted to be a procrastinator, but I never got round to it.
- It may be true that all power corrupts, but you can't light the gas stove without it.
- I rang the Gas Company the other day. I had to press so many buttons, by the time I got through to the right department I forgot what I was phoning for.
- Just as I thought I was winning the rat race along came faster rats.
- I bought all this junk because I had an itchy nose. I scratched it at an auction.
- The decorator uses a big, wide roller when he's paid by the job. But a much smaller one when he's paid by the hour.
- We had a terrible day yesterday. There was a power cut and we had to brush our teeth by hand.
- I lived in a place so small the mice were hunchbacked.
- They were made for each other. He's a proctologist and she's a pain in the butt.
- He's so tall he has to climb a ladder to comb his hair.
- The long bearded old man asked at the Lost Property Office "Anyone handed in my razor yet?"
- You can always turn a negative into a positive. Like if you've got insomnia get a job as a night-watchman.

MONEY

When I told my wife off for spending more than I earn she said she's just following the government's example. I won't say she overspends, but yesterday her credit card refused to come out of the ATM machine. It was seeking asylum. My wife and I operate a system of checks and balances. She writes out the cheques and I try to balance them. Thanks to my wife's spending we can count what's left of our savings in a round figure. Nought. I have to face up to the fact that the only way my wife and I can make both ends meet is by sleeping back to back. They say money talks. In our case it just says goodbye.

It used to only be cars that went from 0 to 60 in ten seconds. Now it's supermarket prices. Nowadays if you want a Swiss Roll you need an account in that country to pay for it. In order to carry a bag of groceries out of the supermarket you now need to carry two bags of money in. Money isn't going as far in the supermarket as it used to. Now I visit one aisle and it's gone. If you get in the line that says "Five Items or Less" at least one of them has to be a £50 note.

Food manufacturers were faced with the choice of raising their prices or reducing the amount in the packet. So most of them chose both. I still remember when "high rise" made you think of a block of flats, instead of prices at the supermarket. When a supermarket advertises an item at 20% less, you can be sure it'll be the size rather than the price. My wife used to cry a lot in the cinema. Now she cries even more in the supermarket.

I don't know how much I've got left in my bank. I haven't rattled it lately. I really think banks are being ruthless with their charges. Back in the days of Bonnie & Clyde it was people robbing banks. Now it's the other way around. Sometimes I think all the banks care about is money. With banks collapsing all around the world you never know if the bank you're with will be saved. We're like the turkey hoping whoever wins him in the Christmas raffle will turn out to be a vegetarian. It used to be money that folded, now its banks. Banks say they are doing so badly now, if you put money in, you can claim it as a charity donation. The government can easily solve the cash flow problem. It just has to get the bankers to spend their bonuses.

Our government bailed out the banks with a no-interest loan. It's called no interest because the banks have no interest in ever paying it back. Small businesses are still struggling to get bank loans. These days the only thing banks will give you credit for is trying. If your business is failing it's no use asking the bank for a loan. They won't lift a finger. They lift two. Some banks are determined not to hand out money unless you've already got some. It's like a restaurant refusing to serve you food unless you bring your own. I asked my bank manager how I stand to get a mortgage. He said "You don't stand. You get on your knees." I'm not sure who actually owns the banks these days. So now when I go in to cash a cheque, I ask THEM for identification. Today you can't even trust a trust fund.

House prices have been pushed up higher than Dolly Parton's frontage. Forty years ago I paid £20,000 for my house. Today all you could get for that money are the builder's blueprints. I asked one estate agent if he had a house for about £200,000. He said "We may have. What's the size of your dog?" He said "First tell me what you can afford. We'll have a good laugh and start from there." Statistics show that 67% of Britons say this is the perfect time to buy a house. It's the same 67% who are trying to sell theirs.

I'm not proud of it, but I made my first obscene phone call today. It was to my financial advisor. He assured me my savings would be flush. He didn't say "right down the drain." If I invested in all his hot tips I'd wind up with more attachments than a vacuum cleaner. Only time I get more for my money these days is when I put a coin in a weighing machine. In today's financial climate some companies have to scrap their usual retirement plan and replace it by taking up a collection among the staff. The company's new Health Plan is to give all their employees an apple a day. Why is it that anything you see going for a song changes its tune the moment you want to buy it?

A man complained because his profit-sharing business went broke because the government was taking too big a share of the profit. Just think, someone somewhere at this moment is working out a way to pass their increased costs onto us. When my kids were young they thought money grew on trees. Then they grew up and learned the truth. It comes out of ATM machines. I'm sure, if my ship ever did come in the tax people would be there to unload it. These days a person is lucky if they reach the end of the month before reaching the end of their money.

Phone calls are costing me a small fortune because my wife's on the phone to her mother every day. Next time I'll marry a woman whose mother has an 0800 number. It seems all's fair in love and war, but not banking. I hate inflation. Why, only five years ago I could live beyond my means for half what it costs today. Rising costs are the price we're paying for reckless thriving.

Invest your money in taxes. They're the only thing guaranteed to go up. Nowadays the only two that can live as cheaply as one is a schizophrenic. Everyone these days seems to be in debt. Even the Lone Ranger says "I owe Silver!"

Greece too has its internal problems. I heard of one Greek father who told his son "Alexis, it's about time you learned the value of a Euro. It has none." Talk about being overpaid. I heard of a top bank executive that was actually given a boat. Turned out to be a mistake. He was supposed to be given the boot. The way things are going they'll soon be selling bank shares in the pound shop.

Our lives are run by the professionals. My doctor tells me what I have to live with and my accountant tells me what I have to live without. My brother's careful with money. He's always looking for a bargain. He once went into a pound shop and asked if they sell cars. Seems that old saying what goes up must come down, doesn't apply to electricity bills. I didn't even need to turn the electricity on. The bill alone gave me a shock. Thanks to the rise in prices I now have a wallet with an echo.

They say money can't buy happiness. Today it can hardly buy anything. My local supermarket's put up a notice "No one under £21 admitted." The government has failed to stop inflation. Apples now cost so much it's cheaper to see the doctor. Just a year ago £30 would feed a family of five. Now it couldn't even feed a child of five.

Everything's going up these days. Prices…taxes…women's hemlines. Thanks to inflation, it's only ten years since we used to dream of earning the wages we can't live on today. I saw a man this week shamelessly flaunting his wealth. He bought a first class stamp. House prices have gone down again. Soon the only thing likely to be left up in most houses is the toilet seat.

The money situation has got so precarious our currency notes will soon say "We promise to OWE the bearer...." I saw an advert for a credit card. It said "Imagine the problems you'd have if you lost all your travellers cheques overseas. Especially if your wife thought you were in Newcastle on business." This isn't so much a fiscal year as a farcical one. For the past week my wife and I have been having candlelit dinners. We're not romantic, just saving on electricity.

A Chancellor of the Exchequer is someone who neither sows nor reaps. He just rakes it in. The cost of living today is ridiculous. And with rising taxes your take home pay is hardly enough to get you there. London's West End now has 120 new pay toilets where your 30p allows you ten minutes. They're very popular with foreign visitors who've set up home in them. Well, at £1.80 an hour it's a lot cheaper than a hotel. Its true money can't buy happiness. It's too busy buying foreign footballers.

The recession's so bad magicians are eating their rabbits. The government says two can live on £10,000 a year. It doesn't say two what. Those of us saving for a rainy day are now facing the monsoon season. Cameron promises us a higher standard of living. The question is will we be able to afford it? It isn't easy for us old folk to survive on a state pension. Mind you, there are millions who think our state pension is great. Trouble is they all live in the Third World.

The Chancellor says our economy is starting to look up. From the position it's in it's the only way it can look. The High Street shops are doing so badly they have to give incentives for people to buy. IKEA for instance has a new offer. Every time you buy its flat pack furniture they give you a rocket scientist to help assemble it.

It's over forty years since decimal currency was introduced in Britain and we still have one worth 10p. It's the £1 coin. The bad news this week is that our British currency is losing its value. The good news is that most of it's in other countries hands anyway. The only way a university graduate can make money now is by getting a job in the Royal Mint.

My brother's financial situation got so bad he sold his house. Heaven knows what his landlord will say. It's easy to tell that mortgage rates have risen because I saw an old street beggar with a sign "Home

Owner- Please Help." I got something this week I thought was an offer to buy my house. Turned out to be just the phone bill.

The only laugh we've had in our house since we got a mobile phone is when we look at the small print in the contract. Everybody's trying to get money from you. Today I phoned the speaking clock and it tried to sell me a watch. Right now my finances are in such a bad state people think I've been advised by The Treasury. I had no idea how expensive things were till I lost my credit card and had to pay in cash. I see one leading department store is continuing to offer "Quality and low prices." It's up to the customers to decide which they want.

Waiters are complaining their tips are down. People used to leave big tips under the plate. Now they're so small they leave them under the toothpick. It's got so bad Soho prostitutes are having a two-for-one sale. If anyone believes our economy has turned the corner, they must be round the bend. Cameron has come up with a great plan to reduce our electric bills. He keeps us in the dark.

When it comes to money I'm afraid we're all in the same boat. The Titanic. My advice to people short of money is to borrow off a pessimist. At least they don't expect to get it back.

There are dozens of books on the market about how to make money. What's needed is one on how to make a living.

ADDITIONAL GAGS

- We can't afford a holiday this year. In fact, we can hardly afford to stay home.
- Mervyn King and I have both managed banks, but mine was just a piggy.
- I was at home last night watching a good comedy. No, it wasn't on TV; it was my wife trying to balance her budget.
- An old man came up to me at the cash machine and ask me to check his balance. So I pushed him over.
- He's so dodgy, every time he plays Monopoly and buys a hotel; he puts it in his wife's name.
- I received my electric bill in the post this week. I tell you, it beats taking prune juice.

- I'm looking to buy a house because I want a roof over my head. I just hope I can afford the walls and floor as well.
- Cost me a fortune to ring the speaking clock. Just my luck, the operator had a stutter.
- The Bank of England's vault is impregnable. Nobody can get into it. It was invented by the same chap who thought up those child-proof tops for Aspirin bottles.
- The government's taking away our pensions and many of our benefits. Soon the only thing the government will leave us with is our opinion of the government.
- Jimmy Carr goes to Switzerland every winter. Not to ski. He just visits his bank account.
- The saying "Take the money and run" doesn't apply to bank executives. They take the money and stay…to take lots more.
- Many big firms are now downsizing their workforce, just so they can upsize their profits.
- Money today is like a New Year's resolution. Easy to make but hard to keep.
- He's so rich he has his cheques returned marked "Insufficient banks."
- Prices have risen so fast my local supermarket's now put its food in the Luxury Goods department.
- The best way to economise is to take all the money you've saved for a rainy day and move to the desert.
- The economy has got so bad that many shops with a "GOING OUT OF BUSINESS" sign now actually are going out of business. Nowadays the only time my wife and I make ends meet is when we're in bed.
- So far the worst part of 2014 is realising that 2013 prices were a bargain.
- As the bank manager said when he got his huge bonus "Debt, where is thy sting?"
- Americans have the Super Bowl. We have the super bill.
- My local supermarket has a carry-out service. I took one look at the bill and they carried me out.
- As far as finances are concerned. If I retired this very minute I'd have enough to live on for the rest of…today.

- Our £5, £10, £20 & £50 notes have a silver streak down the middle. They ought to make it elastic to make the money stretch further.
- I hear Dustin Hoffman's now giving advice on shares. You can learn about the Footsie from Tootsie.
- I taught my son the value of the £1. Now he wants his allowance in Chinese yen.
- Taxes, fuel and food prices are all costing more. I guess that's the price we pay for living in a free society.
- It's not easy supporting the government and a family at the same time.
- The governor of the Bank of England forecasts a change in the economy in four years time. That's assuming we still have an economy in four years time.
- On the subject of inflation I'd like to put in my six pennyworths.
- In my house hot air escapes through the roof. What also went through the roof was my heating bill.
- We're all living longer now. We have to, to pay off our debts.
- I went to the bank to raise a loan but all I raised was a laugh.
- West End stores are so anxious to please people they are even gift-wrapping items for shoplifters.
- Now that bank executives are having their bonuses cut, there's doom at the top.
- My business has got so bad I no longer need to lie on my tax return.
- My brother has a big following. He's followed by the tax man, the gas man, the man from the electricity company and four other debt collectors.
- We used to worry that our cheques would bounce. Now we worry that the bank will.
- My local betting shop has a sprig of mistletoe over the door so you can kiss your money goodbye.
- Last year my doctor put me on a diet. This year my accountant did.
- There's always something to be thankful for. For instance, if you can't pay your bills be thankful you're not a creditor.
- Old bank accounts never die. They just lose their balance.
- There was a chap with so many credit cards he was bankrupt for six months before he found out.

- My local library won't lend to accountants because they have a reputation for keeping books.
- A job applicant told the prospective employer that the last firm he worked for paid for longer holidays, longer coffee and lunch breaks and all travel expenses and gave a generous bonus too. The employer naturally asked "Why did you leave?" He said "I had to. They went bankrupt."
- Just recently my financial advisor has been hit by the recession…and quite a few of his clients.
- We used to go to Las Vegas and come back broke. Now it's the supermarket.
- I took out a fire and theft home insurance policy. I've just found out I'm only covered if the house is robbed while on fire.
- There's a new book out called "How to Be Happy with No Money." Trouble is, if you've got no money you can't buy the book.
- The estate agent said for £50,000 he could find me accommodation in a spot overlooking Hyde Park. Turned out be a bench.
- Harrods summer sale now has a half hour interval to carry out the wounded.
- We used to have creeping inflation. Lately it's moved up to jogging.
- With ever rising prices my supermarket's become a supermark-up.
- What do you give a man who has everything? Answer: A calendar to remind him when the payments are due.
- My wife has a black belt in summer sales.
- My financial advisor is a golf nut. Yesterday he phoned to tell me he just broke 80. I said "I know. I'm one of them."
- I can remember back to when a £1 a plate meant a new set of teeth.
- I told my bank manager I'd come to see him about a loan. He said "Good. How much can you lend us?"
- Not only is it more blessed to give than receive, but it's also more expensive.
- My accountant is available 24 hours a day. All I have to do is make a call and the warden brings him straight to the phone.brings him straight to the phone.
- He's so wealthy he could pay off the national debt on his credit card.
- They say money isn't everything and that's true. But it comes in handy if you've lost your credit card.

- I may not be master of my own home, but I'm certainly the paymaster.
- My mother was so money-conscious when I was born she gave me a bill for nine months rent.
- The trouble with our household budget is that while I'm earning money five days a week my wife's out spending it seven days a week.
- He told his new girlfriend he was a coin collector. Turned out he was a beggar in the street.
- Anyone who thinks this country has free speech has never paid their mobile phone bill.
- Woolworths used to corner the market. Now they haven't even got a market on the corner.
- Money may not bring happiness, but what it does bring is relatives and beggars.
- There's one bank so exclusive it doesn't have a security camera. It hires a portrait painter.
- I've just read the small print in my insurance policy. Apparently if you lose a leg, they don't give you money. They just help you look for it.
- I hear Richard Branson is so rich he used £20 notes on the floor to train his puppies.
- I finally found a house in my price range, but there's a hold up. The dog won't move out.
- Perhaps money can't buy happiness, but at todays prices who could afford it anyway?
- Britain is still the land of opportunity. Where else can you earn enough to owe so much?
- I'm saving my money because one day it might be worth something.
- There are lots of books on the market telling us how to manage when we retire. What we need is one that tells us how to manage TILL we retire.
- My stockbroker tried to jump out of the window, but the warder stopped him.
- The sound investments of today are the tax losses of tomorrow.
- The new credit card slogan is "Due unto Others."

- Most fathers agree that if it wasn't for their wife and kids they wouldn't be what they are today…broke.
- For Father's Day kids should give their Dad cash. It's probably the one thing he hasn't got.
- Bankruptcy is a fate worse than debt.
- Because of my investments in the stock market I now sleep like a baby. I get up every two hours and cry.
- I'm going through a really bad time. Even my bills come postage due.
- Using a credit card is a convenient way of spending money you wish you had.
- He who pinches pennies isn't likely to get the opportunity to pinch pretty women.
- In the financial world money talks. Today it's mostly Chinese.
- Nowadays there's a way of transferring money that's even quicker than electronic banking. It's called marriage.
- I've never regretted getting married. It gives me a legitimate reason for getting drunk.
- Now he's come into money he's like a TV set – better off.
- By the time we get our furniture paid for we'll be able to see it as antique.
- Credit cards have made buying much easier, but paying much harder.
- My house provides little security for my family and a lot of security for the bank that provided the mortgage.
- Money can't buy everything, which is why we have credit cards.
- The Chancellor of the Exchequer can use more many than he has…..and usually does.
- Some of us are living on borrowed time. But even more of us on borrowed money.
- I lost a small fortune in the market today. My shopping bag broke open.
- Bill collectors must be really popular. People keep asking them to call again.
- I've read dozens of books on how to make a million. What I want now is one how to make a living.
- I've just read something that will last forever. My mortgage contract.
- All I have ready for a rainy day is a newly washed car.

- I wouldn't mind helping to reduce the national debt if it would increase my own.
- Things were so bad we had to take out a second loan to pay the interest on the first loan.
- We should all follow Noah's example. He kept afloat when the rest of the world was in liquidation.
- We had to take out a second loan to pay the interest on the first loan.
- I wouldn't mind helping to reduce the national debt if it wouldn't increase my own.
- With the current high cost of buying a house, newlyweds can now be as much in love as they are in debt.
- Every union member knows that time is money. Especially overtime.
- They call it a living wage. But who can live on it these days?
- Supermarkets are a great place to shop. They allow shoppers to go broke in one store.
- The answer to the question "What's up?" is "Everything!"
- It's not hard keeping up with the neighbours. What's hard is keeping up with the payments.
- A person living beyond their means should learn to act their wage.
- You don't have to be a miser to hold on to your money, you need to be a magician.
- A £1 nowadays goes a lot further than it used to. That's because you have to carry it around for ages trying to find something it will buy.
- The newspapers used to tell us what's going on. Now it's what's going up.
- I still remember the days when charity was a virtue instead of an industry.
- If money could buy happiness you can be sure the government would put a tax on it.
- The bank calls it instant credit, but actually its instant debt.
- As Britons we owe a lot to our forefathers, but now we owe a lot to everybody.
- A poor businessman is one who goes bankrupt and doesn't make a penny on it.
- With his country's huge national debt we'll have to settle up before we can settle down.
- I made a killing in the stock market today. I shot my broker.

- I've got so many debt collectors they come to my house in a car pool.
- The bank loan now stands at just 5%. That's not the rate; it's the amount of people who get one.
- The most obscene thing I ever read was…the figures on the gas meter under the stairs.
- Looks like every banker in town is having a bonus of contention.
- I see the value of the £ has gone up everywhere but here in the UK.
- My rich uncle made a mistake in his will. He left his money to medical science and his body to me.
- As an investor I used to be bullish. Then I was bearish. Now I'm brokish.
- The estate agent told the client "Yes, there was a house in your price range, but it burnt down in the Great Fire of London.
- They consolidated all their debts so now they have just one bill they can't pay.
- This week I had an out-of-money experience.
- These days I have to be satisfied with just being merry. I can't afford to eat and drink.
- My bank manager said he'd lend me all the money I want under certain meteorological circumstances, like when hell freezes over.
- During the January sales Harrods changes the sign on their doors from "Push" to "Shove."
- She'll never invest because of her hearing problem. Every time her Broker says "Buy", she puts the phone down.
- My bank manager said he'd lend me all the money I want under certain meteorological circumstances, like when hell freezes over.
- I'd give up work tomorrow if it wasn't for all the people in the community to whom I owe so much. My doctor, my plumber, my dentist, my gardener…..
- Change is inevitable, except when you're trying to get it out of vending machines.
- The two trays on the debtor's desk were labelled "IN" and "IN DEEPER" To put money in the stock market these days you don't need to be a bull or a bear. Just an ass.
- The estate agent was studying a file with last year's house prices. He loves nostalgia.

157

- You can't buy happiness, but if you've got enough money you can rent it.
- My bank's logo is a black horse. It should be a skull and crossbones.
- He has that feeling of not belonging. His house doesn't belong to him. His car doesn't belong to him. His TV set…..
- They say you have to spend money to make money. I've done all the spending, when do I start making?
- They say you have to spend money to make money. I've done all the spending, when do I start making?
- My bank's logo is a black horse. It should be a skull and crossbones.
- I went to one of those financial companies that consolidate your debts, so you wind up with just one you can't pay.
- He has that feeling of not belonging. His house doesn't belong to him. His car doesn't belong to him. His TV set…..
- Our financial position is fluid and it's flowing straight down the drain.
- She's got a piggy bank and the pig's suffering from malnutrition.
- Thanks to the new pension arrangements my piggy bank's suffering from malnutrition.
- I was happy when the Boss said that from now on I'll find twice as much money in my pay packet until he said it's because they're paying every fortnight instead of weekly.
- I'm part of the silent majority. I'd rather be part of the solvent minority.
- The only reason most couples have a candle-lit dinner these days is because they can't afford the electric bill.
- You have to spend money to make money. Ask any counterfeiter.
- The reason we're broke now in our old age is that my husband's peak earning years coincided with my peak spending years. She's got a piggy bank and the pig's suffering from malnutrition.
- I hired the Hubble telescope to read the small print in my insurance policy.
- Young kid says to his mother "The sink's blocked. It must be all that money Dad says has been going down the drain."

MUSIC

Today the Rock 'n' Roll bands play music so loud, if Van Gogh was still alive he'd cut off BOTH ears. All that loud music is dulling the senses of our youngsters. I was listening to some rock 'n' roll yesterday. I had no choice. It was blaring out from the car in front of me. I was actually playing my stereo at 2 am in the morning when the little old lady in the flat next door started shouting "What's the matter with you? Turn the bass up!".

The Rolling Stones are back and charging less for their concerts because they no longer have transport costs. They're all old enough for bus passes. Have you noticed that you never see Mick Jagger at a Blood Bank? There's a good reason. You can't get blood out of a stone.

I hear that after forty years Gerry and the Pacemakers is regrouping, but with a changed name. From now on it'll be Gerry WITH The Pacemakers. And at Boy George's last concert he had a big crowd trouble. He couldn't get one. Previously he hired bouncers to keep people out. Now it's to keep people in.

To me, opera is a group of people singing what they should be saying. And a jazz band is just five men on stage playing a different tune. I've found out why, in ballet, they do all that prancing about on tip toe. It's to avoid waking the audience.

Bruce Forsyth says he's never been a fan of chamber music. Like Bruce's hairpiece it goes over his head. I think it's odd that some folk singers who have a mansion, a yacht and a Rolls Royce, should still be singing protest songs. The Brit Awards are now considering a new category. Bands who mime best to their records.

ADDITIONAL GAGS

- As Elton John said to David Furnish when they first met "Hi Honey, I'm homo."
- Lately I find Lady Gaga obnoxious. She used to turn my head. Now it's my stomach.

- The drummer couldn't stay at the party for long. He said he had to beat and run.
- The poor fellow had a displaced organ. He swallowed his harmonica.
- I don't know what's strangest, the music my kids listen to or the fact that they like it.
- They have music for everything these days. Even music to murder by. You feel you want to murder the guy playing it.
- Whoever decided to call it "Garage Music" should have put a "b" in the middle. That stuff leaves a bad taste in my ears.
- Cliff Richard's been singing for so long, when he started there were only six records in the Top Ten.
- Dolly Parton's records keep popping out of their jackets.
- Perhaps music does make the world go round, but whiskey does it quicker.
- As the bad musician said "For those of you who love Beethoven, I will now play Mozart."
- A Diva is a singer who not only takes great pains she causes everyone else to have pains too.
- I don't mind facing the music. What I can't stand is listening to it.
- That singer hasn't had a hit since Joan Collins was a virgin.
- Rock bands don't dress smartly as they used to. They now look like they'd cut more throats than records.
- Lots of singers have initials after their names. For instance Barry Manillow p.s. The p.s. stands for plastic surgery.
- It took Brahms six months to put his lullaby on paper. Every time he played it he fell asleep.
- His voice is flatter than Sammy Davis's nose.
- He calls himself a musician, but all he's ever played is second fiddle to his wife.
- He plays by ear and listens the same way.
- The woman diner told the naked violinist "No. My request was to pay In the Mood."
- A wife's favourite tune is one she can make her husband dance to.
- They're charging £75 for a ticket to seer Barry Manilow. I guess you can call that paying through the nose.

- He was such a bad singer they suggested he donate his vocal chords to silence.
- Bing Crosby turned up for a gig with his head bandaged. It was all those pennies from heaven.
- As the music producer said to the young songwriter "It should be a hit. I can't understand a word of it."
- I've always loved Andrew Lloyd Webber's songs, even before he composed them.

OBESITY

I'm overweight because, like plants I gravitate to the light. In my case it's the light that comes on when I open the fridge. It's a well known fact that too many square meals can make you round. You wind up going the weigh of all flesh, with your two hips in different post codes. When you have your portrait done, instead of a paintbrush they use a roller. A recent survey showed the average male weighs 12 stone and the average female 10 stone 12 pounds. The disturbing thing is that the survey was taken of school kids.

You know you're overweight when you dream of being as thin as Eamonn Holmes. When the local scouts use your old mac as a marquee When you sit on a rowing machine and it sinks. When you get in the bath and there isn't room for the water. When you get a hangover just sitting on a chair. When the police offer you a job as a road block. When an insurance agent tries to sell you a group policy. When your doctor says you need more exercise and suggests every day you do a five mile waddle. If it takes two tailors to go round measuring your waist and after an hour they haven't yet met. If you're a bride who needs a crane to carry you over the threshold. If you're a woman at the opera and no-one will leave till you've sung. If you're a woman with a two piece bathing suit who needs a ten piece one to cover her body.

The doctor said my body was fit as a fiddle. Unfortunately also shaped like one. He said if I continued to eat and drink I'd never be merry. The first thing I had to give up is reading. Especially menus. He said I should lose three and a half stone. God, that's enough to start another Ronnie Corbett. I got so weight conscious I even plucked my eyebrows before I stepped on the scales.

Actually I'm now near enough to the weight I should be and I freely admit I could not have done it without my wife's help. Her cooking ruined my appetite. Another important factor in my weight loss was those little childproof bottles of diet pills. I was burning up 500 calories just trying to get the caps off.

I've got into the habit of having a salad each day to keep my weight down. Followed by a banana split to keep my spirits up. Weightwatchers is a school for overweight people. Dawn French went there on a scholarship. They told her she could eat anything she likes as long as it doesn't contain calories. They said she must stop putting sugar in her coffee. So now she puts it directly into her mouth.

My trouble is I gain weight when I should be gaining height. My wife admits it's all her fault. She put me on a pedestal instead of a diet. She thought exercise would help so she got me one of those exercise bikes which she said she picked up for a ridiculous figure.....mine. I was feeling depressed. And it didn't help when friends kept telling me to keep my chins up. I first tried losing weight with Slim Fast which I quite liked. It went so well with my Jaffa cakes. But I soon I came to realise that the only slim thing about my figure was the chance of keeping it that way.

One former Hollywood starlet who once appeared in a Playboy centrefold has now got so fat Playboy can appear in her centrefold. Child obesity is a big problem now. I blame that on the parents. Some mothers are deliberately feeding their kids sweets to ruin their appetite. In Britain today we seem to have a serious overweight problem, even among monks who have had to change the wording of their daily prayer. They've dropped the bit about giving us this day our daily bread. It's now our every-other-day bread. Sadler's Wells is leading the fight against obesity. Its next production will be Plum Fairy without the sugar.

They've just invented a non-fattening doughnut. It's just a hole with nothing round it. Getting fat doesn't depend on the minutes you spend at the table. It's the seconds. Most people go on a diet because of hindsight. I'm not saying my wife's fat, but Weight Watchers makes her pay double. Weight Watchers now gives clients an award for shedding pounds. It's called the No-belly prize. My wife went on an acupuncture diet. She didn't eat any differently. She just lost weight through leakage.

She claims it's not her fault; she was born with big bones. As a baby she was so big three rival firms competed for the talcum powder concession.

Someone told my wife that black makes you look slim, so now she hangs around with Lennie Henry a lot. She spends a good deal of time in perfume shops hoping they'll come up with one that makes you smell thinner.

They say three's a crowd. Well, my wife doesn't need the other two, she's a crowd by herself. I'm not saying she overeats, but last Christmas she ate a whole turkey in one sitting. And that was for hors d'oeuvres. She's in denial insisting she's not getting fatter. She says the rest of the world is shrinking. She tells people she's down to one drumstick a day. What she doesn't say is it's from an ostrich.

When we first married my wife used to throw her weight around. Now it's all she can do to drag it around. She weighs herself often and actually thinks she's fooling the machine by lifting one foot in the air. Her sister's even fatter than her. When she got married, it took three relatives to give her away. She can never understand why she isn't losing weight, because she does a lot of jogging. She jogs to the pizza hut, the cake shop and the ice cream parlour. You'd never believe it now, but once she was so thin, she got a run in her stocking and her leg fell out. She was that thin our dog kept trying to bury her in the garden.

ADDITIONAL GAGS

- Old soldiers are supposed to fade away. My old sergeant weighed 29 stone. He did the opposite.
- I'm expanding so fast my wife no longer puts me on a pedestal. She puts me on a weighing machine instead.
- Americans have always eaten too much. They blame it on their constitution which says they have the right to life, liberty and the pursuit of heaviness.
- A fat guy I know always stands on his head when he weighs himself. He has to. If he stands the right way up he can't see the numbers.
- My wife not only kept her schoolgirl figure, she doubled it.
- She's so fat she's living beyond her seams.

- He was worried about being fat so he went to a hypnotist, and it worked. Now he doesn't know he's fat.
- Nothing stretches slacks like snacks.
- My wife would look more spic if she had less span.
- Obesity in Britain is really widespread.
- I never have trouble watching my weight. It's out there where I can see it.
- Some people go to a great length to cut out their great width.
- Cruise food may not be expensive, but it's certainly expansive.
- She's on a very strict diet. The only time anything goes in her mouth is when she's forced to eat her own words, swallow her pride or when she puts her foot in it.
- The diet doctor said if I continue to eat and drink I won't be merry.
- The dietician gave my wife pills to take on an empty stomach. Trouble is, she eats so much her stomach's never empty.
- The diet doctor said my wife's in a stable condition. What he actually said was she's built like a horse.
- My fat wife let it all hang out. Now she's trying to tuck some of it back in again.
- Wearing a mini skirt is fine, as long as the woman has a mini figure to match it.
- He wears a plaid waistcoat so he can keep a cheque on his stomach.
- The best way to lose weight is to read the ingredients on the labels.
- The fat, ugly woman was raped, but the police can't establish a motive.
- When they weighed my wife at Weightwatchers she said "Don't forget, that includes the mascara and lipstick I'm wearing."
- She got on the scales like she was about to step on a landmine.
- The doctor said he needed exercise and should try parallel bars. So each day he walked from one bar to another.
- She's so fat when she asked her hubby to put sun lotion on her back he used a roller.
- She's so fat because she's a glutton. The only woman I know who can go from zero to the fridge in just 2.5 seconds,
- She watches her diet when she's travelling. Last year she managed to do France on only 1500 calories a day.

- My wife says she's not fat, she's Rubenesque
- I've got a weight problem. My wife's on a reducing diet.
- I was surprised to see ice cream on the diet sheet. But it does say you have to use a chopstick instead of a spoon.
- She's the kind of person who likes to have her cake and eat yours too. I used to be afraid of height. Now that I'm on diet, it's width.
- Talk about fat, her figure was 105-90-105 even before we turned metric.
- I belong to a diet group called Appetites Anonymous. If you feel hungry, you phone up and they send someone round to eat your meal for you.
- As the husband sang to his wife with the fluctuating weight "I'll be loving you all weighs."
- As the dietician said to her overweight client "I'd like you more if I saw less of you."
- My overweight wife bought a new dress which fits her like a glove. It sticks out in five places. She looks like twenty pounds of potatoes in a ten pound sack.
- She's on a seafood diet. When she sees food she eats it.
- A fat lady was sitting next to me on the bus when two old ladies got on. She turned to me and said "Why don't you get up and let one of those old ladies sit down?" I said "Why don't you get up and let them both sit down?"
- She's so fat every time she skips it registers eight on the Richter scale.
- The doctor said I'm gaining too much weight and need to exercise more. He suggested every day I take a five mile waddle.
- John Prescott is complaining about the shape this country's in. That's only fair. For years this country's complained about the shape John Prescott's in.
- They showed a 40 stone man on TV this week. He said when he was born he weighed seven pounds six ounces. Now he eats more than that for breakfast. I'm not surprised he's so fat. Other people count sheep at night. He counts cream cakes. He's so fat police keep coming up and asking him to disperse.
- The actress was so desperate to lose weight she not only had her eyebrows plucked, she

- even had the dentist remove her fillings.
- You know you're overweight when you get a hangover by just sitting on a chair.
- My neighbour's so fat he works for the police. They use him as a roadblock.
- She's a big hearted girl, with hips and stomach to match.
- I'm not saying she's fat. But she's two inches taller than her husband just lying down.
- She's so fat when her husband puts his arm around her he has to make two trips.
- She's put on so much weight, once a month they pull her through the Mersey Tunnel to clean it.
- I won't say she's fat but she's just been offered a job modelling beer barrels.
- He's so fat when he has his shoes shined he has to take the shoeshine boy's word for it.
- She's gained so much weight when she entered for the Miss England contest she had to represent three counties.
- She's so fat she has to take a shower in a car wash.
- My wife says she's determined to lose 140 lbs. Me.
- I won't say my ex-girlfriend's got fat, but now for a bikini she wears a hammock and two beach umbrellas.
- She's twice the woman she used to be and she's got the bathroom scales to prove it.
- Nobody loves a fat man or a flat woman.
- Dawn French has a side-line now. It's sponsored slimming. She's charging a fiver for every pound she loses. She's got enough weight to make her richer than Bill Gates.
- She had a forty inch bust, but the boys weren't interested because she had a forty inch waist as well.
- She's a fat girl. Eats sugar and spice and everything twice.
- One murderer was so fat the judge sentenced him to the electric couch.
- I won't say she's fat, but when she sunbathes on the beach you can hear the fat sizzling.
- She's so fat when she sits down it takes five minutes for her loose skin to settle.

- As a baby she was so fat she was born on the sixth, seventh and eighth of May.
- I took her to a Chinese restaurant. She ate so fast her chopsticks caught fire.
- The only way she could touch her toes is if she let her fingernails grow.
- The doctor gave the fat women a calorie counter. She ate it.

POLITICS

MP's are still in the news for cheating on their expenses. I heard of one MP who whenever he drinks to someone's health, sends the bill to the NHS. There's been a complaint about a leading Labour MPs mishandling affairs. The complaint came from the father of the miss he was handling. That's not just confined to one party. One lecherous Tory MP was thrown out by a prostitute because his opposite number insisted on equal time.

MPs have a special reason to appreciate the summer break. It gives them the opportunity to spend time with their loved ones, before going home to their wives. The papers used to be full of names of politicians cheating on their wives. Now they find it easier just to print the ones that don't. One MP was refused planning permission to add a room to his house because, they said, he already had a bit on the side. When they televise parliament the chamber is usually almost empty. Not surprising. Most MPs are probably in church confessing.

An MP has written a new book called "Political Ethics and How to Avoid Them!" History has shown that not all politicians are as honest as they should be. One former MP claims to have served under four Prime Ministers. That's how long a sentence he got. The fact that he cheated on his expenses has been put down to a lack of judgement….. on the part of the constituents who voted for him in the first place.

Parliament still remains one big happy family. That's because so many members employ their relatives. Yes, several MPs are still flouting the rules by employing their wives, mothers, sons, daughters, uncles and cousins. In fact, one MP's just resigned so he could spend less time with his family.

This government's managed to get a lot more people working full time. Most of them investigating the sleaze among MPs. Parliament is saying there are now a tremendously high number of benefit fraudsters. And they should know, because most of them are in parliament. Half our MPs are lawyers. The other half are liars. They spend a lot of time making laws and even more time breaking them. Looks like some members of Parliament think MP stands for My Perks.

What this country's always needed is a good laugh, so it's fortunate we have David Cameron. People say, in these troubled times you'd have to be mad to want to be Prime Minister, which proves we have the right man in the job. Cameron says we're a classless society and refutes the idea that it is the rich who run the country. He says "Britain belongs to you and me." He's got £28 million, so I think more belongs to him than me. He insists it's not his policy to soak the rich. He's out to soak everybody. Every time the Prime Minister's on TV telling us we're in good shape, they have to use sub-titles, because none of us can believe our ears. The way things are at the moment, Cameron's in an awkward position. He can no longer guarantee jobs. Especially his own. But he is very worried about the 2.8 million unemployed, because come Election Day they'll have nothing to do but vote. He's trying everything he knows to stop houses being repossessed. Especially Ten Downing Street, by the Labour Party. But for now, David Cameron is still continuing to lead the country.....up the garden path.

I'm told this week a card sharp was spotted being smuggled into Number Ten. I think Cameron's planning another cabinet reshuffle. There's probably no truth in the rumour that a group of Tory back benchers pinned mistletoe to the door of Number Ten in the hope of kissing David Cameron goodbye. Many MPs didn't want Cameron to go to the International Monetary Fund. Even more didn't want him to come back.

They're making so many cuts now that Cameron, Clegg and Osborne are being called The Three Scrooges. As joint leaders Cameron and Clegg have finally got their act together. I think its Laurel & Hardy. Cameron's not too bothered about the national debt. He figures it's big enough to take care of itself. Our Prime Minister knows how to make a long story short. He cuts out the facts. He's actually a great speaker. He never has much to say, but he says it so well. I really believe our Prime

Minister is the only man who can ensure a victory at the next election.....for the opposition. Cameron was asked if he ever read the Labour Party's manifesto. He said "No. I never read fiction."

He was then asked if he thought the members of the shadow cabinet were all clones. He said "Yes." He thought they said clowns. A recent opinion poll showed Cameron losing popularity with the public. He shrugged it off with "You don't want to take notice of what the public think. I don't." It's a great pity Cameron and Clegg seldom see eye to eye. In fact, I doubt they even see ear to ear. It's Nick Clegg's fault with all his mistaken pronouncements. I blame it on his wealthy family background. He was born with a silver foot in his mouth. Even some Lib Dems think Clegg's so full of wind they should name a hurricane after him.

They say talk is cheap, but not when it comes out of the mouth of George Osborne. Our Chancellor of the Exchequer's trying to convince us we're in a bull market. And nobody knows more about bull than him. Up till now the only useful thing in the Chancellor's red box has been his sandwiches. No matter how much he rakes in he's never satisfied. I bet if he'd been at The Last Supper he'd have asked for a doggy bag. The philosophy behind the Chancellor's budget is that if he can bring a smile to just one person's face, he's failed in his job. He doesn't care about old people. The only time he ever helped the aged was when he once loosened a bottle top for a pensioner. Osborne says a successful economy is our goal. We're still battling the immigration problem. A recent street survey asked whether the government has done enough to stop illegal immigrants. 34% said yes, 45% said no, and the rest didn't answer because they couldn't speak English. Personally I don't mind so many immigrants coming to Britain. I just think we should do a deal and send them our MPs in exchange.

What parliament really needs is a strong leader of the opposition. And when the name Miliband is mentioned you immediately think of charm, leadership, a great orator and all the other qualities he lacks. Having said that, I'd like to be the first to congratulate him on a great speech…if he ever makes one. The last speech he made had MPs on the edge of their seats. They couldn't wait to get up and leave. After the first minute I began to envy my foot. It fell asleep. The only way he'd ever get a standing ovation is if they put drawing pins on the seats. He's so dull that if he gave a fireside chat, the fire would go out. Ed blames his lacklustre speeches on his team of writers. He says they've been damning him with faint phrase. As opposition leader he should be putting together a strategic plan. I'm beginning to doubt he could even put together a flat pack from IKEA.

The government has given us two good reasons to worry about tomorrow. Yesterday and today. America has fifty states, but we just have three. Confusion, delusion and desperation. With the current regime in power I think we've as much chance of turning the corner as an Eskimo in an igloo. I'm convinced there's no problem that the government, if it sets its mind to it, can't ignore. I still remember when cabinet members used to pass the budget instead of the buck.

For years the fascist party's been trying to stir up trouble between the blacks and the Jews. At one point it got so bad Sammy Davis wouldn't speak to himself. In one constituency the British National Party got 32 votes, so it demanded a recount. It couldn't believe it got so many. One fellow complained that the BNP's name was too confusing. He wanted it to be renamed the Bleach National Party because they only want things white. In the Middle

East a general election just ensures one thing. A general will get elected. In China they hate re-electing their President because he is always so moody. He alternates between sweet and sour. And with their human rights policy the poor fellow doesn't know whether to run on his record or away from it. The Chinese now have a booming economy and it has made them so arrogant. I bought a toy from China this week. On the box it said "This Way Up – Yours!"

Ed Miliband's leader of the Labour Party, but some think he could serve the country better as an anaesthetist. His speeches put so many people to sleep. But it has to be said Ed Miliband's speeches have raised a lot more enthusiasm for the party. Not HIS party, the Conservatives. If Nick Griffin represents the far right and Ed Miliband represents the far left, then I guess Dolly Parton represents the far out.

I never used to believe in reincarnation till I realised that Scrooge came back as George Osborne. Statistics show that Chancellors of the Exchequer are notoriously bad tippers. Seems they're never as free with their own money as they are with ours. Thanks to WikiLeaks we now know what our government's been up to. So in future they're holding cabinet meetings inside the cabinet.

Gordon Brown's recently published book explains the strategy he used in handling the country's economy. Thanks to that strategy, few people can afford to buy his book. Staff at Downing Street say Gordon Brown was famous for losing things. Mostly his temper. Just before Gordon Brown lost the election he was asked if he'd like to buy a burial plot. He said "No thanks, I'm in a deep enough hole already." With British Summer Time coming to an end, we'll soon have to turn back the clock. I bet both Gordon Brown and Tony Blair wish they could do that.

Tony Blair is still touring the world. Apparently looking for someone who likes him. If it's true that man profits by his mistakes it would explain why he's now a multi-millionaire. Tony Blair makes a million pounds a year lecturing. I wouldn't mind, but his subject is the Evils of Capitalism. He recently turned down an offer to appear on a TV reality show. Apparently he doesn't know what reality is. There's a lot to be said for Tony Blair, but not in mixed company.

There's an old adage that says "If you can't say something good about a person, become a newspaper columnist." Newspapers love knocking politicians, especially Tony Blair. The only good thing they've said about him is "Good riddance." Some say we went to war because Blair fooled the British people. That wasn't necessary. We were already fools for making him Prime Minister in the first place. I read somewhere that Tony Blair gets paid £10,000 to give a talk. I think most of us would pay him double that amount to shut up. Blair led us into war. His heart, as he says, may have been in the right place, but I don't think his brain was.

Of the millions Blair has earned last year he only paid about £33,000 tax. That's hardly a tax, more like a tip. The waiter asked Tony Blair if he wanted his steak rare, medium or well done. That's the first time Blair has heard the words "Well done" in years. Tony Blair is the one that manufactured the evidence that led us into war. I suppose we shouldn't really complain. It's the only thing that's been manufactured in Britain for years.

The Iraqis put a price on Blair's head. I think a dunce's cap would have been more appropriate. The Prime Minister says he is determined to rid parliament of any MPs that tell lies. I think he's afraid of the competition.

It's the government's handling of Iraq and Iran that have made us irate. MPs won't work longer hours. None of them will stand for an all night sitting. A certain government department labels all its documents "Top Secret" so it knows they'll be leaked.

Most M.Ps claim to be working so hard they only get one hour's sleep a week. And that's during Prime Minister's Question Time. They've stopped serving coffee in the House of Lords. It was keeping members awake. Parliament's now added a cafeteria to its restaurant. It's for self-serving politicians. One MP didn't turn up to vote because he said he'd gone down with something. Turned out what he'd gone down with was his golf clubs to the links.

Thanks to the government cutbacks my nest egg now wouldn't even make an omelette. In my financial state all I can get out of an ATM is an IOU. The government's biggest problem is spending. It seems to be paying this year's bills with next year's money. If the government wants to make genuine cuts, it should start with its campaign promises. After all, when all is said and done, a lot more is said than done. The government's continual fight with the unions over money is being called The War of the Rises. Our biggest problem is we're dependent on the state for our independence. The government's idea of beating inflation is to spend all its money and then borrow some more. It makes things easy for the millionaires. The only time they're affected by a cut is when they're shaving.

The Russians have the best idea. They put their weirdoes in Siberia. We put ours in parliament. Some people just don't understand the nuts and bolts of politics. It's easy. The nuts are the ones in parliament. Under our present administration GB stands for going broke. If you're one of those people who think things can't get worse, just wait until tomorrow.

I'm not naming which political party leader but one of them suffers from arthritic hands. It makes it difficult to uncross his fingers after he's made a promise. The trouble with the United Nations is that it's run by a bunch of foreigners. I think it's great that we're living in a democracy where we can choose which of the three main parties we want to bankrupt our country.

A recent survey showed that sixty per cent of Poles thought they'd be better off working in the UK. The other forty per cent are already here. I hear University students have put up a new sign outside parliament. It says "Politicians crossing – aim carefully." One man who could do something to help our unemployment figures is Santa Claus. He should give out toys made in Britain instead of China and Hong Kong. Our economy is being ruined because we're importing too much stuff from abroad. I shouldn't be surprised if next year's winner of the Miss England contest isn't a girl brought in from China because she's cheaper. Today the only way you can get money out of this government is by pretending to be a foreign country. Getting the economy right is our goal. Trouble is, we need a new goalkeeper.

We used to just have maternity leave. Now in most cases it's turning out to be eternity leave.

In the next election the big winner will be either Cameron or Miliband. And either way, the big loser will be us. Politicians always promise us change. And as soon as they get in they change what they promise. As far as politics is concerned I used to be a "don't know". Now I'm a "don't want to know." I'd like to see more truth from our politicians. Like when someone asked a leading cabinet minister whether he honestly thought his party could get this country back on its feet, he said "We can certainly get it back on its feet, but I'm not too sure about honestly".

Even as a baby everyone knew Vince Cable was going to be a politician. He already had his foot in his mouth. The government's policies have some MPs revolting. I'm not surprised. I've been revolted by some of them for years. It's about time we in the UK realised we have a dope problem. We're being run by dopes.

The government's kept to its promise not to introduce new taxes. Instead it is increasing the old ones. We all have our little problems, like the senior politician who told his GP. "You've got to cure my snoring. It's disturbing my colleagues at cabinet meetings." With all the backstabbing between the political parties you never know whether to vote for the underdogs or the dirty dogs. A lot of people who were having trouble living within their income are now having even more trouble living without it. Every time I make ends meet, the government moves the ends.

The government has finally done something about the unemployment figures. It's increased them. The current rate of inflation means that half your income goes on living expenses. Same with the other half. Most of our top politicians were born too rich to ever have had a proper job. But I heard of one that went down the mines at 12. Mind you, he was up again for lunch at 12.15.

Today in Parliament gives politicians a chance to speak their minds, proving that most of them don't have one. I hear they've just installed electric hand driers in the House of Commons' loos. At last all that hot air is being used. I think it would be a good idea to let whichever party loses the next election to run the country. After all, they claim to know all the answers.

There's a war on now against benefit cheats. The government's trying to convince them that crime doesn't pay. Now if only they could convince them that working does. The government's had its conflicts with the Railwaymen's Union, but by the end of it eight out of ten trains were running normally. The other two were on time. Government cutbacks are now so stringent official documents will no longer dot the i's so they can save on ink.

Every week my local Tesco has a loss leader. It's like the Liberal party. Their leader's a complete loss. The government's giving millions to other countries to stabilize their economies, which is probably destabilising our own. Today our biggest export is money.

The national debt is growing daily. It'll soon be as high as Paul McCartney's alimony payments. Do you realise we have three ex-Prime Ministers still alive? That means they're either living longer or we're getting rid of them quicker.

They're now trying to devise a strategy to reduce the number of immigrants coming to Britain. That's probably unnecessary. The way things are going, who'd want to come here anyway? There are still too many conflicts going on around the world. I saw a sign outside an army recruiting office "Six Wars- No Waiting." The trouble with our two political party leaders is one thinks he's got great imagination and the other imagines he's great.

Last time I was on holiday I got through all three party's manifestoes. I had to remind myself next time to bring more toilet paper. They say a country gets the politicians it deserves. What did we ever do to deserve this lot? Our Chancellor of the Exchequer is so worried about the state of our economy he stays awake at cabinet meetings thinking about it

The government's policies haven't done much to stamp out poverty in this country. But they've done a hell of a lot to stamp out wealth. The Bank of England Governor keeps telling us we're heading for another recession. That man's so negative he could be sponsored by Kodak. We do have to make cutbacks, but our Defence Minister is determined our troops won't be short of weapons. This week he was seen doing a deal at Toys 'R Us. I'm one of those people who used to believe in the hereafter, but with this government I don't even believe in the here and now.

All the government's promises have turned out to be as meaningless as a transvestite burning his bras. With the state this country is in they ought to replace the House of Lords with the House of Lourdes. Where I live we have just about the only MP who's never drank, smoked, gambled or cheated on his wife. Unfortunately, since his election he hasn't done anything else either. Our politicians promised equal pay for women. Let's face it, these days the only way a woman can get a man's salary is by marrying him.

The government had plans to make 10,000 jobs in the UK vacant, but the Polish immigrants refused to give them up. When I told my wife the government's new white paper contained some good syntax, she said "My God, are they taxing that too?" The parliamentary expenses scandal is still with us. Latest gag making the rounds is "What's the difference between a Corus worker and an MP? Answer: "A Corus worker makes iron and steel and an MP. doesn't make iron."

Halloween used to be the scariest day of all. Now it's the day of the General Election. Now we don't vote for one party as much as against the other. I don't belong to any organised political party. I'm a Labourite. Yet another politician has resigned over an illicit love affair. He had to. In public life if you live it up, you can never live it down. Many MPs are very gifted men. And MI5 are trying to trace who those gifts came from. Some M.Ps are claiming to work staggered hours. That's usually the first two hours after a liquid lunch. We used to say the amount of our national debt was chicken feed. Now it's gone from Trill to a trillion. In a general election now, it's a choice between two. Heads or tails.

In political circles Nick Clegg's known as Mr. Champagne, because he gets up people's noses. Happily, Obama is being credited with more intelligence than George Bush. They say when Bush was told his proposed meeting with Putin was in jeopardy, he kept looking at the map to find where jeopardy was. I start off each day by reading the interesting bits in Hansard. Well, it's an easy way to time an egg. Cameron and Clegg's views are as far apart as Eric Pickles' hip pockets.

Rumour has it that Bill Clinton threw a charity party and invited 100 pretty women. When asked what the cause was, he said "'Cause my wife's out of town." Bill was said to be courting the ladies while his wife was campaigning to be President. She was hoping while he was groping.

In 1901 American President Teddy Roosevelt said his foreign policy was "Speak softly and use a big stick." At least, they think that's what he said. He spoke so softly no one could hear him. Figures show our government's giving millions away in foreign aid. I'm surprised we have so many illegal immigrants. Surely they could get more money from us by staying in their own country. Thanks to this government I'm no longer worried about the cost of living. I'm now more concerned about the cost of borrowing. The recession is still with us and biting hard. It means more redundancies. Santa's already been told he's getting the old heave ho-ho-ho.

How can we trust our MPs. I mean, how much can they know if they're calling each other honourable? Politicians have a habit of shaking your hand before an election and your confidence after it. They quickly change from persuasive to evasive. I've half a mind to be a politician, because that's apparently all you need. Politicians often say "Let's be clear about this..." You'll notice they never say "Let's be specific." It seems a true politician is a man who can say absolutely nothing and meant it sincerely. We now know that John Major had a four year affair with Edwina Currie and Presidents Clinton and Kennedy had dozens of girlfriends, which proves people don't go into politics just for the money.

Ed Miliband's now putting more fire into his speeches. He'd do better putting more of his speeches in the fire. I personally find his speeches quite refreshing, I always feel better after a nap. I've noticed that his audiences are never less than polite. They always cover their mouths when they yawn.

There's an air pollution problem over the Chancellor of the Exchequer's house. All his predictions have gone up in smoke. I knew the Treasury was in trouble when I was due a tax refund and all they sent me was a lottery ticket. Our country's economy's doing so badly, even the people who make "Going out of Business" signs are going out of business. The only people that buy British these days are foreigners. They bought British Gas, British Steel, British Leyland…

I refuse to criticise the government when I'm on a cruise. When you're in the middle of the ocean you don't talk about a sinking ship. I hear scientists are busy searching for signs of intelligent life on Mars. They'd do better searching for it among our MPs. I'm sure that if some MPs say what they really think, they'd be speechless.

ADDITIONAL GAGS

- My wife would make a great politician. She has the knack of never getting to the point.
- The cheapest way to have your family tree traced is to run for political office.
- Its funny how some politicians can speak at great length about something they say leaves them speechless.
- It was in November 2012 that President Obama was sworn in. Ever since then he's been sworn at.
- The government keeps pestering us to save money. I'm all in favour of that. After all, one day it might be worth something.
- The Chancellor of the Exchequer is living on borrowed time, because he's caused so many of us to live on borrowed money.
- Most railway workers have an excellent attendance record. They haven't missed a strike in years.
- If I ever need a heart transplant I hope I get the Chancellor Of The Exchequer's. It's hardly ever been used.

- When several unbalanced people get together once a week it's called group therapy. .But when they meet in Downing Street, it's called The Cabinet.
- With this government, to err is human. To repeat it is policy.
- David Cameron's a damn good talker. It's listening he's no good at.
- We've been tightening our belts for ages. What I want to know is if there is life after dearth?
- The Chancellor of the Exchequer says we ought to export more. I entirely agree. So let's export the Chancellor.
- If as we're led to believe, we're riding on cloud nine. It must be one of those clouds that drifted over from Chernobyl.
- As the Chinese guide told the Western tourist "Of course we have elections here in China. In fact, I had one in bed this morning."
- I got a letter from a politician. I knew it was from a politician, it was signed "Insincerely Yours."
- The politician's speech was having a simultaneous translation…..into rational.
- It's been pointed out that most members of the cabinet were educated at Eton. That seems like a good enough reason to close the place down.
- Ed Miliband says his aim is to make David Cameron look like Gordon Brown. And David Cameron's aim is to just make Ed Miliband look like Ed Miliband.
- As David Cameron's refused to implement Lord Levenson's suggestions for a new law, his Lordship's decided to become a footballer. That way he's more likely to get something passed.
- David Cameron's wife won't let him cook at home. She knows everything he comes up with is hard to swallow.
- Every school kid has the chance to become Prime Minister. And those that play truant are already qualified to be MPs.
- Last week David Cameron played golf and was asked by the club's golf Pro what his handicap is. He said "Nick Clegg."
- This present government is all talk and no action. Reminds me of my first date.
- Overweight government minister Pickles is worried about the terrible shape the world is in. I'm more concerned about the terrible shape he is in.

- The European Community's always imposing new health and safety rules on us. I wouldn't be surprised if the next thing they want from us is hand rails on Mount Snowdon.
- Ed Miliband gives his wife his speeches to proofread. Then he goes back half hour later to wake her up.
- The Health and Safety people have gone too far this time. Their latest demand is that Jack puts a flashing light on his beanstalk.
- Politicians are not lazy. Most of them work a lot. It's a pity their policies don't.
- Most Conservative MPs refer to Tony Blair as Mr. Peanut shell. They think he's a nutcase.
- Cameron's famous for giving out classified information. He's always telling the unemployed to look up the classifieds and find themselves a job.
- The BBC has banned any more jokes about the Conservative Party cabinet. It figures there's enough jokes there already.
- Politicians always tell us there's no such thing as a free lunch. That's usually after they've just been given one.
- Tony Blair would have been good at running a Burger King. He was experienced at dispensing whoppers.
- If Cameron doesn't face the big issue, he could wind up selling it.
- I'm all in favour of politicians providing more jobs. But not just for their relatives.
- There are so many wealthy people governing us, they're now including Gucci in the retail price index.
- How come when MPs vote themselves a rise they never ask where the money's coming from?
- Economists say we're due for a weak recovery. But they never say which week it will be.
- David Cameron would make a great astronaut circumnavigating the Earth. After all, he's been going round in circles for years.
- When Peter Mandelson heard Ed Miliband had won the leadership of the party, he was speechless. So already it's done some good.
- Old politicians never die. They just steal way.
- The Conservative party is a group of people pulling together in opposite directions.

- I'm all in favour of a higher percentage of women in parliament. It frees more men to do an honest day's work.
- David Cameron exercises every day, but he'd still love to lose 12 stone…..Nick Clegg.
- Every baby born in Britain today is guaranteed liberty, opportunity and a share of the national debt.
- It's amazing how long a politician can talk without letting on what he's talking about.
- My MP's served three terms. Two in parliament and one in Wandsworth Prison.
- We're pouring a small fortune into the Middle East so we can keep getting Arab oil to put into our Japanese, Italian and German cars.
- One politician complained to the Press Council that newspapers were telling lies about him. They said he should be thankful they weren't telling the truth.
- David Cameron wanted to show he's a man of the people, so when he went on holiday he travelled tourist class on British Airways. He told them he didn't want any special treatment. He just wanted to be treated like any other passenger. So they lost his luggage.
- Give a politician a free hand and he'll put it in your pocket.
- They asked a politician what he thought of Putin. He said "I can't say. I've never puted."
- There's a campaign going on now to encourage us to buy British. Trouble is we can't get the Japanese, Chinese and Arabs to sell.
- Britain has places in each town where gambling is positively encouraged. They're called Polling Stations.
- Some MPs have absolutely no inkling of foreign affairs. They have all their affairs in England.
- We learn quickly from our mistakes. Especially after a general election.
- We need the best clergy available. With this government someone has to pray for our country.
- Just think, if it wasn't for the money we pay our politicians they'd have to work for a living.
- I don't think our country's finances are in a healthy state. I've just had a tax refund with a note saying "Please don't cash this cheque till next Thursday."

- A politician is someone who can say absolutely nothing and really mean it.
- If Prime Minister Cameron makes a big mistake he won't get re-elected. But if the voters make a big mistake, he will.
- There would be more women members of parliament if it wasn't so much trouble putting make-up on both faces.
- He got in the Guinness Book of Records as the only man to stay awake during the whole of an Ed Miliband speech.
- The political candidate had absolutely nothing to say, but I had to listen to him for half an hour to find that out.
- Cameron has gone power mad. He ate in a restaurant in Brussels and when the bill came, he vetoed it.
- I'd like to put an advert in The Times saying I am no longer responsible for debts incurred by this government.
- George Osborne's doing a wonderful job. He's brought poverty within the reach of all of us.
- I heard Ed Miliband's last speech and I must say he was never better. Which is such a pity.
- I hate political jokes, mainly because too many of them get elected.
- There are lots of MPs after Ed Miliband's job as leader of the Labour Party. That's like competing to be captain of the Titanic.
- We're thankful for the way Osborne is handling our economy. In fact, we couldn't be more indebted.
- I saw David Cameron out on the golf course and asked him what his handicap was. He said "Nick Clegg!"
- I heard that David Cameron had a secret popularity poll taken and wants to ensure its kept that way.
- When politicians sit down to dinner it's usually forks on the left and knives in the back.
- When Miliband was told the labour voters wanted him out of office, he said he didn't believe what the voters say, which is only fair, because they don't believe what he says either.
- I looked high and low but couldn't find an honest politician. Obviously I didn't look low enough.
- Fifty per cent of MPs are lawyers, which is useful to keep the other fifty per cent out of jail.

- The political candidates who didn't get elected are sitting around doing nothing, same as the ones who did get elected.
- Thanks to this government there's a new social class. The nouveau poor.
- Osborne's doping a great job solving problems we didn't even know we had.
- Ed Miliband's wife is taking skiing lessons so she can go downhill with her husband's career.
- Wasn't it Tony Blair who said "I have but one lie to give to my country."?
- A recession is when one loses one's job. A recovery will be when George Osborne loses his.
- In a democracy you can eat dinner while watching TV. In a dictatorship while you're eating dinner TV watches you.
- Figures don't lie. Unless of course, they're public figures.
- As a pensioner I don't mind that the Chancellor of the Exchequer's doing nothing for us. It's what he's doing TO us that bothers me.
- I had a cousin who lived in Zimbabwe; he managed to escape in an usual way.....alive.
- In Russia they guarantee freedom of speech. But not after the speech.
- Thieves broke into President Mugabe's house and stole the results of the next election.
- No matter what we British invent, the Russians will say they invented it first and the Japanese will make it cheaper.
- Ed Miliband's just had a secret popularity poll and hopes to keep it that way.
- Every Member of Parliament is entitled to his opinion. If only we could find out what it is.
- Some political candidates never get elected because nobody knows what they have done. Others DO get elected for the very same reason.
- Thanks to this government's policies the British people are downtrodden. Mind you, I've never known a rime when they were up-trodden.
- In a democracy everyone talks and nobody listens. In a dictatorship everyone listens and nobody talks.

- The one thing the Russians have more than us is shortages.
- The political candidate said "I have listened to the voice of the people. But I've decided to run anyway."
- Life is what you make it and this current government has made it….worse.
- With government nothing's as bad as it seems. And with this lot it's worse.
- What a pity Moses isn't around to lead our government out of the wilderness.
- I've just read the stock market report. It says that helium is up, feathers are down, paper is stationary, knives went up sharply, mining equipment hit rock bottom, toilet paper also touched the bottom, babies napkins remain unchanged and pencils lost a few points.
- A further analyst report says the Japanese Origami Bank has folded, the Bonzai Bank has cut back some of its branches and the Karaoke Bank is going for a song.
- Times are not as bad as they seem. They couldn't be.
- During his term in office ex-President Clinton had some near misses. And some Misses he got far too near.
- Clinton's made a fortune out of his lectures. His working life is now said to be all profit and lassies.
- Thanks to our government lots more houses are being put up….in price.
- The politician has all his speeches immediately translated into French, German and rational.
- Most of our top politicians went to Eton. Cameron, Clegg, Johnson……Isn't it about time they wised up and closed that place?
- Mrs Thatcher brought in the poll tax, but it was Blair's government that brought in the Poles.
- I don't know why everyone criticises the Lib Dems, they haven't done anything.
- Richard Nixon will always be known as the man who took crime off the streets and put it in the White House.
- Ed Balls outlined his economic policy. Fortunately no one took any notice, so no harm was done.

- Sure the government have made prices rise. They say if you want economy you have to pay for it.
- Woman tells political canvasser at her door "I don't have any opinions about the political candidate, but I'd be happy to give you my opinion of my neighbours.
- A government survey shows that 91% of illegal immigrants come to Britain so they can see their own doctor.
- When the politician realised his speech was riddled with obvious half-truths he realised he had to re-write it, to make it less obvious.
- I had a chat with my bank manager about granting mortgages. He loves to reminisce.
- The defence budget proves that our government's still making bombs that can end the world and the BBC is still producing shows that make it sound like a good idea.
- There are so many foreign immigrants in London the government is considering opening a British Embassy here.
- With inflation rising faster than wages, soon the only content of my wage packet will be 'dis'.
- Sometimes Members of Parliament have to make very tough decisions, like which member of their family to let go.
- Gurus can explain the meaning of life, but no one can explain the UKP's policies.
- Government departments waste so much money hiring consultants to consultants to find the right consultants.
- The only way some political candidates can get elected is by fooling all the people all the time.
- The politician said "I used to be open and honest and tell the truth about myself, but it left me too open to blackmail."
- It's the British people who should take the blame for this government's mistakes. After all, it was us who elected it.
- On the Cabinet Minister's desk are two trays. They're labelled "IN ONE EAR" and "OUT THE OTHER".
- Cameron may be a great Prime Minister but he's no good as a cabinet maker.
- Nick Clegg is a most astute, intelligent, perceptive politician. That's not my opinion. It's his.

- I don't know why the government's building more nuclear weapons. We haven't even used the ones we've already got.
- This week we had a power cut. That's nothing new to Ed Miliband. He's been powerless for ages.
- We'd better not go to war with Germany and Japan again. Most of our defence weapons rely on computers made in those countries.
- The message from the economy is "Owe Now – Pay Later."
- He went to Yale so he could be a key man in Washington.
- As ex-Prime Minister Maggie Thatcher proved the best man for the job was a woman.
- He's an honest politician. Ends all his letters with "Insincerely yours."
- He's a lousy politician. He can't even fool a few of the people a little of the time.
- They asked a politician what he does for a living. He said "As little as possible."
- A recent poll showed that 75% voted for Cameron as the lesser of two evils. The coalition between the Tories and the Lib Dems means together they can pool their ignorance.
- In hospital Patton got lots of "Don't Get Well" cards from people after his job.
- He's so two-faced he can sing a duet all by himself.
- The Chancellor of the Exchequer said "I'll get this country back on its feet again if it costs us every penny we have."
- The trouble with this country is too many people are complaining about the trouble with this country.
- One politician got into trouble for not declaring the income he got from selling the fiction rights to his expense account.
- When Bill Clinton's daughter got married they spent a fortune on security. Most of it was to protect the bridesmaids from Bill Clinton.
- Nick Clegg went to Whipsnade and visited the panda there. It made a lovely picture. On the one hand you had a creature that's almost extinct and on the other hand you had the panda.
- Ed Miliband's going to take a break – a week off to rewind. As against his predecessor Gordon Brown who never wound at all.
- The treasury tells us that retail sales in the High Street are up again, which is good news for the country. The country being China from

where most of the goods are imported. In the past decade there have been thirty major mistakes made in 10 Downing Street. 32 if you count Blair and Brown.
- Nigel Farage says it's fundamentally wrong allowing the EU to tell us what to do. He thinks HE should tell us what to do,
- One MP turned up for a debate on the NHS carrying a human skull in his hand. Mind you, there's nothing new in that. Parliament's been full of empty heads for years.
- Gordon Brown wrote a book about his time in office. He agonised every word. Same as his readers.
- I enjoyed that picture in the paper of Ed Miliband eating a bacon sandwich. I prefer seeing what's going into his mouth to hearing what's coming out of it.
- The Russians are said to be withdrawing their tanks from the Crimea. It's said to be the first time Putin's pulled back since Angela Myrtle tried to kiss him.
- Among politicians there's a three-party system. Lots of them have three parties a night.
- He's non-political. The only party he supports is Tupper wear.
- The Chinese constitution is great. It grants every citizen the right to say what he thinks. And the government the right to shoot him for it.
- The trouble with the Chancellor of the Exchequer is he always puts our money where his mouth is.
- The politician asked her for his air fare back because there'd been a mistake. He thought they'd said it was a "frequent liar" offer.
- What this country's economy needs is a long term quick fix.
- As I see it the whole of Europe is broke, but we're less broke.

PUNS

Sixteen publishers have rejected my autobiography. Ah well, that's the story of my life. Investment pundits tell us that 7's up, duck feathers are down and yo-yos are up and down.

Banks tell us money doesn't grow on trees, yet they all have branches. In Japan the Geisha girls have their own theme song "Someone to Wash over Me." Undertakers avoid going to Venice because they don't want to run into more Titians.

Did you hear about the foreign consul who was let off a charge of drunken driving because he claimed dipsomatic immunity? As the American bank manager told the lady when she asked for a loan "Frankly my dear, I don't give a dime." As Toulouse Lautrec said to the Parisian prostitute "Not tonight, dear. I'm a little short."

Mortgagers are demanding larger deposits now. So, to feather your nest you need enough down. Did you hear about the couple that got married in a public lavatory? It was a marriage of convenience. The cost of a holiday on a ship proves the old saying Beggars Can't Be Cruisers. We're living in a class ridden society, except of course for the weather which is the same for everybody. Even the Queen wrote in her diary "Reigned again today." As one ghost said to the other "Thank heavens for little ghouls."

I bet my butcher £100 he couldn't reach the meat off the top shelf. He refused the bet because the stakes were too high. Doctors put a postman in quarantine because they heard he was a carrier. Ronnie Corbett was spotted asking directions to the Small Claims Court. An Indian streaker was arrested and charged under the Obscene Public Asians Act. A woman taught her pet bird to swear and was arrested for contributing to the delinquency of a Mynah.

Did you hear about the cannibal eating a German, who complained there was a Herr in his soup? Did you hear about the cannibal who said his favourite food was baked beings? Did you hear about the driver on the M1 who got a phone call saying his wife was having an affair, so he pulled over and found a hard shoulder to cry on? My son refuses to accompany me to Brent Cross, Westfield or Metro shopping centres because, he says "If you've seen one you've seen a mall."

Petrol prices have risen again. Buying fuel is getting to be fuelish. Did you hear about the transvestite who was suffering from delusions of gender? Thanks to my wife all my shirts are crumpled. She has an ironing deficiency.

As the Egyptian said when he prepared the mummy for its tomb "That just about wraps it up." I heard of one supermarket that refused to serve a man from Croatia. They said "We don't serve Czechs." Did you hear about the nurse at the dermatitis clinic who got the sack because she wasn't up to scratch? Theatre ticket prices are keeping customers away. There's even a rumour that Sadler's Wells is going ballet-up.

Way back in the days when Jonah was having a whale of a time, Goliath was getting stoned and the Tower of Pisa became a listed building..... Bob Monkhouse put in his will that he wasn't to be cremated, because he didn't want to make an ash of himself. In Buckingham Palace the Queen swept down the staircase, dusted the curtains and polished the furniture. They've just stationed four armed guards outside Ten Downing Street. It's the first time I've seen guards with four arms.

A mathematician and chef got together and divided the circumference of a pumpkin by its diameter. Do you know what they wound up with? Pumpkin Pi. Nigel Kennedy says he only plays the violin to scratch a living. I'd never buy a detergent to unclog the sink. It's just money down the drain. Groucho Marx told the restaurant waiter "Bring me some hominy grits. On second thought, leave out the grits and just bring me the hominy".

Waiter, that food's given me ptomaine poisoning. It started at my main toe and worked its way up. Groucho told his bank manager "If you can't float me a loan, at least float me a kidney." The man who invented the alphabet retired when all was zed and done.

Why bother to learn history? It's just a thing of the past. Avoid people with colds because they'll sneeze right atchoo. Did you hear about the newspaper reporter who suffered from Reuter's block? The acupuncturist who was congratulated on a jab well done. The choreographer who wants to stamp out Flamenco dancing. The drummer on a cruise ship who was warned to keep proper time or be thrown overboard. He had to decide whether to sync or swim. The council gardener who worked his lawnmower by computer. When they asked him to mow the lawns, he said "I modem yesterday." I watched Princess Diana's funeral on TV with all those thousands of orchids and lilacs. I thought to myself "Oh what a beautiful mourning."

Xavier Hollander's writing a book confessing about tapping in to other people's e-mails. It'll be called "The Happy Hacker." The French are launching a new family version of the Citroen car. It'll be called The

Hatchback of Notre Dame. Metallurgists have discovered a metal you can only rely on for six days a week. On the seventh day it rusts. The vet who will make a horse call, but only if the animal is coming down with a colt. Thieves caught trying to steal harvest crops from a farmer's field were charged with attempted reap. I just read my grandfather's will. It was a dead give-away. The group of fishermen playing poker agreed to put their cods in the table.

There were eight women in a lifeboat and one was expecting a happy event. The other seven wanted to help her, but they were all in the same boat. My girlfriend dumped me when she heard I had only nine toes. She wanted a man she could count on. I told the guard on the train I'd booked a sleeper. So he gave me a three foot block of wood. As the male tortoise said to the female "Your pace or mine?" Our next speaker has spent the last ten years studying the habits of kangaroos. Professor, would you hop onto the stage please.

ADDITIONAL GAGS

- In this morning's mail there was a letter from Ireland. I knew it was from Ireland, on the envelope it said "Opened in Eire." The candle maker's wife decided she'd had enough, so she gave him two wicks notice.
- Did you hear about the Siamese twins in Australia who were separated at Perth?
- Did you hear about the art dealer who got into debt because he ran out of Monet?
- Did you hear about the drug peddler who got caught because he opened a joint account?
- My wife painted the walls in our house. I looked upon her work with mixed emulsion.
- Too much German beer might upset your stomach, but it affects your liver worst.
- I moved into an old castle, but they couldn't install central heating. Ah well, you can't have archaic and heat it too.
- Did you hear about the drug dealer who got caught because he opened a joint account?

- What drinks and falls off horses? A wine-stoned cowboy.
- There are very few professional ping pong players because the game only offers a little net profit.
- The crossword puzzle compiler was feeling down because his girlfriend wouldn't come across.
- A lunatic sexually attacked a nurse and escaped from the asylum. Next day the newspaper headline read "NUT SCREWS AND BOLTS."
- In Hawaii men make passes at girls who wear grasses.
- Girls take birth control pills in order to avoid an issue.
- Did you hear about the cannibal detective who grilled all his suspects?
- Did you hear about the newspaper deputy editor who was eaten by the head cannibal and ended up as editor-in-chief?
- The Spanish girl jilted at the altar said "You should have seen the Juan that got away."
- The cop trying to meet his weekly target needs arrest.
- Would you call a napping bull a bulldozer?
- A driver wrote the history of his car. It was an auto-biography.
- As the letter said to the postage stamp "Stick with me and we'll go places."
- As one fishmonger said to his rival "Let's put our cods on the table."
- As the receptionist at the Fertility Clinic said to the female patient "The doctor will seed you now."
- As the ancient cloth seller said to his female customer "How about one for the woad?"
- A carpenter always does his level best.
- A plumber is a drain surgeon.
- A confession article in a magazine is where people write their wrongs.
- A tree surgeon whose business was doing so well decided to branch out.
- Lovers have been known to commit EROS of judgement.
- The truth should be as clear as a bell, but it isn't always tolled.
- Did you hear about the drug manufacturer who became a pillionaire?
- To a Cannibal one man's meat is another man's person.

- A bigamist is a man who leads a double wife.
- An IOU is just a paper wait.
- As Rip Van Winkle once said "It's a great life if you don't waken."
- Writing poetry is fun as a hobby but not as a living. Rhyme doesn't pay.
- A shotgun wedding is a case of wife or death.
- A grandfather clock is an old timer.
- Our neighbour's holiday ended a month ago, but we're still suffering the slide effects.
- A bigamist is a man who keeps two himself.
- My son wanted to be a writer but he can't spell. So instead he's taking a course in pharmacy so he can be a farmer.
- One time there was a father tomato, a mother tomato and a baby tomato. They went out walking, but the baby tomato kept lagging behind. So the father tomato stepped on him and said "Ketchup!"
- My brother says that missing his goals is just a misdemeanour. The more he misses the meaner he gets.
- Did you hear about the Colonel who went to the VD clinic because he was having trouble with his privates?
- The midget asked the doctor if he could fit him in for an appointment that day. The doctor said "Yes. But you'll have to be a little patient."
- At the lumberjack's birthday party the guests all sang "For he's a jolly good feller."
- As the tailor said to his apprentice "If you can't stand the pleat, get out of the stitchin'"
- We left handers should stand up for our rights.
- The Grim Reaper came for me last night, but I fought him off with a vacuum cleaner. Talk about Dyson with death!
- A widow went to the cemetery to plant flowers on her late husband's grave. She roamed around for four hours looking for it. Apparently she'd lost the plot.
- I attended the funeral of a tennis player who was struck on the forehead by a very fast ball. It was a fantastic service.
- A lady was cautioned by the police for dating under age cub scouts, so she decided to cut back. She's now down to two packs a day.

- It was easy to tell the fellow was a lecher. When a pretty girl passed him wearing a Hula skirt he said "I think it's time for me to hit the hay."
- Did you hear about the male bee who split with his boyfriend when he realised she was after him for his honey?
- A member of The Samaritans was sacked after he got a call from a suicidal man who said he'd tied himself to the railway track and was just waiting for the next train. The Samaritan told him to keep calm and stay on the line.One man went to see a psychiatrist because he thought he was a goat, and he'd been that way since he was a kid.
- I start a new job in Seoul next week. Why did I choose Seoul? It's a Korea move.
- The AA motorcyclist whizzed past me zig zagging across the road. He was obviously heading for a breakdown.
- In the microchip business you have to learn to think small.
- I think people who falsely claim whiplash are a pain in the neck.
- Two wrongs don't make a right. But two wrights made an aeroplane.
- Avoid clichés like the plague. They're a dime a dozen.
- All women's libbers should be put behind bras.
- The gunsmith was fired. The lumberjack was axed and the transvestite got a pink slip.
- Robin Hood's Friar Tuck cooked himself an egg for breakfast. It went out of the frying pan into the friar.
- I went to visit a nudist camp, but they had nothing on.
- This clairvoyant could see into the future right up to 2150. She has extra sensory perception.
- I wasn't impressed when she said her husband was a six footer till I saw he had six feet.
- Did you hear about the alcoholic cowboy who was arrested for drunken droving?
- As Eddie the Eagle said "I've got to stop taking risks. My feats are killing me.
- The Mona Lisa has the eyes of a woman in Louvre.
- The prostitute said she hates rainy days when she can't go out and ply.
- My wife never stops talking. I've given her the best ears of my life.

- My wife breast fed our babies. It was a case of sucking up to the Boss.
- The lecher invited the girl up to his apartment to see his itchings.
- I write, therefore I AMB.
- My crazy family and I live in a four bedlam house.
- A wife is a woman who has been dis-missed.
- He loves it when his wife has babies. He's a fresh heir fiend.
- There's a new magazine out now especially for gardeners. It's called Weeder's Digest.
- My next door neighbour's a backward musician. He's cymbal minded.
- As one cow giving birth said to another "It only hurts when I calf."
- A pessimist is a person who knows the moaning of life.
- A burglar arrested for stealing beehives was caught during a sting operation.

QUESTIONS

Why is it that nuisance callers never get the wrong number?

Is a witch doctor expected to make hut calls?

Why is it that when you fast, it goes so slowly?

Would you call an ugly air hostess a plane Jane?

Why is there no meat in mincemeat?

Was there ever a Father Goose?

Did all couch potatoes watch MASH?

What's an inchworm called under the metric system?

Did the cow that jumped over the moon do it because the milkmaid had cold hands?

Do people who work in a microwave factory more quickly?

Do American bankers celebrate Thankslending?

There's a Natural History Museum. But where's the unnatural history museum?

Does one fly tell another "Your human is open"?

Why don't people who snore wake themselves up?

Do double glazing salesmen start out selling single glazing?

Do dermatologists start from scratch?

Why don't people with bad coughs go to the doctor instead of the theatre?

Why do theatregoers put on their best clothes just to sit in the dark for three hours?

Can an accused Peeping Tom get off by claiming to be part of the Neighbourhood Watch?

Where did the man who invented patents go to register his idea?

Why is it always people with bad breath that become dentists?

Does a hummingbird hum because it can't remember the words?

If you give a banker a cheque for a wedding present, do you have to show two forms of identification?

Is a fencing club an epee centre?

Is it a plastic surgeon's job to pick your nose for you?

When the girl who was the apple of your eye gets old, is she a Granny Smith?

Does an undertaker with no customers have a stiff shortage?

Would you expect something in mint condition to have a hole in it?

Should you play poker with Dolly Parton when you know she already has a winning pair?

When the inventor of the drawing board messed things up, what did he go back to?

If a woman's work is never done, why doesn't she start earlier?

Is it true most Sunday drivers are actually Friday drivers still looking for a place to park?

Is it true most pantomime villains quit because they get hissed off with the job?

Is it true that when Bill Clinton was President he had a Girl Friday…and two girls every other day of the week?

Is it true you can have your library ticket endorsed if you're caught speed reading?

In Spain when a bull loses they cut off its ears. But if the matador loses, what do they cut off?

Would an in-continental breakfast contain prune juice?

Has Old McDonald been cautioned for keeping a noisy farm?

Why it that you never find out there is a drummer in the flat above till after you've signed the lease?

Is the KGB agent who forgot to plant a hidden microphone in the British Embassy a silly bugger?

Is a rare coin something you have left over after you've paid your taxes?

Does the name Quasimodo ring a bell?

Is someone who works the lights in a disco a quick flasher?

Does a belly dancer do navel manoeuvres?

How can a country with over a million divorces every year call itself the United States?

Will they ever stamp out flamenco dancing?

Was the man who trained his pet rabbit to service 25 females a day trying to make a fast buck?

Is it bad luck to be superstitious?

Why is it nobody ever orders a wet martini?

If Australians want their boomerangs back, why do they keep throwing them away?

How does a leopard know if it has measles? Do Texas oilmen send each other "Get Well" cards?

Do Ubangi children sit on Santa's lip?

Why do we never see the headline "PSYCHIC WINS LOTTERY"?

Why is the man whom invests all your money called a Broker?

Why isn't there a mouse-flavoured cat food?

If flying is so safe, why do they call the airport the terminal?

Why don't they start swimming races with a water pistol?

Why is it the school bus always breaks down on the way home and never on the way TO school?

Does a caterpillar have kitten pillars?

RELIGION

The vicar's sermons were so boring they always took up the collection beforehand. The vicar asked the Sunday school kid if he knew why Joseph and Mary had to stay in the stable. He said "Yes. It was because the innkeeper wouldn't accept American Express." With the current financial constraints churches are having problems. My local vicar's introduced an eleventh commandment "Thou shalt donate to the church."

A young lady told her mother that her new boyfriend was a botanist. The mother said "It doesn't matter what religion he is, as long as he's nice." Did you know that Jehovah's Witnesses don't celebrate Halloween. They don't like strangers knocking on their door and annoying them. Several priests have had to resign over child abuse. Now they're all afraid to use the expression "I'm going to the little boy's room."

The reason Tony Blair turned Catholic is so he could confess all his sins. Priests say they're still dealing with as many confessionals as always. But most are now coming in by email. Even churches are now making cuts. My local confessional has got an express cubicle for ten sins or less. I feel sorry for priests. It's such a hard job. They have to give up their sex life and listen to all those people talking about theirs.

I'm told the Vatican is very happy about all the women who want to be priests. It's just not happy about all the priests who want to be women. For Lent some people give up meat, some give up drinking and many more just give up Lent. If God had meant us to fly he'd have given us airline tickets. As the Trappist Monk's mother said to him "I don't care if you did take a vow of silence. I'm your mother, you should have called."

ADDITIONAL GAGS

- All the people that work for this man wish he was the Pope. Then they'd only have to kiss his ring. Mind you, even then he'd probably keep it in his back pocket.
- As Moses said to God on the mountain "Let me deliver these first ten and see how it goes."
- She goes to church regularly every week. Not Sundays, Thursday is when they have Bingo.
- The church was flooded. It's the first time I've seen people really walking on water.
- As one Israelite said to Moses after he read out the Ten Commandments "Oh yeah? Says who?"
- What isn't generally known is that after the flood Noah opened a pet shop.
- Atheism is a non-prophet organisation.
- There are some new religious films out now "The Holy Ghostbusters" "Amen in Black" "A Pew Good Men" and "A fistful of chollars."
- Moses spent 40 years on the road. I hate to think what his expenses sheet looked like.
- As one Biblical Jew said to another "Our headaches are over. Here comes Moses with the tablets."
- In today's climate David would never have slain Goliath. They'd have sat down at the negotiating table.
- Since we've had a woman rabbi we all sing from the her book.
- Moses looked at the burning bush and asked "Who speaketh unto me?" And a voice came back saying "Well it ain't Smokey the bear."
- He always keeps the Ten Commandments. He keeps them at home in a drawer.
- The church cleaner was sacked because she used stain remover on the windows.
- The Italian eleventh commandment is "Honour thy godfather."
- Today everything's organic. Even the music in the church.
- The church belfry has two ropes. They're marked "DING" AND "DONG".

RIDDLES

What's the difference between Fulham Football Club and a tea bag? ANSWER: a teabag stays in the cup longer.

What's the common denominator between a 3-pin plug and the English football team? ANSWER: They're both no good in Europe.

What's the difference between Jose Mauhrino and a jet engine? ANSWER: A jet engine eventually stops whining.

What's the most dangerous food known to man? ANSWER: Wedding cake.

Where do you find mangoes? ANSWER: Wherever woman goes.

How much did the millionaire leave when he died? ANSWER: Every penny.

What do you call a budgie run over by a lawn mower? ANSWER: Shredded tweet.

What's the best part of a joke on boxing? ANSWER: The punchline.

What is the quietest sport? ANSWER: Bowling. You can hear a pin drop.

What word starts with an "E" and has only one letter in it? ANSWER: An envelope.

Why did the Texan buy a dachshund? ANSWER: Because another cowboy said "Get a-long little doggie."

What did the horse say when he finished eating his hay? ANSWER: "Well, that's the last straw!"

What do you call a cat who's eaten a lemon? ANSWER: A sourpuss.

What did the tortoise say when the hare beat him in a foot race? ANSWER: You turned the fable on me."

What's the difference between a sigh, a Rolls Royce and a jackass? ANSWER: A sigh is "Oh, dear!" A Rolls Royce is too dear. And a jackass is you dear.

ROYALTY

Prince Charles took Camilla for a day out at London zoo. He particularly showed her the elephants. He wanted her to see something with bigger ears than he has. Prince Charles is in a flap about modern architecture. Mind you, with his ears he can't help being in a flap. Prince Charles has been criticising modern architecture again. That's Charles for you. Even when he talks to his plants he winds up having an argument. Prince Charles is so rich when he can't sleep instead of sheep he counts polo ponies. It's said that even when the Queen was a little girl she rode her rocking horse side-saddle.

While playing polo Prince Charles fell off his horse. Luckily his ears broke the fall.

As the king's chef said to the four and twenty blackbirds "I suppose you're wondering why I called you all here?

The bathroom towels at the royal palace are marked "HIS" HERS" and "HEIRS".

Our queen is so rich she has six crowns. One on her head and six in her mouth

ROYAL MAIL

This week I had my mail chewed up by a tortoise. Well, it's an improvement on having it delivered by one. Only Scandinavia can guarantee next day delivery. The nights are six months long. They tell me post offices will accept all credit cards except American. They just don't recognise the word "Express." It would be appropriate if the next three faces on stamps were Buddy Holly, Marc Bolan and John Denver. None of them reached their destination. The postal workers went on a three day strike. It was a waste of time. Nobody even noticed.

Postage is up again. Soon we'll be buying stamps that are blank, leaving the Royal Mail to put whatever price it likes on them. First class stamps have gone up to 63p. With the current delivery rate at Royal Mail that works out at almost 10p a day. Our Prime Minister would love to have his face on a postage stamp. He'd enjoy people licking his backside.

I thought Royal Mail was doing so well when it started putting two extra windows in all its Post Offices. Then I found out it was just to handle the complaints. Royal Mail keeps reminding us to write FRAGILE on our delicate parcels. It gives them something to aim at.

I think our government ought to merge with Royal Mail. It won't stop inflation, but it'll certainly slow it down. I gave my postman his tip in an envelope and he lost it.

ADDITIONAL GAGS

- Royal Mail is going to increase charges again by making us pay by the weight. Not of the letter, this time it's the postman.
- There are three good reasons why the mail in Alaska can guarantee next day delivery.
- They're efficient, they're motivated and their nights are six months long.
- Did you hear about the lady postman who had an eleven month pregnancy? Yet another case of late delivery.
- Old postmen never die. They just fail to deliver.
- My brother's a pall bearer for Royal Mail. He works in their Dead Letter Office.
- Did you hear about the woman who eloped with a postman and had to wait hours at the church for him to catch up?
- I don't so much mind Royal Mail losing my post, but this week it lost my postman.
- If postage costs rise any higher they'll soon be putting Dick Turpin's face on the stamps.
- The very first letter had a penny black stamp on it and was posted in 1840. Royal Mail says it should be delivered any day now.
- I long for the old days when a Special Delivery letter arrived ahead of the normal mail.
- If you're holidaying, send your post cards before you go and, with a bit of luck, they'll arrive before you get back.
- For Christmas I gave my postman a ticket for the zoo, so he can watch the tortoises whiz by.Postage is going up yet again. If only Royal Mail's delivery was as quick as its price rises.

RUGBY

My wife knows nothing about sport. When I took her to a rugby match she wanted to know why they were fighting over the ball. She said "Why don't they don't give each team a ball of their own?" At one time I fancied myself as another Laurence Dallaglio, mainly because he pulled all the girls. They were mad about his tackle. Mike Tyndall's another rugby player who had everything going for him. Money, prestige and the love of a beautiful woman. That is, until his wife found out.

SEX

Some philosopher once said that sex is great for improving the memory. I wish I could remember his name. I'm finding sex difficult as I get older. In fact, at my age I can hardly keep my socks up. Talk about sex after forty, I can't even manage it after lunch. I still remember the first time I asked my father about sex. I said "Where can I get some?" My dad never actually told me about sex. In fact, till I was fourteen I believed I came from Woolworth's, because everything else in the house did.

My wife insists on turning out the lights when I want to make love. That doesn't bother me. It's her hiding that seems so cruel. We used to talk during sex. Now it's instead of. We often made love to the tune of "Staying Alive". Now it's "Staying Awake." I don't want to give away too many personal details, but once when we were in a hotel she ordered a wake-up call. I wouldn't have minded, but it was our wedding night. We would have had the obligatory cigarette afterwards, but my lighter didn't work either.

I'm proud to say that even though my wife and I have just celebrated our fortieth anniversary, we still make love like we did at the start. Once a year. As far as lovemaking is concerned my wife has her own little word for it. "No." She calls our lovemaking boreplay. I love the sound of laughter, but not while I'm making love.

Did you hear about the Page Three girl whose cups runneth over to Page Four? She was so big-busted, when the local disco advertised for two bouncers she got the job. There's one famous actress who's had her breasts enlarged twice. If she does it anymore she'll need planning permission. I hear that Dolly Parton's changed her theme song to "All I Want for Christmas is my Two Front....." Thanks to Dolly Parton my cousin has an enormous water bill. Every time he sees a picture of her he has to take a cold shower.

As one young starlet said to another "I never did or said anything to give him the idea I was a pushover. He must have read my mind." Her mother told her all about the birds and bees, but it was too late. She'd already been stung. I know a girl who's had TOP SECRET tattooed on her breasts because she doesn't want them to fall into the wrong hands. She should have been like the girl who only ever dates chess players. She figures they'll take hours to make a move. She was a right prude. We used to call her Venus De Milo because she had a hands-off policy.

The recent population explosion is down to the fact that too many young girls are keeping their fingers crossed instead of their legs. There's been a big increase in teenage pregnancies and the government is definitely doing something about it. It's sending them Mother's Day cards.

When Clinton had sex he always wore protection. A bullet proof vest in case her husband walked in. To you and me love forty is just a tennis score. To Bill Clinton it was his monthly target. As a President, he was definitely hands on. He says from now on he'll give up looking for new girlfriends. He'll just recycle the old ones.

As the prostitute said to her satisfied customer "It was a business doing pleasure with you." One fellow was honest with his wife about dating a prostitute. He didn't actually say that. He just said he was taking out the trash. I read of one famous politician who had a clandestine meeting with a prostitute and had no idea there was a hidden camera in the room. He found out next morning when the hotel manager said "I hope you enjoyed your stay last night as much as we did." In Soho I bumped into an ex-girlfriend who's now on the game. I said "Hello, what are you up to these days?" She said £100 a night."

They now have sell-by dates on condoms. Actually most women don't worry about dates on condoms. They just want condoms on their dates. One condom manufacturer is making condoms with our national flag on them. It's supposed to help when they play the National Anthem.

A recent survey showed that 16% of men who had pre-marital sex regretted it. And that the 84% who didn't have sex regretted it even more. Today women often play with men on the snooker table. Anyone wishing to play snooker has to wait till they've finished. Women like a lot of foreplay. To a man, foreplay is counting up to four and then he starts to play. Anita Lonsborough did the breast stroke and got two medals in the Olympics. My brother stroked a breast and got two years in Pentonville prison. Alice in Wonderland kept crying "I'm late! I'm late!" and her mother was sick about it.

The government in Spain is trying to cut down on all the illicit sex in Ibiza. They're using a Spanish fly swatter. A young woman complained that her boyfriend had her confused. "He tells me how good I look, and then he wants to turn out the light." All you read in the papers these days is about banking and bonking. They're even dropping the titles of "Woman of the Year" and replacing it with "Other Woman of the Year." And they're changing that song to "I want a girl just like the girl who lived with dead old Dad."

Where unprotected sex is concerned, one and one makes three. I've always wondered why, if sex is such a natural phenomenon, there are so many how-to books on it. Love has been described as the Comedy of Eros. I finally found a girl who cooks like my mother. Unfortunately she looks like my father. It's a fact that the battle of the sexes will never be won while there's so much fraternising with the enemy.

They used to say "Make love- not war." I'm married, so I do both. Have you noticed how stage plays today are mostly about sex? Playwrights who used to bare their souls are now baring their actors. Seems like the only place there's any covering up now is in government circles. To me, TV represents sex and violence. Every time my wife catches me watching sex on TV, she gets violent. I personally hate sex in the cinema. That's because I tried it once and the seats folded up. It caught me unawares, very painful.

Men used to want to marry virgins, not any more. Now they say let Captain Spock go where no man has gone before. An Arab terrorist found he'd been tricked when he got to heaven. He was met by 70 vegans. Even footballers unashamedly kiss and hug each other after a goal. If they do

203

that on the field, I'd hate to think what they get up to in the changing room.

Everyone's at it. Even Delia Smith's husband is known to curl up with a good cook. Men often leave the straight and narrow for a girl who isn't built that way. At the supermarket I stood behind two housewives discussing sex, "I'm ashamed to admit it, Sandra," said one, but I caught my husband making love." "Don't let that bother you" her friend replied. "I got mine the same way." It's no fun kissing a girl over the phone. Unless you're right there in the booth with her.

Most men wonder what life would be like without sex, and then they get married. I once got friendly with a promiscuous woman on a cruise and when we parted she said "If you ever want some fun and games, ring this number. I did. Turned out to be Toys 'R Us.

Madonna's supposed reputation for promiscuity came into doubt when she was asked to write a new book entitled "I only ever loved one man" The publishers wanted to add "At a time." Joan Rivers says she was so naïve about sex that when her mother explained the custom was man on top and woman underneath, she went out and bought bunk beds. The government's doing too little to end the boom in teenage pregnancies. "After all" they say, "to heir is human." My parents punished me for lying. And they were the ones who said it was the stork that brought me. The doctor told his young female patient "In the language of the birds and bees, you've been pollinated."

My wife's bi-sexual. If I want sex I have to buy her something. The problem is she's so indecisive about sex. She can never make up her mind whether to fake a headache or an orgasm. She's even taken to playing the National Anthem in our bedroom to get things to stand up. It doesn't work. It's not my fault parts of me aren't patriotic.

My brother's a man ahead of his time. He has premature ejaculation. He went to the Premature Ejaculation Clinic, but they sent him away. He turned up too early. Yesterday he went to Boots and bought a whole year's supply of condoms.....two. The folks down at the Sperm Bank must think he's a sailor. They keep referring to him as semen first class.

I had a blind date with this girl who told me she was in the communications business. I found out later she was a call girl. Actually they don't call them "call girls" any more. Now it's "maid-to-order." I thought I had everything till I met her. Now I have herpes as well. Most nights she can be found hanging out in restaurants. That's her other job, she's a topless waitress. I won't say she's oversexed, but she's just bought a T-shirt with the slogan in Braille. She became a nymphomaniac because she believes chaste means waste. But she does stand by her principals of never having sex with strangers. She always asks their name first. She's so different from my last girlfriend who knew nothing about sex. She's so ignorant; when her pet rabbit died she thought she was pregnant. Mind you, I'm no expert. All I know about sex is I'm not getting any.

My wife says that as a lover I remind her of James Bond. She says on a scale of one to ten I'm an 007. When I told her that sex is a driving force, she said I should stop and ask directions. She's even installed a mirror over our bed because she likes to see herself laugh. My wife's got a new hobby now, she's into group sex. Trouble is, she won't let me join the group. I asked my wife if there was anything I could do to make her sex life more interesting. She said "Yes. work late."

A lecher's a man who spends six days sowing his wild oats and then goes to church on Sunday to pray for a crop failure. My neighbour's a real lecher. After he's taken a girl out to dinner he grabs everything but the bill. He says he hates going out with girls who use four letter words, like can't, don't and won't. He's been banned from the fairground because they caught him smuggling an anchor into their Tunnel of Love.

After his divorce he was a free male. Then he joined an escort agency and became a fee-male. His first client was a schoolteacher, who he found very hard-going. She kept making him do it over and over again till he got it right. The only time my wife said the earth moved during sex was when we were in Italy and there was an earthquake.

ADDITIONAL GAGS

- She found the perfect way to keep the wolf from the door. She meets him in the alley.
- Clinton's always been a smart man. They say he has six new suits a year. Mostly paternity.

- The young lady complained that when she was a kid she was always being told off for leaving the lights on. Now, with her boyfriend, she gets shouted at for turning them off.
- Did you hear about the prostitute who had to go for her thousand male check-up?
- Did you hear about the promiscuous Russian film starlet who thought Alexander was great and Ivan was terrible?
- One film star admitted that he used to be pre-occupied with sex, but that's all changed. Now he's occupied with it.
- We ought to be able to control the population explosion the same way as farmers in the EU. Pay men not to plant their seeds.
- When the wife discovered her husband in bed with the au pair, he said "It's your fault. You told me to find something to do to take my mind off smoking."
- Joan Rivers says "I was such an ugly baby my mother never told me about sex. She figured I'd never need to know."
- Some days it pays to stay in bed. At least, that's what my local hooker says.
- Women are getting more litigation conscious these days. In the old days if you said goodbye to a girlfriend she took it to heart. Now she takes it to court.
- With postage as expensive as it now is you should see what my girlfriend charges me to play Post Office. And she isn't even first class.
- My wife's an animal. All she wants to do is sleep and make love. Unfortunately both at the same time.
- Ronnie Corbett married a very tall girl. It's worked out fine, except when they make love he has to make two trips.
- The young model is so thin she knows she'll never be a Page Three Girl. But she's hoping to be a Page One and a Half.
- I hear the government IS thinking of putting a tax on sex. That's not necessary. I already find it taxing enough.
- The travelling salesman's wife divorced him just because he had an unscheduled lay-over. She found out who he'd been laying over.
- The girl said about her last date "He started on a shoestring and worked his way up. So I slapped his face."

- Ours was a very long wedding night. We lost our place in the sex manual.
- Her husband didn't come home for supper. He said he was grabbing something at the office. Turned out to be his secretary's breasts.
- My wife hates sex. You should have heard the way she screamed at the girl I was in bed with.
- After our first date she said "I hope you're not one of those fellows who say they'll call.. and do."
- I have a service contract on everything in my house. The TV set..the video recorder…the washing machine…the fridge…About the only thing that doesn't get serviced is my wife.
- The Travelling salesmen asked the brothel-keeper "Are the ladies of the house in?"
- In Britain we count sheep. In Australia they mount them.
- I've no objection to people being perverts, as long as it's done in good taste.
- She worked her way through college…..one boy at a time.
- Julian Clary's just written a new book. It's called Fifty Shades of Gay.
- As the prostitute said to the man in bed with her "Alright, I'll give you a discount. But only because you're my husband."
- Sex means never having to say you've got a headache.
- Have you noticed how people don't make obscene phone calls anymore? Now they write them down and look for a publisher.
- When my friend's wife caught him cheating for the fifth time this week, she said "What's your excuse this time?" He thought for a moment, and then said "I'm trying to get into The Guinness Book of Records."
- In cigarettes it's mildness. In wine it's age. And in a Volkswagen it's almost impossible.
- The Gay Lib has its entrance in the rear.
- The paedophile wasn't at all superstitious. He didn't care if the girl he slept with was thirteen.
- As one girl described her latest boyfriend to her pal. He's nothing to text home about.
- First he bought his girlfriend a bikini. Then he tried to talk her out of it.

- My Dad always believed that all questions about sex should be answered frankly. So whenever the subject came up he'd say "Go ask Frank."
- In their school sex lesson the kids were told to remember that one mistake leads to a mother.
- This poor soldier posted his girlfriend a proposal every day for a year. When he got home he found she'd married the postman.
- He was a normal straight man till he graduated from university. After he put on the gown he found he liked dresses.
- I want to donate my body to science when I'm dead and to Dolly Parton while I'm still alive.
- As the young starlet said of the ageing Hollywood star "I didn't care about his mind wandering. It was his hands that bothered me."
- The old man wound up in hospital because he tried to keep up with the Joneses. They were a honeymoon couple.
- I'm not saying that man's a pervert, but he approaches women on the street with an open mind and raincoat to match.
- When he bought his secretary a fur coat it wasn't to keep her warm so much as to keep her quiet.
- She refused his offer of a post-sex cigarette because, she said, her husband doesn't like her smoking.
- She complained about her name being written on toilet walls, but only because they got the phone number wrong.
- Anne Boleyn was the first woman in history to go topless,
- Among the gay community, true love's a many gendered thing.
- He thinks he's so sexy; he sits in front of the mirror all day playing strip solitaire.
- In Elton John's house his young son was heard singing "I Saw Daddy Kissing Santa Claus."
- Last Christmas, instead of a turkey, Elton had a goose.
- He couldn't get it up. Now he takes Viagra he can't get it down.
- I caught my wife in bed with my best friend. I'll kill that dog.
- When a man is bald at the front it means he's a thinker. When he's bald at the back it means he's sexy. And when he's bald back and front that means he just thinks he's sex.
- My girlfriend's an outdoor lover. Mind you, she's pretty good indoors too.

- The least sexy people are fat men and flat women.
- People at nude conventions get very little coverage.
- Even at his age he still pays for sex. But now he gets a refund.
- She speaks eight languages but can't say "No" in any of them.
- Bill Clinton said he could read women like a book. And he did most of his reading in bed.
- You know you're a loser when, at your bachelor party they show a porn video and your future wife's in it.
- She thought all men were created equal till she went to a nudist colony.
- If you break the mirror over your bed, you'll have seven years bad sex.
- He's mad about money and women. He tries to make them both go as far as possible.
- At the last count there were 950 million Chinese. Don't their women ever get a headache?
- I asked her what gave her the impression the man she dated was a psychiatrist. She said "He asked me to lie down on the couch."
- "He asked me to lay down on the couch."
- After sex on our honeymoon my wife said "At least we've got the "For Worse" part over with."
- He was a premature baby. Born three weeks before his parents got married.
- Since we gave up sex my wife refers to our water bed as Lake Placid.
- I'm not saying she's promiscuous, but she reached the age of consent three hundred consents ago.
- One school kid boasted to his mate "I know how babies are made." "That's nothing" said the other "I know how they're not."
- Men often make passes at girls who drain glasses.
- Sex can shorten your life. Especially if her husband comes home early.
- I got a letter from the local library saying they're going to cancel my library card unless I bring back the librarian I took out two months ago.
- I've just found out the sexy footman in Downton Abbey is a breast man.

- He's so naïve, on his wedding night he had to use cue cards.
- I've discovered a new birth control method. My wife takes off her make-up.
- The Hollywood actress never had an Oscar, a Tony or an Emmy, but she had lots of Tom, Dick and Harrys.
- The most frightening thing a wife can hear when she's making love is "Honey, I'm home."
- My girlfriend and I had a wonderfully romantic night. The moon was out and so were her parents.
- I've just read in the paper there's a new device out that can cut down a man's sexual desires. That's not new. I've been married to one for thirty years.
- My wife says her burning ambition is to have sex in the back of the car while I'm in the front driving.
- She was absolutely furious with her boyfriend when she found out he was cheating on her…with his wife.
- He always kisses with his eyes open…so he can see in case his wife comes in.
- She insisted that nothing goes on until the ring goes on.
- I was very disappointed with the book "Everything You Wanted To Know About Sex"i t didn't tell you where to get it.
- The woman told her friend "I never slept with my husband before we were married. How about you? Her friend said "I don't know. What's his name?"
- My daughter's going out with a chauffeur. We know he's a chauffeur because when he takes her to the pictures he makes her sit in the row behind.
- I told a friend that sex in my marriage has become boring as I know my wife's every move. He said "Don't complain. At least your wife moves."
- Love they neighbour, but draw the blinds first.
- One woman tells another "The chap I was out with last night said he wanted some old fashioned sex. So I introduced him to my grandmother."
- I invited this girl up to see my etchings and it worked. She bought three of them.
- Sex will always be popular because it has no calories.

- When us men exchange spouses it's called wife-swapping. But when native girls do it it's called passing the buck.
- He was happy when he heard his secretary was giving him clothes for his birthday, till he found out it was a paternity suit.
- Lady Godiva was the world's greatest gambler. She put everything she had on a horse.
- She got the job as a stripper because she proved to be unsuitable.
- My brother and his wife spend a lot of time making love, which is why they rarely see each other.
- On our wedding night I gave my wife the best performance of my life. In fact, I darn near woke her up.
- The boss set his brand new secretary a test. He said "If I give you £5,000 minus 12%, what would you take off?" She said "Everything, but my earrings."
- Sex may be a sin. Mind you, the way some do it it's a crime.
- Our local Townswomen's Guild held a swap party to which members were asked to bring along things they no longer wanted. Most of them brought their husbands.
- Sex is nothing new in the cinema. But now they have it on the screen as well.
- I'm dead against wife-swapping parties. It's such a disappointment when you get your wife back.
- The young lad was told by his dad about the birds and the bees, but it was a waste of time. He didn't know any birds or bees.
- She has boyfriends by the score...and most of them do.
- At school she was voted the girl most likely to.
- If at first you don't succeed, try again. She'll expect it.
- I want to thank the supply teacher who volunteered to stand-in for my wife during our honeymoon.
- She confessed to her father that she had posed nude for her boyfriend. "But" said her dad, "you're not a model." "No" she said "And he's not an artist."
- I'd been dating this girl for years and didn't know she was married....till my wife told me.
- Guns kill people, but not as much as jealous husbands do.
- I know a girl whose big ambition in life is to have a king-size bed...with a king already in it.

211

- When the sexpot was told that 65% of married men had extra marital affairs, she said "Never mind the statistics, just give me their names."
- When an Oriental woman walks several paces behind her husband it's a sign of respect. When a Western woman does it means her husband's being trailed.
- When I first courted my wife her Dad insisted we keep the light on. It wasn't that he didn't trust me. He had shares in the electric company.
- As far as seducing girls was concerned he tried everything. Chocolates, flowers, perfume, jewellery….they all worked.
- As the sexy girl said to her male admirer "If you had three wishes, what would be the other two?
- Lots of women dress to please men. And even more undress for the same reason.
- It's said that Bill Clinton had eight new suits a year. Six of them paternity.
- Clinton always believed in life, liberty and the pursuit of women.
- I was a boy scout till I was sixteen, then I went scouting for girls.
- If, when you kiss your girlfriend her lips are like fire and she trembles in your arms, ditch her. She probably has malaria.
- Two's company, three's the result.
- Most strip clubs make you pay a no-cover charge.
- When a lecher talks about the good old days he really means the nights.
- Joan Collins says dialling a number on her mobile is like getting married. She usually winds up with the wrong party.
- She has the reputation for giving men the glad aye.
- He saw a sign in the road "Yield", so he took it home and put it on his wife's side of the bed.
- One man stopped going to the nudist camp because they put the prices up. His final words to the manager were "You've seen the end of me."
- She slept with so many young men she was known as Miss-under-stud.
- If a lady says no, she means maybe. If she says maybe, she means yes. And if she says yes, she's no lady.

- Some actresses agree to do a sex scene if it's integral to the part. She'll do it if it's integral to GETTING the part.
- I told my son that storks bring babies. He said "Someone ought to tell Mum, she's been bringing them herself."
- I once had sex with a policewoman. She gave me a ticket for speeding.
- My daughter said her boyfriend is very protective. He always wears a condom.
- Does Playboy magazine come in braille?
- She only has sex during the safe period. When her husband's out of town.
- It's not true that condoms guarantee safe sex. A friend of mine was wearing one when he was shot dead by the woman's husband.
- If you're wearing a durex and you have a kid you can send Durex back the condom…And the kid.
- He refers to her as his overnight bag.
- The actor was arrested for playing a rapist. He did it with too much feeling.
- They met in the days of flower power. He was the one that deflowered her.
- Lady Godiva drove through Coventry advertising the local nudist camp.
- As far as sex is concerned she said she'd only do it for love. So he gave her a diamond bracelet which she loved.
- Clinton said "I never slept with that woman. We never even had a nap together."
- He has a fear of sex. He's afraid he won't get any.
- As Grumpy said to his fellow dwarfs "Snow White's door is locked again and I can't find happy."
- She wore a skirt made out of a union jack and he kept saying it was time to raise the flag.
- The beaches in Brighton are divided into two sections "NUDES" and "PRUDES."
- As the homosexual Roman said to his fellow countrymen "Friends, Romans and countrymen, lend me your rears."

213

- I thought he was a transvestite because he came to work wearing his wife's clothes. Then he explained he'd got out the wrong side of the bed that morning.
- She sat on his sunglasses and broke them, He wouldn't have minded but she was wearing them at the time.
- The man went to watch a belly dancer because he was tired of contemplating his own navel.
- Love is just around the corner. Unless, of course, you live in an igloo.
- The lecherous boss had all the yes-men he needed. Now he's looking for a woman who'll say "Yes."
- Her husband caught her on the beach with the lifeguard practicing mouth to mouth resuscitation.
- The Hollywood producer told the starlet "Don't look on it as a casting couch. Look upon it as more of a launching pad."
- She claimed on her car insurance because she got pregnant in the car.
- I'm not suggesting she was promiscuous, but what she put in her boss's suggestion box was the key to her flat.
- Most girls hold up their thumbs to get a lift. She holds up her bra.
- I bought a sex magazine and found the pictures in it are not only obscene, they're impossible.
- He's always looking for ways to try out new things, like the vasectomy he's just had.
- His idea of oral sex is making an indecent phone call.
- The politician involved in a sex scandal was re-elected. His constituents were just pleased he was screwing someone else for a change.
- She not only belongs to the world's oldest profession, she was one of its founders.
- His wife doesn't object to him spending all day at work painting nude women. But she gets annoyed when he takes the work home with him.
- She calls Dolly Parton a Hunchfront.
- About native woman with bare big bosoms. Her country might be underdeveloped, but she certainly isn't.
- As the young boy said to the young girl "I'll be the bird and you be the bee."

- When the husband opened his wardrobe and found his wife's lover in there, she said "Oh, darling, I forgot to tell you. I've rented out the cupboard."
- I'm not saying he's a philanderer, but when they play "Come All Ye Faithful" he stays where he is.
- The old prostitute said to her colleague "His cheque came back marked "insufficient fun.""
- Most people have their WELCOME mat by their front door. She has one by her bed.
- The single mother said "I don't know who the father is. He's got Bill's eyes, Roger's nose and Bert's chin."
- I'm not saying she's lousy in the bedroom, but every time we make love I have to shoo away the vultures overhead.
- Lady Godiva was arrested for not wearing a safety helmet.
- As the Palmist said to the lecher "You'll go to parties and meet lots of girls…you'll be invited to orgies of all types…and one more thing. Get your grubby hand off my knee."
- The ignorant girl got pregnant through an immaculate misconception.
- She's rich because her number came up…on the men's toilet wall.
- She says she's one of the now generation, but all I get from her is "Not now."
- The porn star had to have a cue card which read "In-out…in out…in out…!
- The prospective secretary was rejected because the boss found out she had a record for lateness, gossiping and chastity.
- When the wife found her husband in bed with another woman he said "Well, you wouldn't let me have a night out with the boys."

SHOPPING

Thanks to my wife, I've just read a book with a very sad ending. It was my cheque book. You see, my wife and I have different hobbies. Mine's playing golf and hers is shopping at Harrods. She goes to every Harrods sale. In our house it's known as the Charge-of-the-Wife Brigade. She's great at sign language. When she shops she signs for everything. She reckons she has the perfect monetary plan. She buys now, I pay later. If she doesn't stop spending soon, when I die all I'm going to leave her is alone. Before we were married it was all billing and cooing. The cooing soon stopped, but the billing's carried on.

For our last anniversary all I gave my wife was a card, but it made her happy. It was American Express. All this country needs to boost its economy is to let my wife loose with a credit card. She refers to me as her poor husband. And she ought to know, she's the one that made me poor. I used to take her on package holidays, but not anymore. She came back with too many packages.

My wife's very careful with money. She's the only one I know who buys shoes one at a time. Once she wanted to buy me a ring for my birthday. I still remember the jeweller's exact words "Yes Madam we do have cheaper rings, but they're holding up the curtains." The only time I've known her waste money was when she thought I was having an affair with another woman and hired a private detective. She wanted to know what this other woman saw in me.

ADDITIONAL GAGS

- The shoe salesman said he'd only agree to serve my wife if, in the middle, she let him have a coffee break.
- When my wife goes shopping it's like magic the way she can make money disappear.
- My wife is always out shopping. One day she stayed at home and two stores went out of business.
- My wife's just had plastic surgery. I cut up her credit cards.
- My wife gets letters marked "Return to Spender."
- The only thing my wife does on time is buy things.
- My wife went out to buy a new car and came home with just the chassis. She refused to pay for the accessories.
- If I ever give my wife credit for anything, she immediately goes out and spends it.
- My wife put her credit card into the ATM but it wouldn't come out again. It was seeking sanctuary.
- My wife was told she had to cut down on watching so much TV. So she bought a set with a 9-inch screen.

- She had her credit card suspended for reckless shopping.
- My wife's a treasure. Trouble is she thinks I'm the treasury.
- As the woman said when she tried on the dress in the shop "This is just what I was looking for. Let me know when you have it in the sale."
- The wife said to her friend "My husband works hard to bring home the money, so the least I can do is show my appreciation by spending it."
- Cowboy says "Yes, I was caught in a stampede once. It was sale time at Harrods.
- The only time my wife went out without buying a thing is when someone stole her purse.
- Every time my wife buys a labour saving device I have to work overtime to pay for it.
- She got a medal for being wounded in the Harrods sale.
- My wife never sends me shopping for groceries because last time I came back with two items that had to be cooked.

SHOW BUSINESS

What an obese figure Jo Brand has! She's the only one I know who wears a cross-your-knees bra. She went into a women's wear shop and said "I'd like to see a swimsuit in my size. The salesgirl said "So would I!" She bought a pair of jodhpurs because it's the only piece of clothing that goes out where she does. You couldn't help noticing Jo in her school picture. She was the front row. She's so fat; when she got married she had to walk down the aisle single file. When her husband carried her over the threshold he had to make two trips. As a comedienne, in her act she guarantees a hundred laughs. A hundred and two if you include her face and figure. I heard that she willed her body to science and science is contesting the will. I must admit I'm no fan of Jo Brand's anti-male jokes. Personally I think her best cracks are the ones in her make-up. Last year she was voted top female comic, which proves nothing's impossible. Just implausible.

Even as a young girl it was clear Dolly Parton had a great future ahead of her. She was cautioned by the police last week. They saw her driving her car with her top down. She played an incompetent secretary in

9 to 5, but it wasn't her fault. She couldn't get close enough to the typewriter. She tried her hand at being a schoolteacher, but that didn't work. Every time she turned round she wiped the blackboard. She's was also useless at golf. With her figure she could never see the ball. Actually she has tiny feet, which is understandable. Things don't grow well in the shade. Dolly realised long ago that certain things were impossible for her. Like becoming an accordion player. She now lives in Hollywood and you can tell which door is Dolly's house. It's the one with the big knockers.

Sir Terry Wogan says that resigning from his morning BBC radio show was the most painful thing he's ever done. Not true. The most painful thing was his recording of The Floral Dance. It was Wogan's record of The Floral Dance that made one music lover come out of a five year coma. He got up to switch it off.

Jonathan Ross's fans are protected by law under the Endangered Species Act.

The marriage between Lisa Minnelli and David Gest lasted just six days and seven fights. Dean Martin used to make a deposit at the bank every day. The bottle bank. Eighty four year old Tony Bennett may have left his heart in San Francisco, but now leaves his teeth in a glass of water. Before Orville, Keith Harris had a dog dummy. He got rid of it because, when he threw his voice, it wouldn't fetch.

Ronnie Corbett is so short he can milk a cow standing up. If he pulls his socks up it acts as a blindfold. He can only make love if someone puts him up to it. He plays polo a lot and you can tell which his horse is. It's the one with lifts on its horseshoes. But he insists he's never been superstitious. He thinks nothing of walking under a black cat.

When Cher wore a stunning very low cut gown to a premiere a woman in the crowd asked "I wonder who made her dress?" The woman next to her said "Probably the police." Clint Eastwood has a beautiful new girlfriend. She makes his days and he makes her nights. And all for a fistful of dollars. Telly Savalas went bald at the age of twenty. He had premature Kojakulation. Show business stars have to accept substantial wage cuts. Many can't get work at all. One year they're starring and next year the second 'r' is replaced by a 'v'.

Did you hear about the actor who changed his name to EXIT because he wanted to see it in lights? So many of these so-called celebrities are writing books. I'm surprised. I didn't think some of them could even read one. Next time at the Academy Awards I'd love to see a Hollywood actress be honest and say "I wouldn't be up here accepting this Oscar if it wasn't for the hard work behind the scenes of one man…my plastic surgeon." A new West End nightclub has just opened which claims to have four bouncers. They're two topless waitresses.

The Village People are too old for TV and now doing so badly they're actually living in the YMCA. I know of one Hollywood actor who spends two hours every day reading his fan mail. And four hours every day writing it. Playboy chief Hugh Heffner says at his age just the thought of sex makes him cry. For him now it's all hankie with no panky.

ADDITIONAL GAGS

- Angus Deayton's always been one for the ladies. When he was born the nurse slapped him before the doctor did.
- He had so many affairs, when he was on This Is Your Life they used a blue book.
- Anne Robinson and Joan Rivers both had plastic surgery. They're going to star together in a sequel to The Untouchables. It's called The Re-Touchables.
- Joan Rivers claims she's had so many facelifts she now goes to a gynaecologist for her migraine.
- In Joan Collins' bathroom she has towels marked "Hers" and "The Latest."
- Joan Collins says she doesn't need to get married any more. She's now collected enough wedding rings for her charm bracelet.
- When Joan Collins was told her ex-husband was on the phone, she said "Which one?"
- Joan Collins claims to have been happily married for forty years. Mind you, it took her six marriages to do it.
- They asked Joan Collins how many husbands she's had. She said "You mean, including my own?"
- Joan Collins has managed to keep her figure from all the exercise she gets walking up and down wedding aisles.
- Joan Collins has signed more marriage certificates than autographs.

- Joan Collins says she believes in large families. She thinks every woman should have at least three husbands.
- I want to live long enough to find out who finally winds up with Joan Collins.
- Joan Collins has walked down the aisle so often they're trying to make her pay for the carpet.
- Joan Collins says she owes her long career to people too numerous to mention. Her ex-husbands.
- Dawn French wore all white to a party and the hostess screened a movie on her.
- Dawn French went to America and found another female wearing the same size dress. It was the Statue of Liberty.
- There's a new Dawn French doll on the market. You don't need to wind it up; it just eats its way out of the box.
- Dawn French was ejected from the beach at Brighton. She was providing too much shade.
- Obese Dawn French never eats between meals. For her there IS no between meals.
- Dawn French is twice the woman she used to be. And she's got the bathroom scales to prove it.
- Equity threw a big party for Dawn French's birthday. She was the big party.
- I'm not suggesting that Dawn French is overweight, but this week she donated her bra as a shelter for the homeless.
- Show business doesn't make for successful marriages. I guess the only perfect couple I know in Hollywood is Dolly Parton.
- Watching Dolly Parton squeeze into a parking space is almost as much fun as watching her squeeze into a sweater.
- As Barbara Windsor said to Dolly Parton "This town ain't big enough for the four of us."
- Bruce Forsyth broke a mirror and ended up with seven years bad jokes.
- A Bruce Forsyth joke is no laughing matter.
- Bruce Forsyth doesn't have an enemy in the world. He's outlived them all.
- Bruce Forsyth is so old he once did a Shakespeare play and Shakespeare himself was in the wings prompting him.

- I'm not saying Bruce Forsyth is old but the picture of him on his driver's license is by Van Gogh.
- 87 year old Bruce Forsyth – a barely living legend.
- When Bruce Forsyth told a joke on Strictly Come Dancing he had the entire audience open mouthed. All yawning at the same time.
- Strictly Come Dancing is shown in 26 African countries and Bruce Forsyth was older than most of them.
- George Washington couldn't tell a lie and Bruce Forsyth can't tell a joke.
- In his earlier years, Bruce Forsyth never came out on top, but his hair did.
- I'm not saying Bruce Forsyth is old, but as a kid he had a pet dinosaur.
- Before she died Liz Taylor, who'd put on so much weight, was going to do a sequel to one of her films. It was to be called "Fat on a Hot Tin Roof."
- Bernard Manning was a difficult man to work with. Even when he did a one-man show he couldn't get along with the cast.
- Ken Dodd is the fastest talker in Show Business. They're even talking of putting an impression of his tongue outside Grumman's Chinese Theatre.
- Ken Dodd was one of the most sought-after comedians in the country. Mostly for tax evasion.
- I've never seen a bad word said about Jonathan Ross. It's usually a whole page.
- The trouble with Jonathan Ross is his initials are JR and he really thinks he is.
- Jackie Mason is an ordained rabbi, which is handy. If a joke dies he can conduct a memorial service on the spot.
- Self-deprecating comedian Rodney Dangerfield built himself up by running himself down.
- Phyllis Diller used to be a pin-up girl. They pinned her picture up in prison to deter sex offenders.
- They asked Mae West how she managed to keep her youth. She said "Under lock and key and too exhausted to leave."
- Arnold Schwarzenegger's so egotistic. His body's gone to his head.

- Mickey Rooney's been married nine times. He's now truly spouse broken.
- Nigella Lawson's favourite drink is marriage on the rocks.
- George Burns won the case when a girl sued him for breach of promise. He said at his age there wasn't anything he could promise.
- Ex-president Clinton's getting lazy. He now only dates girls that are already pregnant.
- Dean Martin was such a big drinker, when he died and was cremated it took them a week to put out the flames.
- Because of all the swearing they put the Lee Evans shows on late at night. He's kept more people awake than black coffee.
- Just think, if you and I had dandruff it would be a nuisance, but to Duncan Goodhew it would be a thrill.
- If you want to see a woman who has her hands full, watch Liz Taylor's masseuse at work.
- I bumped into Duncan Goodhew at the barber shop. He was there reminiscing.
- Paul McCartney says if his music company ever goes broke he might consider re-marrying Heather Mills for his money.
- Paul McCartney's so successful two of his gold teeth just turned platinum.
- Jo Brand's just been voted the top sex symbol, for men who don't care.
- You can tell which man was Dolly Parton's dancing partner. He's the one with the sunken chest.
- Anne Robinson has a dimple in her chin. Before the face lifts it was her navel.
- Even circus clowns have updated their act. Now the laughs they get are canned.
- They've never found out who the Unknown Soldier was, but they now know the unknown pervert was Jimmy Savile.
- The tightrope walker at the circus had an accident. It was his own fault for drinking too much. That night he was tighter than the rope.
- Madame Rambert was a very strict disciplinarian. She kept all her ballet dancers on their toes.
- Some show off actors are called hams, which doesn't really apply. Hams can be cured.

- One actor got a bad review and wrote a note to the critic which said "I am sitting in the loo and your review is in front of me. Very soon it will be behind me."
- The old Thespian flirting with the young starlet asked her "Where have you been all my life." She said "Most of it at home teething."
- Very few actors have full time employment. It's the luck of the game. One day you're delivering a soliloquy and the next day a pizza.
- There must have been a lot of good in Bernard Manning because none of it ever came out.
- Show Biz has its ups and downs. One day you can be an unknown failure and the next day a known failure.
- The best way to study body language is to watch a belly dancer.
- Modern comedians are either lewd or rude and usually both.
- An actor realises his career is over when the only time he's invited to appear in public is in police line-ups.
- At the audition the casting director told the young actress "I'm afraid you won't do." She said "Who said I wouldn't?"
- In Show Biz the girls marry for either love or money....but not for long.
- She's a lousy actress. During the rape scenes she can't stop smiling.
- Lots of old artistes now have the familiar billing "Stars of stage, screen and police investigations."
- One film actress has played prostitutes so many times; the producers don't pay her in the regular way anymore. They just leave the money on the sideboard.
- My wife says my lovemaking skills remind her of an intoxicating liquor. Old Grandad.
- Despite the child abuse allegation, Woody Allen may be popular with most of the USA but certainly not with the PTA. He's being accused of being in Miss Saigon.
- The juggler had a very novel act. First he juggled with ten very sharp knives. Then, as an encore he juggled with ten fingers.
- He was a sword swallower with a difference. He always put mustard on it to give it more taste.
- Fame seldom lasts. One day you're at the top and next day in the tip.

- They're obviously very hygiene conscious here. The dressing room they gave me has twelve sinks.
- He's a true comedian. He even smells funny.
- Julian Clary's always in the pink. That's his favourite colour.
- To a man happiness is bumping into Dolly Parton very slowly.

SIGNS

Outside a bakery "THANK YOU FOR NOT DIETING."

Outside the Inland Revenue office "IT'S BETTER TO GIVE THAN TO DECEIVE."

Outside the Maternity Hospital "WE DELIVER."

Outside a church "IN BUSINESS SINCE YEAR ONE."

On the door of a street phone booth "TEMPORARILY NOT OUT OF ORDER."

Outside an American petrol garage "THE BUICK STOPS HERE."

Outside Weight Watchers "CLOSED FOR LUNCH 12.55 TO 1.00 PM."

On the door of the Sheriff's office displaying pictures of Bonnie & Clyde. Under Clyde the word "WANTED" and under Bonnie "DESIRED."

On the wall of a pet shop "ANY REMARKS OF THE PARROT ARE HIS OWN AND DO NOT REFLECT THE OPINIONS OF THE MANAGEMENT."

On the wall of a ladies hairdresser. "TOPIC OF THE DAY – HOLIDAYS AND DATING."

Outside a self-service restaurant "24 TABLES - NO WAITING"

Outside the Beauty Parlour "DON'T WHISTLE AT THE GIRL COMING OUT OF HERE, SHE MAY BE YOUR GRANDMOTHER."

Outside the barber shop "DURING ALTERATIONS CUSTOMERS WILL BE SHAVED IN THE REAR."

Outside the second hand shop "WE EXCHANGE ANYTHING, HAIR DRIERS, TOASTERS, STEAM IRONS. BRING YOUR WIFE HERE FOR A BARGAIN."

Outside the golf club "TRESPASSERS CAUGHT COLLECTING GOLF BALLS WILL BE PROSECUTED AND HAVE THEIR BALLS REMOVED."

Outside a computer shop "OUT FOR A QUICK BYTE."

Outside a maternity ward "TO HEIR IS HUMAN."

On the door of a maternity labour ward "PUSH, PUSH, PUSH!"

Outside a Nudist Camp "WE NEVER CLOTHED."

Outside a taxidermist "WE KNOW OUR STUFF."

On the notice board of an Adult Education Centre "DYSLEXICS OF THE WORLD UNTIE."

Outside A Poetry Society "FREE AND BLANK VERSE SPOKEN HERE."

Outside a Bridal Shop "WE PROVIDE EVERYTHING FOR THE BRIDE, EXCEPT THE GROOM."

Outside the RAC office "WE DON'T CHARGE AN ARM AND A LEG FOR A TOW."

Outside the Income Tax Office "THE CUSTOMER IS ALWAYS WRONG."

Outside a furrier "FUR COATS MADE FOR LADIES FROM THEIR OWN SKIN."

Outside a fenced field "THE FARMER ALLOWS FREE ACCESS, BUT THE BULL CHARGES."

Outside a former topless restaurant "OUR WAITRESSES ARE NOW BEHIND BRAS."

In the launderette: "WHEN WASHING STOPS, PLEASE REMOVE ALL YOUR CLOTHES."

On a husband's tombstone: "YOU SAID IT WOULDN'T KILL ME TO BE NICE TO YOUR MOTHER."

Held by a man with a placard outside a marriage registry office: "PREPARE TO MEET THY DOOM."

On the door of a dachshund's owner: "BEWARE OF THE DOOOOOOG."

In the window of the Avis Detective Agency: "WE PRY HARDER."

On the door of a fat person's fridge: "YOU ARE HERE – AND SHOULDN'T BE."

Outside a department store at Christmas: "VISIT OUR GROTTO. SIX SANTAS-NO WAITING."

Outside a London tube station: "TEMPORARILY IN SERVICE."

Outside a church: "TRESPASSERS WELCOME "

Outside Weight Watchers: "THINK SMALL."

Outside a book shop: "COOKBOOK LEFTOVERS – HALF PRICE."

Outside a repair garage: "HAVE YOUR ACCIDENT NOW, BEFORE PRICES GO UP."

Outside the tennis courts after the annual tournament: "WIMBLEDONE."

For an astronaut in flight: "NEXT FILLING STATION 3 MILLION MILES."

In the children's section of a book store: "SHOPLIFTERS WILL BE SPANKED."

On the goalpost in a game of hockey: "THE PUCK STOPS HERE."

On a seaside promenade telescope: "ALL YOU CAN SEE - 50p"

Outside a prison gate: "NO VACANCIES."

On a man's leg covered in plaster of Paris: "PAIR OF SKIS FOR SALE, CHEAP."

Outside a tobacconist shop: "THANK YOU FOR STILL SMOKING."

Sign in a church: "THANK YOU FOR NOT SNORING."

Outside a porno cinema: "SUITABLE FOR MATURE DEGENERATES ONLY."

Outside a scout camp: "BE PREPARED – CARRY A CONDOM."

In a supermarket: "EAT, DRINK AND BE MERRY, FOR TOMORROW OUR PRICES MIGHT BE OUT OF REACH."

Held up by a heavily pregnant hitchhiker in a wedding dress: "GET ME TO THE CHURCH ON TIME."

Over a business executive's desk: "EAT, DRINK AND MAKE MONEY."

In a tulip garden: "TIP TOE."

Outside a sports shoe shop "ATHLETE'S FOOT WELCOME."

On an airline check-in desk: "WE TAKE YOUR BAGS AND SEND THEM IN ALL DIRECTIONS."

In a department store: "BARGAIN BASEMENT UPSTAIRS."

Outside the Weather Bureau: "POSSIBLY BACK AT 1 PM, WITH A SLIGHT CHANCE OF 1.30."

Pinned to Dolly Parton's bra: "THIS IS A STICK-UP."

In a hospital waiting room: "EXPRESS LANE – TWO SYMPTONS OR LESS."

Outside a castle: "KEY IS UNDER THE MOAT."

Outside a fish shop: "TODAY'S SPECIAL – SQUID PRO QUO."

Outside the Job Centre: "WONTED – SYNE PAINTOR HOO CAN SPEEL."

Outside a doctor's surgery: "DR. ROBERT SMITH & GEORGE ROBERTS HIS LAWYER."

Outside the penicillin injection centre: "PLEASE ENTER BACKWARDS TO SAVE TIME!"

Inside a brothel: "PLEASE PAY WHEN SERVED."

Outside a Chinese restaurant: "MEN AT WOC."

Outside sperm bank: "OUT TO REST.

In a maternity ward: "NO CHILDREN ALLOWED."

Outside a church: "IF YOU LOVE TO SIN, JOIN OUR CHOIR."

University English students protest sign: "DWN WTH VWLS."

Outside a pawn shop: "DROP IN AT YOUR INCONVENIENCE."

Outside the assertiveness training centre: "BARGE RIGHT IN."

On the wall in the Tax Auditing Office: "THANK YOU FOR NOT GETTING HYSTERICAL."

Outside a psychiatrist's office "SATISFACTION OR YOUR MANIA BACK."

Outside the post office: "WE SELL STAMPS – FINANCING ARRANGED."

Outside the launderette: "BRING IN YOUR SINGLE SOCKS AND WE'LL MATCH THEM."

In the middle of a swamp: "PARKING FOR FROGS ONLY. OTHERS WILL BE TOAD."

Outside a physical fitness centre: "HAZARDOUS WAISTS DUMPED HERE."

Outside a toy shop: "DOTING GRANDPARENTS WELCOME."

On a tin can: "DON'T SPILL THE BEANS OR EVERYONE WILL KNOW."

Outside a boxer's dressing room: "OUT TO PUNCH."

Outside a fast food restaurant: "QUICHE ME QUICK."

Outside the pollution fighting bureau: "THANK YOU FOR NOT CHOKING."

On the back of a wedding car in Hollywood "JUST MARRIED. HIS 5TH. HER 3RD."

On the cover of a bible "HANDLE WITH PRAYER."

At Heathrow Airport "THANK YOU FOR NOT HI-JACKING."

Outside a florists shop "ON VACATION. MEANWHILE SAY IT WITH WORDS."

Outside a restaurant "COME IN AND EAT BEFORE BOTH OF US STARVE."

Outside a restaurant. "IF YOU REALLY LIKE HOME COOKING – GO HOME."

Outside a Beauty Parlour. "WE CAN GIVE YOU A NEW LOOK, IF YOU'VE STILL GOT THE OLD PARTS."

Outside a Strip Club "HERE THE BELLES PEEL."

Outside a bar "PLEASE DON'T DRINK ON AN EMPTY WALLET."

Outside a poultry shop "BETTER LAID THEN NEVER."

On a prostitute's tombstone "SHE SLEEPS ALONE AT LAST."

In a Russian hotel room "DON'T PUT YOUR CIGARETTES OUT IN THE POTTED PLANTS. YOU'RE LIABLE TO DAMAGE THE MICROPHONE"

Outside a mortuary "GOOD MOURNING"

Outside a mortuary "EQUAL RITES FOR WOMEN."

Outside a Nudist Camp "CLOTHED FOR THE WINTER."

Outside a Clock Shop "CLOSED FOR TWO WEEKS TO UNWIND."

Outside a condom factory "LOVE THY NEIGHBOUR – FREQUENTLY"

Outside a brothel "EVEN GEORGE WASHINGTON SLEPT HERE."

Outside a greasy-spoon restaurant "ALL YOU CAN KEEP DOWN - £5."

Outside a flooded church "TEMPORARILY OUT OF SERVICE"

Outside a church "THOU SHALT NOT PARK."

Outside a diet clinic "SATISFACTION GUARANTEESD OR YOUR TUMMY BACK."

Outside Weightwatchers "OUT TO DROOL."

On the side of a yacht "REDUCED FOR A QUICK SAIL."

On the M1 motorway "LAST CHANCE FOR FRESH AIR BEFORE REACHING LONDON"

Hitchhiker Priest's sign "WHITHER THOU GOEST."

On a tombstone "HAROLD KELLY 1956-2011. Beneath it "WIDOW KELLY 886 9643"

Outside a brothel "FEEL FREE TO COME IN AND HAVE A FREE FEEL."

On the wall of a prison clinic "SWIPE A NUMBER AND BE SEATED."

Inside door of a comedy club "EXIT- LAUGHING."

Outside mirror factory "REFLECT

On tree about missing dog "HE'S A FLEA BITTEN MUTT WITH ONE EYE AND JUST THREE LEGS AND ANSWERS TO THE NAME OF LUCKY."

On the Managing Director's door in a tyre factory. "THE BIG WHEEL".

On the buttons of a skyscraper's lift "WAY UP" and "WAY DOWN"

On the twin doors of the restaurant kitchen "TO" and "FRO".

Outside the Stock Exchange "BEWARE OF FALLING SHARE PRICES."

Outside greetings card company "ROSES ARE RED- VIOLETS ARE BLUE – GONE TO LUNCH – BACK AT TWO."

Outside Christmas tree sellers "NO DOGS ALLOWED."

Outside a gun shop "TRESPASSERS WILL BE SHOT."

Outside ladies hairdressers in Mayfair: "IF OUR EMPLOYEES DON'T MAKE YOUR HAIR CURL, OUR PRICES WILL."

Outside a diet clinic. "REAR TODAY – GONE TOMORROW."

On the road outside a school "WATCH YOUR SPEED. DON'T KILL A CHILD." Underneath in a child's handwriting was "WAIT FOR A TEACHER."

In a toyshop. "IF YOU SEE SOMETHING YOU WANT, THROW A TANTRUM."

In a café. "COURTEOUS AND EFFICIENT SELF SERVICE."

Outside the corset manufacturer "WE MAY BE BUSY BUT WE'LL ALWAYS SQUEEZE YOU IN."

In a shoe shop "ANY WOMAN BUYING THE FIRST PAIR SHE TRIES ON GETS A 20% DISCOUNT."

On a tombstone "NEVER SICK A DAY IN MY LIFE. AND NOW THIS."

In Wall Street "DANGER – FALLING STOCKS."

Outside a loan company "FOR THE MAN WHO HAS EVERYTHIJNG – BUT HASN'T PAID FOR IT."

Outside a pet shop "GIVE A PET AS A PRESENT – NO ASSEMBLY REQUIRED."

Outside the Breast Enlargement Centre "LIFE BEGINS AT FORTY."

On a child psychologist's door "OUT TO DIN DINS."

Outside private doctor's surgery "SPECIALISES IN DISEASES OF THE WEALTHY."

SKI-ING

I wanted to be a skier, but I decided against it. My career's headed downhill fast enough as it is.

Ski-ing is the only sport where you spend an arm and a leg to break an arm and a leg.

SPORT

I hear the Brazilian police are very worried about the 2016 Olympics being sabotaged. They've had a tip off that someone was going to put glue on the relay race batons. I've always been a lover of sports. Even as a school kid I used to play hooky to play hockey. I tried every competitive sport going. Even tiddly winks. But I was disqualified for being too tiddly.

I think parents should encourage their kids to take up bowling. That'll get them off the streets and into the alleys. I still remember back to the days when amateurs were paid big money to stay as amateurs

ADDITIONAL GAGS

- The nearest I ever got to being sporty was when I had athlete's foot.

- I've been taking fencing lessons. I'm going to build one round my house.
- If you're unable to hear a pin drop, it's best to give up bowling and find another hobby.
- You can tell an angler's stretching the truth by the way he's stretching his arms.
- I attended the funeral of a tennis player who was killed when a fast ball hit him on the forehead. Everyone said it was a lovely service.
- I heard of one cricketer who even wears his face protector in bed. He has to. His wife sleeps in those iron curlers.
- The widow of a fanatic sports fan had him interned with his face buried in the sports page because that's the way she always remembered him.
- After five hours fishing I finally caught the big one. Pneumonia.
- When he goes fishing his wife gives him something to put his catch in. A goldfish bowl.
- It was a 423 yard drive to the hole, but with my first stroke I cut that down to 421.
- Roses are red, violets are blue. Horses that come last are made into glue.
- Aston Villa said at the beginning of the season they'd be the team to beat this year. And sure enough, everyone beat them.
- People laughed at the seaside when they saw me doing the Australian crawl. They said I should have got in the water.

STINGY

He's so stingy, every Christmas he sends just one card and tells the recipients to pass it on. As far as charity is concerned he always gives till it hurts. It's not his fault he has a low pain threshold. I won't say my wife is stingy, but for our wooden anniversary she gave me a toothpick. My sister-in-law's so stingy she never goes out shopping. All she does all day is sit in front of the TV set. And to show you how stingy she is, she never turns it on.

He's so stingy when his wife said she wanted to see the world he gave her a map. For her birthday she wanted something in fur, so he bought her a kitten. The dress her ordered for her was the right size, but the cheque he sent was two sizes too small.

ADDITIONAL GAGS

- This man's so stingy; he's the only one I know who has his hearing aid on a party line.
- He deliberately proposed at Christmas so he could get the engagement ring out of one of the crackers.
- He's just bought himself a carrier pigeon, so he can save on postage.
- He's so stingy he won't even laugh unless it's at someone else's expense.
- He has nothing but respect for the lifeboat association. They found that out when they asked for a donation.
- He's generous person. When it comes to giving he'll stop at nothing.
- With him charity begins at home and always stays there.
- I was in a restaurant with him and he performed an unnatural act. He paid the bill.
- He's the carefree type. Doesn't care about anything as long as it's free.
- He's so stingy the only thing he ever threw out was a debt collector.
- He's a man of rare gifts. No one's ever had one from him.
- His wife said she wanted to see the world, so he bought her a map.
- He's so cheap; if he pays you a compliment he wants a receipt.
- He deliberately rides on the underground during rush hour so he can get his suits pressed.
- He loves to take things for gratis.
- He's so stingy; to him happiness is a "No Tipping" sign.
- He's really stingy. I asked him how many cigarettes he smokes a day. He said "Any given number."
- He's so stingy he never took out a girlfriend. The only thing he's ever taken out is his teeth.
- He's so stingy; in restaurants he orders asparagus so he can leave the tip for the waiter.
- He's so stingy he only once gave a waiter a tip. And even then, the horse lost..

- He's so stingy; when his son was born he handed round cigar butts.
- He's a lady killer. He starves his dates to death.
- He doesn't care how he's treated as long as he is.
- When there's a call for charity he is the first to put his hand in his pocket…and leave it there.
- He's so stingy he's been saving all his toys for his second childhood.
- In our democratic country a person can grow up to be whatever they want. He grew up to be stingy.
- He's so stingy when he plays monopoly and buys a property; he never pays the asking price. He makes them an offer.
- After he throws a penny in the wishing well he wishes fir his penny back.
- With him charity begins at home….and stays there.
- I had a stingy landlord who believed in live and let live. And you should see the termites he let me live with.
- I complained there was a leak in the bathroom pipe, so he put a curtain round it and called it a shower.
- I complained about the smell of gas. All he did was give me a gas mask..
- He invited me and six other friends round for tea. We not only shared a pleasant afternoon, we shared a teabag as well.
- The slowest trip known to mankind was Tommy Cooper's hand to his pocket.
- He changed his name because he bought a second hand shirt and wanted to fit the monogram.
- He's the kind of guy who has an embarrassment of riches, but it never embarrasses him.
- He's so stingy; he's having acupuncture treatment to take the pain out of giving.
- Some people economise so they can save for a rainy day. The way he cuts back you'd think he was saving for a monsoon.
- When the hotel said he was paying so much for the room because it has a spectacular view, he asked "Can you bring the price down if I promise not to look out the window?"
- He's so stingy; he told all his friends "Any time you happen to be passing my house, I'd certainly appreciate it."

- He's really stingy. For his wife's birthday he told her to go the dress shop and pick up an expensive gown. But not to be caught doing it."
- He's so stingy the food he buys is low in calories and high in discounts.
- He's so stingy even the pencils he buys are unleaded.
- He's a very generous man, donates a £1,000 cheque to charity every week. But he wants to do it anonymously, so he doesn't sign it.
- He's so stingy, for their anniversary he gave her a photo of a bunch of flowers.

TELEVISION

Scientists are still trying to find out how old our planet is. No chance. They can't even find out how old Bruce Forsyth is. If Bruce Forsyth had starred on Strictly Come Dancing much longer his initials B.F. were going to seem very appropriate. I'm told he's actually 85, but you'd never know it till you hear his jokes. And I can tell you, a Bruce Forsyth joke is nothing to laugh at. Bruce was on TV just one day a week. After that he needed the other six to rest.

Despite all I've said against Jonathan Ross, I'm delighted they've given him a Sunday night TV programme. That's the night I go out to the cinema. Jonathan Ross was once voted top TV anchor man, which is not surprising. After all, an anchor is something that drags you down. No one can ever accuse his shows of being in good taste. But the BBC would love to have Jonathan back. It would save putting up the licence fee. They'd get enough money just from his swear box. On his shows they had to bleep out so many swear words it's like watching TV in Morse code. There's a rumour that Jonathan Ross volunteered to go out to Iraq to entertain the troops. But the army said no. They figured our soldiers had suffered enough already. Millions of Britons now go abroad to avoid the bad weather. Or maybe it's to avoid Jonathan Ross? I bet he gets more pan mail than fan mail.

Dozens of countries have bought our version of Strictly Come Dancing. When the Russians saw what little our girl dancers wore, they sent us food parcels. Those Russians say they have better dancers than us. But that's a load of Bolshoi. Swiss scientists conducted that big bang experiment to try and explain the earth's mysteries, like how Russell

Grant stayed so long on Strictly Come Dancing. He said he did it to keep in shape. If I had that shape, I certainly wouldn't want to keep it. For a whole season the biggest thing on TV was Russell Grant's stomach. He was such a lousy dancer while he was on the show they reinforced the rules. And the dance floor. With his rotund figure every dance he did was like the Okey-Kokey. He kept shaking it all about. That Craig Revel Horwood's an odd character. I tried to meet him through a friend, but found he didn't have any. For the next series they're introducing a new dance called The Politician. It's one step forward, two steps back and then sidesteps.

TV's got so bad lately; kids are actually getting on with their homework. The only good thing about television is it gives you a great reason to go out more. More and more people are now recording modern TV comedy shows so they can play them back the next day to insult their own intelligence. Some shows are so bad my Sky box refuses to record them. When I watch many of today's TV shows I find it hard to forgive John Logie Baird. Most of them seem to be aimed at the 18 to 35 group. That's not their age, it's their IQ.

Actress Penelope Keith ranted on about the state of comedy on TV. She said the shows not only use four letter words, they act them out. When I watch all those sex shows on TV I'm shocked, I'm revolted…I'm jealous. When I was a kid we didn't have TV. We had to listen to the radio and imagine all the sex and violence. The producer of Panorama says next week he'll be looking at pornography…and doesn't want to be disturbed. The BBC is cutting back on plans for more of its late night comedy shows. It's nothing to do with economy. It's just suddenly had a bout of good taste.

Graham Norton was supposed to have had a show at 3pm on Christmas Day, but the BBC cancelled it. They didn't want two queens on at the same time. A lot of TV presenters are gay. In addition to Graham Norton there's Paul O'Grady, Dale Winton and Evan Davis. Seems on TV, to get IN you have to come OUT. Gay comedian Julian Clary says he'd love to have been one of the famous TV comedians. He didn't care if it was either Cagney or Lacey.

TV advertising gets me angry. The commercial breaks are now so long the show's producers are demanding equal time. ITV's trying to win back audiences by giving us more stars to watch. In one night I saw Bruce Forsyth, June Whitfield, Michael Parkinson and Twiggy. And that was just in the commercials. Most of the adverts on TV now are for holidays abroad. I think it's a plot to get us out of the country to make room for more illegal immigrants. They keep interrupting those holiday commercials for a newsflash. Usually to tell us the travel company in the advert has just gone bust. I watch a lot of television, but at my age I must be slowing up a lot. Last night they got in a couple of words of a commercial before I could turn off the sound. It may be just a rumour, but I heard one leading TV channel's planning instant replays of commercials to target people who left the room during the commercial break. I'd love to see an honest TV commercial that says "Feeling tired, headachy, listless and run down? Then why not turn off the telly and go to bed?" I actually believed one commercial offering something that will combine all your remote control units into one. Turned out to be just a rubber band. I'm always amused when TV commercials say "This offer cannot be repeated." Yet they repeat it in every commercial break. This week I went to buy a digital TV set. When the salesman switched it on for a demonstration there was an advert for the same set 20% cheaper elsewhere. So I went there instead.

I love watching Dragon's Den with those ridiculous inventions like a battery operated battery charger, a fur lined toothpick, an air conditioned sauna and the very impressive pen that allowed a man to write a whole sentence on a single human hair. The Dragons turned him down, but he still went on to make a fortune, writing the print on insurance policies.

There's too much nudity on TV now. Some show more flesh than my local butcher. I watched one sexually explicit show last night and by the time I said "Well, I never!" They already had. They even brought back Star Trek as The Next Generation. There's only one woman in the show and they have a whole new generation. God, she must have been busy!

A lady contestant who won TV's The Apprentice show complained Alan Sugar completely ignored her afterwards. Surely that can't be true, he's known to be very considerate to his employees. He even buys edible boot polish. Lord Sugar wants to be cremated, just so he can have on his tombstone "Now I'M fired!" I always think the real winners of those reality shows are the people who don't watch them. My wife's favourite person on TV is Nigella Lawson who says when she dies she's to be cremated at 350 degrees or until golden brown. There are so many cooks on TV it's no wonder their broth is always spoiled.

My wife's such a TV fanatic, when someone dies in a soap opera, she sends flowers. Kids today are more interested in TV than history. They think BC stands for Before Cable. We had water pouring out of our TV set. It was my own fault for tuning into the English Channel. The X-Factor's given a lot of people with no talent the chance to prove it. Simon Cowell's search for hidden talent has proved one thing. Most of it should have stayed hidden. Recently the programmes have been so bad; I can't wait for the commercials.

Despite all the rubbish that's on, I still get a lot of pleasure out of TV. It keeps my wife quiet all evening. One viewer complained because he spent a whole day switching channels trying to find one without Stephen Fry. TV's now full of those university types. For instance Stephen Fry got a BA at Oxford and Jeremy Paxman got an MA at Cambridge. All I ever got was a BLT at Kentucky Fried Chicken.

Every time I watch the TV news there's a battle raging in some remote place in the world. I'm beginning to think war is God's way of teaching us geography. I keep wondering if a cabinet minister appeared on Mastermind whether he'd give each question an evasive answer.

The BBC's so-called ageist policy has caused many performers to seek work abroad. Prime example is spoon-bender Uri Geller who's now in China bending chopsticks. I blame television for the increase in homicides. Every time Morse or Frost appears on TV there's another murder.

I bought shares in ITV when I heard how much new money they were getting out of showing old films. Rupert Murdoch is trying to find an alternative to newspapers which are said to be on their way out because we're getting all the news on TV. It'll never work. You can't train a puppy by putting a TV set on the floor. Statistics show that 95% of GPs regularly watch Casualty so they'll know what illnesses to expect the next day. What with Casualty, Holby City and Doctors, it's no wonder the BBC needs more money. They're spending a fortune on malpractice insurance.

A woman called in a top medium to help make contact with her husband. He wasn't dead; he was just sitting in front of the TV watching football all season. I still remember when they first introduced TV sets with plasma screens. They called them plasma because you had to sweat blood to afford them. I think it's funny when newsreaders on American TV tell you about all the rapes, muggings, murders, floods and hurricanes and then say "Have a nice day."

I now complain so much about the TV, my wife calls me a grouch potato. I hear the BBC governors want to eradicate all that violence on TV. So now they're going to skip the Ten O'clock News and go straight to the weather forecast. Russell Brand resigned from his BBC show to save face. I've seen his face. It wasn't worth saving. Commercial TV's lost a lot in advertising revenue. Channel Five has the dilemma of spending money on new programmes or hanging on till people actually watch their current ones.

I hear they're planning to turn Party Political Broadcasts into TV Game Shows. Anyone who can figure out what they're talking about gets a prize. I was watching something interesting the other night. Then I turned the TV on. Some TV comedians tell jokes so old their cue cards are on stone tablets. I've been watching television now for forty years on and off. And, to be honest, I prefer it off. Actually I hate watching television, but it's the only pleasure I get.

ADDITIONAL GAGS

- Now that we've spent £400 on a colour TV, my wife refuses to watch anything in black and white.
- I always think it's odd on TV when, after a commercial break, the presenter says "Welcome back" when I haven't been anywhere.
- Steven Fry's never off the screen He was on TV over 150 times during Christmas. I even got him on my electric toothbrush.
- I think it was a mistake for Dan Stevens to leave the cast of Downton Abbey. People will soon forget his name. I mean, look what happened to whatsisname that left Coronation Street last year.
- I spent £150 on TV repairs before I realise my glasses were cracked.

- So many athletes have admitting taking drugs; they're planning a new TV Quiz show called A Question of Snort.
- My favourite TV character has always been the Invisible Man. There was actually more to him than meets the eye.
- These days TV seems to only cater for ignorant people. I'm going to write in and complain. How do you spell BBC?
- People often say to me "So you're a TV scriptwriter? What shows do you take the blame for?"
- He's such a lousy comedian, halfway through his act my TV set switched itself off.
- It's a show that absolutely no one could possibly accuse of being in good taste.
- Strictly Come Dancing has a secret sponsor, Tess Daley's dressmaker. They pay to keep their name a secret.
- TV opens many doors, mostly on refrigerators.
- TV is proof that some married couples would rather look at the set than each other.
- The best thing about being a TV comedian is that you can reach millions of people who can't reach you.
- I saw a film on TV that was so old the cowboy was riding a dinosaur.
- There's so much sex on TV, I always watch the award shows just to see actors standing up.
- See no evil, hear no evil and think no evil and you'll never be able to watch a TV soap opera.
- The one thing you can say about today's TV shows is they take your mind off entertainment.
- You can tell my wife watches all the TV medical shows. She now washes her hands before changing channels.
- They used to say watching too much TV ruined your eyesight. Now they say it ruins your brain.
- Have you noticed on TV they never interrupt a commercial for breaking news?
- Kids have it so easy now. In my day you had to stand up to change channels.
- Today's TV has become a classic example of re-cycling. The commercials demonstrate how to get the dirt out and the shows put it right back in again.

- They're bringing back a pornographic version of Colombo. In every show he reveals what's under his raincoat.
- The defence budget proves our government's still making bombs that can end the world. And the BBC is still producing shows that make it sound like a good idea.
- I hate to think what The Six Million Dollar Man would cost today.
- These days the only way you can tell if a TV show is a comedy is if it has a laugh track.
- I'm against violence on TV. Those gunshots and explosions keep waking me up.
- The only way you can tell if a TV show's supposed to be a comedy is if it has a laugh track.
- I didn't turn the TV set on at all yesterday. It was such a lovely day I didn't want to spoil it.
- Michael McIntyre is on TV too often. Yesterday I even picked him up on my pacemaker.
- I hate watching television, but it's the only pleasure I get.
- During the summer it's all re-runs. Even my dreams.
- It was supposed to be a sitcom, but it was all sit and no com.
- I'm all in favour of the BBC switching to Pay TV, if it means they'll pay me to watch it.
- He was told the camera adds five inches on you, so he photographed his crotch.
- I find the Jonathan Ross Show very educational. Every time it comes on I go in the other room and read a book.
- The Jonathan Ross show is the one in which all the viewers say the same thing "Where did I put my earplugs?"
- Certain parts of the Jonathan Ross Show can be considered tasteless. The rest of the show definitely IS tasteless.
- I've watched most of the Jonathan Ross programmes and I've come to the conclusion they shot the wrong JR.
- I always prefer watching BBC. They usually forecast better weather.
- Half the people who watch his show think its rubbish. The other half knows it is.
- There's so much sex and nudity on TV, even my shock proof watch is embarrassed.

- They tried out a Red Indian on Strictly, but every time he danced it started to rain
- The announcer said "Due to a satellite breakdown Hugh Edwards will now guess the news."
- As the producer of Britain's Got Talent said to the singer who failed the audition "Your act is bad. Unfortunately not bad enough."
- You can tell how rife inflation is when you consider how much we pay for entertainment on TV and how little we get for it.
- You can say one thing about Bruce Forsyth; he knew just the right time to retire from Strictly Come Dancing. But he stayed three seasons longer anyway.
- Bruce Forsyth admits his jokes haven't brought the house down. But they haven't brought his fee down.
- Bruce Forsyth is eighty five and recently attended the National Television Awards ceremony where he received a prestigious award for staying awake. He then made a speech and the audience didn't get that award.
- The heavily pregnant TV actress called the ambulance because her pains were coming two commercials apart.
- The TV commercial voice said "Try our product for one month. If not completely satisfied…try a different product."
- My couch potato housewife tires herself out trying to squeeze all her chores into the commercial breaks
- Did you hear about the TV sitcom star whose dreams during summer are all re-runs?
- I hate so-called modern comedy on TV, but it's the only pleasure I get.

TENNIS

Recently I started watching tennis matches from the centre of the court, just to get out of the habit of saying "Yes." Our tennis players don't do us much credit. The way some of them play they should be had up for contempt of court. I heard of one fanatical tennis fan who was so obsessed his wife took him to a psychiatrist. She said "My husband's got Murrayitis." The medic said "Not to worry, it seldom reaches the final stage." Rumour has it the real reason John McEnroe split from Tatum

O'Neil was a disagreement on their wedding night. Apparently he insisted it was in.

Tennis players don't usually have long marriages, because to them love means nothing.

THEATRE

I saw one show recently that featured a nude wedding. The only good thing about it is you could easily pick out the best man. I've noticed that, with commission, some West End theatres are charging as much as £70 a ticket. That makes the prices just as obscene as the shows. Impresarios are so scared of losing money they're reviving lots of shows from the 1960's. It's a pity they're not reviving the ticket prices too, then we'd all be happy. I'm not a fan of Shakespeare. I think the only time he had a decent plot was when they buried him. On Shakespeare's desk the IN and OUT trays were marked TO BE and NOT TO BE.

ADDITIONAL GAGS

- They had only nude women at the Windmill Theatre. Actually one naked man auditioned, but he was turned down. They said his act was too short.
- The only revivals I want to see in London's West End are the ticket prices from two decades ago.
- I saw a play that was so dirty I think the author copied the script off the wall of the men's toilet.
- I saw a version of King Lear where the leading actor was so bad it would be easy to tell who really wrote the play, Shakespeare, Marlowe or Bacon. Just dig them all up and see which one turned in his grave.
- The part I liked best in the show was when it was over.
- I've never known a play where there were so many four letter words, used by the critics.
- He's so dumb he left the theatre at the interval because the programme said the second act takes place two years later.

- The play was so bad I asked the woman in the seat in front of me to put her hat on.
- Any fool can be a critic, and most of them are.
- The show that was so bad, the only thing keeping half the audience awake was the other half snoring.
- All the world's a stage and my wife's its hardest critic.
- In the modern pantomime when Aladdin rubs the lamp he gets a recorded message "I'm sorry, the Genie isn't in right now. Please leave your name and wish and he'll get back to you as soon as possible."

THINGS YOU DON'T WANT TO HEAR

From your wife: "I told you I was expelled from school. I forgot to say it was the cooking school."

From your wife: "I told the doctor about my pain in the neck. He wants to see you."

From your wife: "Of course I saw the traffic cop, but when you've seen one you've seen them all."

From your wife: "With you it's sex, sex, sex every night. Why can't we occasionally have some fun?"

From your wife: "Let's do something different for our anniversary this year. Let's get a divorce."

From your wife: "Alright, I'll let you speak your mind. It won't take long."

From your wife: "The earth only moved once when we made love and that was because of an earthquake."

From your wife: "I know the magic hasn't gone out of our marriage, because you're still up to your old tricks."

From your wife: "I'm not saying you're not a good husband. I just wish you were someone else's."

From your wife: "Of course my mother's always hanging around. You should have thought about that before we moved in with her."

From your wife: "You're just being reasonable to infuriate me."

From your wife: "When are you going to start earning beyond our means?"

From your wife: "I used to think you were your own worst enemy. Now I am."

From your wife: "I know sex helps you sleep, dear, but can't you wait till we're finished?"

From your wife: "It's the other drivers you want to watch out for. They could be stupid too."

From your wife after your operation "The last thing I remember hearing the surgeon say was "Oops".

From your wife while you're making love: "When are you going to fix that crack in the ceiling?"

From your wife doing a crossword puzzle: "What's a four-letter word meaning slave, other than 'wife'?"

From your wife on the phone: "I told your mother you're watching TV. She said you should sit up straight."

From your wife to your son: "Ask your father first, dear. We have to keep him thinking he makes the decisions here."

From you wife to your naughty son's Headmaster: "You're lucky. I have to put up with his father as well."

From your wife during a row "Can we stop this argument right now? I want to get on with the next one."

From your wife after a row "Now that I've let you have the last word, I'll tell you what I think of it."

From your wife, the day before her birthday "I found where you hid my present and I've already exchanged it."

From your wife who's come home carrying just the steering wheel: "You know how you were thinking of jogging to work…"

From your wife after you've confessed to having an affair: "I'm not upset, dear. Actually it eases my conscience."

From your wife to her friend: "In the 20 years we've been married Brad has never raised his voice to me once, lucky for him."

From your wife to the baker "Do you have something that didn't turn out so good that I could pass off as homemade?"

From your wife "You've been taking lessons from that same golf pro for years. Isn't it about time you sued him?"

From your wife to her ex-convict brother "How long are you out for?"

From your wife who's just crashed the car "It's not so bad. The police car got the worst of it."

From your wife to the restaurant waiter "I'm not ready to order yet. I'm still counting the calories."

From your wife to your school kid son "When you're writing to Santa, don't ask for anything your father has to assemble."

From your wife after you've repaired something "Can you fix it back to the way it was before you fixed it?"

From your wife "Grab your coat and car keys. I'll explain what happened to the roast on the way to the restaurant."

From your wife "Harrods has got a three day sale. I'll see you on Thursday."

From your wife to the traffic cop "Yes, I DID see the sign MAX: 30 MPH, but I thought it only applied to a man named Max."

From your wife "What do you want to complain about for dinner tonight?"

From your wife: "Good news, dear. The airbag DOES work"

From your wife when you're busy with DIY "What time shall I call the ambulance?"

From your wife after she's cooked a new dish: "Well, how do you like it, apart from the taste?"

From your wife after she's crashed the car "I don't suppose you'd believe the garage moved?"

From your wife who's just crashed the car "This is nothing. You should see the other car!"

From your wife to her female friend "I have this terrific recipe for beef casserole. All I have to do is mention it to my husband and he immediately insists we eat out."

From your wife to her female friend: "My husband and I have a great system. I buy and he pays later."

From your wife "Taste this will you, dear. I have my doubts about these mushrooms costing only 40p a pound."

From your wife "Guess what you bought me for my birthday?"

From your wife: "Live within our income? God, has it come down to that?"

From your wife after you've queried her spending "You want to know where all the grocery money goes. Stand sideways and look in the mirror."

From your wife to the traffic cop "I wish you people would make up your mind. Two weeks ago you took my licence away and now you want to see it."

From your wife "Tell me one of your jokes, dear. I can't get to sleep."

From your wife to the marriage guidance counsellor "We seem to be slowly drifting apart. Is there anything you can do to speed it up?"

From your wife after she's spotted the furniture shop sign NO INTEREST FOR A YEAR. "That reminds me, when was the last time we made love?"

From your wife who's been out shopping in the family car "First the good news. The insurance company will pay for it."

From your wife after your son's been naughty "Send him to HIS bedroom? With the plasma TV, the stereo music centre, computer and video games? No, I'll send him to OUR bedroom. There's nothing going on there."

From your wife "I want to borrow the car. I'm leaving you."

From your wife "No John there isn't anyone else. That's the trouble."

From your wife "Look at it this way, my extravagance is just a sign of my confidence in you."

From your wife "Yes, I would like you to teach me to play chess. I'll just get the pack of cards and you can show me."

From your wife "This is the last time you go shopping with me without taking a tranquiliser."

From your wife "You talked me into giving up expensive jewellery and clothes. Next thing I'll give up is something very cheap...you!"

From your wife "What would you like for supper tonight, dear? Braised steak, roast beef, smoked haddock? Or would you rather stay home and have an omelette?"

From your wife after you've paid for the restaurant meal: "The nerve of that waiter! He even charged for those sweeteners I slipped into my handbag."

From your wife to the doctor "I have this shortness of breath. I noticed it when my husband started getting a word in edgewise."

From your wife after another car has crashed into the back of her "I distinctly signalled that I was trying to make up my mind."

From your wife on the phone to your GP "Doctor, I haven't got any mustard for a mustard plaster. Will ketchup do?"

From your wife "I told you to take the kids for a walk. I didn't say bring them back."

From your wife preparing for an evening out: "How come you can wait all day for those fish to bite, but you can't wait a few minutes while I get dressed?"

From your wife before an evening out "It won't take me long to get dressed. Go rotate the car wheels or something."

From your wife: "Save money? On what you earn I can't even spend money."

From your wife "Of course I'd never leave you for another man. Once bitten twice shy."

From your wife: "I'm glad you turned down Fred's offer to wife swap. He's lousy in bed."

From your wife: "This is the last time you go shopping with me without taking a tranquilizer."

From your wife to the milkman: "I'm sorry I can't pay you today, I have a headache."

From your wife: "Whatsisname phoned from a firm called something-or-other. He wants you to ring him straight back."

From your wife to the milkman: "I'm sorry I can't pay you today, I have a headache."

From your wife to the traffic cop: "It's not my fault, officer. I've been in enough accidents to know."

From your wife to the traffic cop: "I know that's my library card, officer. But I thought you might like something to read while I search for my driving licence."

From your wife at the Department Store information booth: "I need to buy a present for my husband. Which way to the bargain basement?"

From your wife: "The doctor said not to worry you, so don't ask about the car."

From your wife to her friend: "I'm looking forward to my husband's retirement. We were never able to afford a maid."

From your wife to her friend: "I'll never send my husband shopping again. Today he came home with two things that needed to be cooked."

From your wife "I think I've found a way to solve our financial problems. I've invited Father Murphy over to help us pray for a miracle."

From your Tax Inspector: "I'm very suspicious. You understood every question on the tax return. How?"

From the car mechanic "At least you can use it for spare parts."

From the car mechanic: My best advice is for you to keep the oil and change the car."

From the car mechanic: "That pfft-pfft noise is nothing to worry about. It's that clang-clang that'll cost you a fortune."

From the car mechanic: "My son wants to thank you for putting him through university."

From the car mechanic "Sure I can fix it. How do you open the bonnet?"

From the car mechanic: "Have some shock absorbers while I make out your bill!"

From the car mechanic: "My advice would be for you to leave the key in the ignition and hope someone steals the car."

From the car mechanic: "Sure I can fix your car for £100. But if you want it done right it'll cost you £250."

From the car mechanic: It's exactly what I thought. I have no idea what the problem is."

From the used car salesman: "When I said it did 30 miles to the gallon I was, of course allowing for a tail wind"

From the used car salesman: "This car was owned by a little old lady who never took it out of her garage. She only used it to carbon monoxide her two previous husbands."

From the car salesman: "This car goes real fast and it has all the gadgets, even a little shelf for the speed cop to rest his pad on."

From the car salesman: "We're the cheapest car sales in town. The only thing is you have to go down to the factory and assemble it yourself."

From the used car salesman: "It's done very little mileage. The previous owner couldn't get it started."

From your garage mechanic "Sure I can cut your repair bill in half. Which half of the car do you want repaired?"

From your car mechanic: "It's your fan belt. It needs a new car."

From the car mechanic "Oh, it's nothing that a fortune can't fix."

From your car mechanic "After stripping down your car I finally found the cause of the rattle. Your grandson was under the seat."

From the garage owner to his mechanic "If he doesn't flinch when you tell him how much, say "plus labour."

From the car mechanic "The clocks go back today. So I've turned yours back 20,000 miles."

From the car salesman "I know I said it comes to exactly £1,200. I was referring to my commission."

From the car mechanic "Have some shock absorbers while I make out your bill."

From the used car salesman "Just sign here where it says "sucker."

From the airline receptionist: "Don't worry sir, I'm sure we'll find your luggage, as soon as we find the plane."

From your air stewardess: "The bad news is we're going to crash. The good news is your luggage is on another plane."

From the girl on your blind date: "You're different from my previous lovers. They were all women.

From the lawyer reading your Granddad's will: "He was such a great believer in reincarnation, he left it all to himself."

From your doctor: "Take this medicine twice a day. If it doesn't make you better, have your next of kin call and tell me."

From your doctor: "Let me rephrase that. Is there anywhere that DOESN'T hurt?"

From your doctor: "I've taken you off everything I can think of. Is there anything you still enjoy?"

From your doctor: "Try these pills. If they don't work, come back to me next week and I'll prescribe something more expensive."

From your doctor: "I'll give you my diagnosis on Monday. I don't want to spoil your weekend."

From your doctor: "In your condition I wouldn't bother to watch the first episode of that two-parter play on TV tonight."

From your doctor: "It's the third time you've come to me about your irritation. It's beginning to irritate me too."

From your doctor:"Of course I'm up to date on the latest medical advances. I've never missed an episode of Casualty."

From your doctor: "You'll have to stop taking everything with a grain of salt. It raises your blood pressure."

From your doctor: "If you insist on a second opinion, come back and see me tomorrow."

From your Doctor: "The good news is you haven't been worrying for nothing."

From your doctor's receptionist "Sorry, the doctor's never available on Wednesdays. That's the day he goes to court."

From your doctor's receptionist: "The doctor can see you now. He's just found where he put his glasses."

From your private hospital doctor: "The drug itself has no actual side effects. But the price might give you a heart attack."

From your private hospital doctor: "I'm giving you a time-activated medicine. It won't start to work until your cheque clears."

From your private hospital doctor "Take one aspirin before you go to bed and two before you open my bill."

From your private hospital surgeon to his student doctors: "When the patient enters, the first thing you look for is the slight swelling beneath the left collar bone. That's where he keeps his wallet."

From your private hospital surgeon: "We're delaying your operation till you've gained more strength in your bank account."

From your hospital surgeon: "Aren't you going to wish me luck? This is my first operation."

From your diet doctor: "You can continue to take everything with a pinch of salt. Except food."

From your hospital surgeon "I've operated on you before. Look, those are my initials."

From the surgeon after your operation "Since it wasn't actually you that wanted the sex change, Mr. Benson, there will be no charge."

From the cashier at the private health clinic "No sir, the hundred the doctor was talking about is his golf score. Your bill will be a lot more than that."

From your Japanese doctor "If the pain continues, commit Hari Kiri."

From the doctor at the private clinic "Yes, your operation IS essential. How else am I going to pay for my cruise?"

From your hospital surgeon "Don't worry about the operation. I've already performed the same one on over twenty patients. God rest their souls."

From your doctor "If I've told you once, I've told you a thousand times, I don't treat people with amnesia."

From your doctor "No, what you have isn't rare at all. In fact the graveyards are full of it."

From your doctor "Alright then, tell me where it DOESN'T hurt."

From your doctor "The good news is you won't have to give up smoking and drinking. It's too late for that."

From your doctor: "The good news is your disease will be named after me."

From your doctor: "You want a second opinion, alright I'll give you one. You're a lousy patient."

From the doctor to your pregnant daughter "You'd better prepare for an additional family member…starting with a husband."

From the nurse after you've given blood. "I've made a slight mistake. I should have taken a pint not a gallon."

From the hospital surgeon during your vasectomy "Forceps…gauze..Scalpel…Ooooops!... Lawyer!"

From the surgeon during your operation: "Ooooops!"

From your doctor's receptionist "I'm afraid the doctor's fully booked right up till his retirement, but if you don't mind hanging on, his son's just started at medical school."

From your doctor's receptionist "Yes, I do have you down for February 20th at 2.30. But what made you think it was for THIS year?"

From your doctor's receptionist: "The doctor's agreed to a house call. What time can you be at his house?

From the doctor at the private clinic "I'm sorry, for £75 all I can do is kiss it better."

From your hospital surgeon: "Promise not to laugh when I tell you what I took out by mistake."

From your hospital surgeon: "We'll have to delay the operation. I forgot to bring my rabbit's foot."

From your nurse at the Harley Street clinic: "You've got ten get-well-soon cards. And nine of them are from BUPA."

From the doctor at a surgeon's private clinic: "We've run several tests and they all prove the same thing. You CAN afford the operation."

From your optician: "If there's anyone here in the waiting room, I'll see you now."

From your psychiatrist: "Of course you have a useful purpose in life. You're paying for my next cruise."

From your Tax Inspector: "We'd like you to come in for an interview tomorrow. Bring your records, pyjamas and a toothbrush."

From your Tax Inspector: "I don't care if you ARE a born again Christian, you still owe us from your life before that."

From the Tax Inspector reading your submitted accounts: "I see we've already taxed your imagination."

From your Tax Inspector: "Did you fill this return out yourself, or did you have an accomplice?"

From your Tax Inspector on the phone: "Hello, this is your partner speaking."

From your Tax Inspector: "Do you mind if I show your tax return to my colleagues? We like to share a good laugh."

From your Tax Inspector: "Our records show you're a man of untold wealth."

From your Tax Inspector: "We'll allow depreciation on your car and computer, but not on your wife."

From your Tax Inspector: "It's the old law of supply and demand. We demand and you supply."

From your Tax Inspector: "I think you may have miscounted your blessings."

From your Boss: "Simpkins, I need your advice. I have to let three employees go. Who do you suggest for the other two?"

From your Boss: "I hate yes-men. Now do you still want to ask me for that raise?"

From your Boss: "You've come to be like a son to me. And since I don't like nepotism, I have to let you go."

From your Boss: "I like your suggestion for getting rid of all the dead wood round here, but I must say I will miss you."

From your Boss: "Go ahead and enjoy your holiday. The bad news can wait till you get back."

From your Boss: "You're the most creative worker I've ever employed. No one's created more problems for me than you have."

From your Boss: "Now about that interesting suggestion I found in the box with your fingerprints on it..."

From your Boss: "You always wanted a longer tea-break. Here's your P45, now you can have them as long as you like."

From your Boss: "I'd be happy to pay you what you're worth, but can't. There are laws against it."

From your Boss: "I know you can do your job in your sleep, but must you?

From your prospective Boss's secretary: "I wouldn't hold out too much hope if I were you. The boss took your CV into the toilet and came back without it."

From your Boss: "We were thinking of cutting out the dead wood and your name came up in conversation."

From your Boss: "We all make mistakes, Benson. Just forget it ever happened when you're out tomorrow looking for a new job."

From your Boss: "So you've decided to take early retirement, Benson. I was wondering when you were going to make it legal."

From your Boss: "From your prospective employee: "My career goal? Your job."

From your bank manager: "If you want bread, go to a bakery."

From your bank manager: "I'm afraid I can't accept this letter from Reader's Digest saying you may already have won £250,000 as collateral."

From your stock broker: "Thanks to that investment I recommended, you now have a small fortune. It's a shame you put in a large fortune to begin with."

From your stock broker: "What's the opposite of eureka?"

From the MC at the Financial Advice meeting: "Our next speaker on tax loopholes has come a long way to be here today. In fact, all the way from Parkhurst Prison."

From a vicar during his sermon: "I'm taking my driving test tomorrow. I want you all to pray for me."

From your little son: "I hope you don't mind, but I swapped my baby sister for a pet rabbit."

From your little son: "Dad, what did you do for money before they had credit cards?"

From your little son: "I didn't go back to school after lunch. I got homesick."

From your little son: "You spanked me last week for telling a lie. Now you want me to tell the rent collector you're not in."

From your little son: "Who took my snowballs? I put them under my pillow last night."

From your son to your wife: "Dad's giving the au pair artificial respiration behind the wood shed and he's doing it all wrong."

From your son who's come home with a black eye: "I DID stand up and fight like a man. But so did she."

From your 9-year-old son to his 8-year-old girlfriend: "I'd ask you to marry me, but we'd have to live with my parents."

From your young son "When I grow up I want to be just like you, Dad. With a few refinements, of course."

From your young son "Mum says I got my hair and eyes from her and she got her frazzled nerves from me."

From your young son "What do you think I'll get from the Tooth Fairy for grandpa's dentures?"

From your young son "I'm writing to Santa now to avoid the Christmas rush."

From your young son to your wife: "Stop screaming at me. I'm not your husband."

From your school kid son to your wife "You say Dad's bringing home his Boss? But I thought YOU were his Boss."

From your school kid son: "You sell stocks and bonds? No wonder there's a policeman at the door. I told everyone you sell rocks and bombs."

From your school kid son "I didn't win the spelling bee, Dad. But I did win the prize for originality."

From your school kid son: "You wanted to see a good school report, so I brought home someone else's."

From your threatening young son: "Dad, don't make me go over your head to Mum."

From your young son to your wife: "Dad has a strange habit. Every time we pass a pretty lady he closes one eye."

From your young son when you have passed through Customs: "He wasn't even warm, was he Dad?"

From your young son: "I would have bought you a Father's Day present, Dad, but I didn't know what size tie you wear."

From your student son: "Look at it this way, Dad. By not making it to university I'm saving you £9,000 a year."

From your young son: "Of course you did better than me at history, Dad. When you were at school there wasn't so much of it."

From your young son: "Before you married Mum, who told you how to drive?"

From your school kid son: "There's a special meeting at the school tonight, Dad. Just the Headmaster, the police and you."

From your school kid son: "You know that radio you bought me for my birthday, Dad? I broke the aerial in half so I can get short wave."

From your young son: "Either you increase my allowance or I'm renting out my room."

From your young son presenting his school report: "So what if the grades are lousy. You always said it's not what you know, but who you know."

From your ten-year-old son: "I don't need any spending money this week Dad. I just sold the film rights to Mum's diary."

From your young son presenting his school report: "Is stupidity hereditary, Dad?"

From your young son to his pal: "Sorry, I can't come out to play. I promised Dad I'd help him with my homework."

From your young son to the poll-taker at the door: "You'll have to come back later if you want Dad's opinion. Mum's not in right now."

From your young school kid son: "I told Mum I failed in sex education. She said I take after you."

From your young son who's just returned from a fishing trip: "I didn't need to catch them, Dad. They were floating on top."

From your school kid son: "It wasn't my fault I flunked the maths exam. The battery in my pocket calculator gave out."

From your school kid son: "So I told Billy no matter how big his Dad is, you could lick him easy."

From your school kid son: "We had our first sex education class today. Boy, has that teacher's got a lot to learn!"

From your school kid son: "Today at school we learnt that 'Go forth and multiply' has nothing to do with maths."

From your daughter dating a member of parliament: "I think he's getting serious, Dad. He bought me a gift he can't claim off expenses."

From your daughter with a black eye: "My date was a perfect gentleman. It was his wife did this to me."

From your daughter to her long haired boyfriend: "Will you please get a haircut. People are starting to think I'm a lesbian."

From her boyfriend to your teenage daughter: "Why would I respect you in the morning? I don't even respect you now."

From your eight-year-old daughter: "Brian and I are playing at being married. Do you have any old chequebooks I can practice on?"

From your marriageable-age daughter: "The wedding rehearsal went well, Dad. Now we're off to rehearse the wedding night."

From your 12-year-old daughter: "The man on the internet asked if I was a virgin. I told him no, I'm a Sagittarius."

From your daughter who's been courting for six months: "He finally mentioned marriage. He told me he's got a wife and six kids."

From your untidy daughter: "I hate it when you tidy up my room. Now I can't find anything."

From your teenage daughter: "Mum says my hair looks like a mop. What's a mop?"

From your daughter after her first date: "You told me to be good. Jim said I was the best he's had."

From your marriageable-age daughter: "Dad, last night Jim finally popped the question. He asked if I was on the pill."

From your pregnant daughter: "No, I didn't object to his laying-on hands. He told me he was a Faith Healer."

From your eight year old daughter: "Never mind about buying me a doll that can walk and talk. Get me one that does my homework."

From your daughter: "Last night he posed the big question. He asked if I was on the pill."

From your toddler at bedtime: "Keep reading, Dad. I'm still about three stories awake."

From your blind date: "Thanks for this evening. It's been a once-in-a lifetime experience...I hope."

From your blind date: "Where have you been all my life, and when are you going back?"

From the girl on your blind date: "It was nice of you to see me home, John. But that's all you're going to see."

From the girl on your blind date: "Yes, it is a nice night for a walk. Why don't you take one?"

From your new girlfriend: "Sure I'm into foreplay. Have you got a pack of cards?"

From your new girlfriend after your first date: "I like your approach. But I'd like your departure even better."

From your new girlfriend: "If you wanted a long neck, you should have gone out with a giraffe."

From your girlfriend: "Yes, I'll agree to marry you if you promise to love me forever, buy me nice things and sleep on the couch."

From the girl you've just proposed to: "Of course I'll marry you. And while you're down there, see if you can find my earring."

From your prospective date: "I'd love to go out with you, Harold, but tonight's my night to do crochet."

From your new bride: "I never learned to cook – just defrost."

From your grandson: "Grandpa, I don't understand. If they didn't have computers when you were a kid, what did you run your software on?

From your grandson playing with your phone: "This is fun, Grandpa. All I had to do was press some buttons and I'm talking to someone in Australia."

From your young grandchild: "Grandpa, guess how many crayons it took to wax your car?"

From your young grandson: "In school today they told us the story of Little Red Riding Hood where the wolf put on Grandma's clothes. Was he gay?"

From your young grandson: "Grandpa, what was fresh air like?"

From your estate agent: "I'll show you the house in the morning. I don't like driving in that neighbourhood after dark."

From the estate agent: "Yes, we DO have a house in your price range, but it's in Ethiopia.."

From your new babysitter: "It'll be fine. Just leave me tea, biscuits and a chair and a whip."

From your new babysitter: "Have a nice time till 11.30. After that have a nice time and a half."

From your kid's schoolteacher: "Five thirds of the class don't understand a thing I say about fractions."

From the shoe shop salesman to your wife: "its simple mathematics, Madam. Seven into six won't go."

From your gas and electric supplier: "We provide a fast, efficient, reasonably-priced service. Which one do you want?"

From the TV newsreader: "Before I read today's news I suggest you sit down with a stiff drink."

From the TV weather forecaster: "If I'd known the weather was going to be this good, I'd have taken the day off."

From the announcer on your TV set: "For those of you who sneaked out during the commercials to put the kettle on, we're repeating them for you!"

From the captain of the plane you're in: "The Lord is my shepherd, I shall not want…"

From the firm you've spent ages on the phone trying to get through to: "Thank you for holding on, your call is important to us. But not so important that we could be bothered to hire enough operators to speed things up."

From the Gypsy fortune teller: "I see a tall, slim sexy blonde…who your Boss is employing to take your place."

From the gun salesman: "I hate to lose a customer, but shouldn't you see a Marriage Counsellor first?"

From the Maître d' at your local Bistro: "Sorry, we don't do tossed salad any more. The last one was tossed at the waiter."

From your literary agent: "I was not only able to put your book down, I was able to throw it in the bin."

From another husband at a wife swapping party: "Do we have to exchange? Couldn't I just give you mine?"

From your visiting next door neighbour: "Will you stop going on about the lawn mower you loaned me six months ago. I'm not here to listen to your problems."

From the woman who lives in the flat below yours: "I've brought some peanuts for your elephant."

From the landlord of your local pub: "If you're drinking to forget, I'll have to ask you to pay in advance."

From the department store lady running the complaints desk: "My husband's left me. My son's a drug addict. I've been diagnosed with diabetes…and you're complaining about a lousy toaster!"

On the golf course about your golf bag. "Your zip's open and your balls are falling out."

From the pet show owner: "I can't refund your money. If the parrot's not speaking it's probably because you said something to offend him."

From a policeman: "I will now inform you of your rights. You have a right to scream when I hit you with my truncheon, you have a right to yell Mercy when I kick you in the ribs…"

From a husband to his wife: "This cheque I'm making out to the Beauty Parlour, what's it for?"

From the restaurant waiter: "I hope you're not in a hurry, we're breaking in a new chef."

From your new bride just after the wedding ceremony: "I forgot to tell you, I'm not pregnant after all."

From the man you've just lent money to: "Thanks for the loan. I shall be eternally in your debt."

From the foreman of the jury at your trial: "Has anybody got a coin?"

From your solicitor: "If you want it in layman's terms, go see a layman."

From one politician to another: "You can stop making promises. You're already elected."

From your wife to the shop salesgirl "I found where my husband was hiding my Christmas present. Is it too early to exchange it?"

From the doctor's receptionist "Sure the doctor makes house calls. Have the deeds ready when he gets there."

From your babysitter on the phone "Is there anything I can use as a tourniquet?"

From the restaurant waiter "You haven't eaten those mushrooms yet, have you?"

From the Customs & Excise Officer "Just a minute. You with the relieved look on your face. Come back here."

From your wife "Sure you can have a night out with the boys, but make sure you don't come home too early."

From your daughter "When I grow up I want to marry someone like you, Daddy, so I can always have my own way like Mummy."

From the lawyer reading the will "Your late rich uncle must have had a sense of humour. He's left all his money to medical science and his brain to you."

From the estate agent "I'm afraid everything in your price range has been condemned."

From your bank manager "Do you mind if our trainee turns you down, he needs the practice."

From your wife to the traffic cop "You don't need to give me a ticket officer, I've already got four I haven't used yet."

From your private doctor "I want to see you again when You've saved up enough money."

From the Estate Agent "You can heat the whole house for only THINGS YOU DON'T WANT TO HEAR:

From the girl after your first date, "Be careful on your way home, Rodney. I wouldn't want you to get robbed of all that money you saved tonight."

From wife who's just driven home from shopping "Good news, dear. The air cushion works perfectly. Unfortunately the car no longer does."

From your school kid son "I got 100 in school today. 50 in English...30 in Maths and 20 in Geography."

From your Boss "You may well be doing the work of two men, Benson, in which case they're both incompetent."

From the Driving School owner to your wife "Don't give up, Mrs. Benson. Just hang in there till I hire a new instructor who doesn't know about you."

From the surgeon after your operation "There was a bit of a mix up, Mr. Benson, but at least you got a new kidney out of it."

From the surgeon during your operation "Clamps!, Scalpel! Sutchers!...Rabbit's Foot."

From your psychiatrist "You've got a split personality so I'm going to have to charge your double. "

From your wife "You never snored when we just lived together."

From the restaurant waiter "The chef would like you to watch out for his contact lens."

From your school kid son "I tried to be good a few times, but my heart wasn't in it."

From the used car salesman "That knocking you hear is a safety device. It stops you falling asleep at the wheel."

From your car mechanic presenting his bill "Just give us the car and we'll call it even."

From your urologist on the phone "Can you hold?"

From your doctor "When I said I wanted a second opinion, I didn't mean yours."

Wife to salesgirl in shoe shop "We're making progress. This is exactly what I wanted before I changed my mind."

From your doctor "No more wine or women, but you can sing as much as you like."

From your babysitter "By the way, I promised little Tommy that if he went off to sleep you'd buy him a five-speed bicycle for his birthday."

From restaurant waiter "This job is murder on my feet. I keep tripping over those rat traps."

From your doctor "Don't make any long term plans. Like tomorrow."

From your Boss "I've called you all here to help me make an important decision. Pick a straw."

From your son to the vicar "That was a great sermon, vicar. And certainly worth the penny my Dad put in the collection box."

From your small son to the car mechanic: "How come you're not wearing a mask if you're a robber like my Dad says?"

TRAVEL

NASA announced its intention to put the first man on Mars. Immediately David Cameron volunteered Ed Miliband. There was one space mission where Neil Armstrong walked on the moon looking for a bush to go behind to spend a penny. He wanted to go where no man had gone before.

I think it's funny when my wife says she wants a holiday to get away from it and then packs so much she takes it all with us. She packs so much the neighbours don't realise we're going on holiday. They think we're moving house

We've reached that time of year when holidaymakers go to the Canary Islands to experience the kind of heat they complained about here in August. With holidays, have you noticed that when the temperature goes down, the price goes up? Holiday surveys show Spain is still the most popular place for us Brits. I guess it's because they're so broke we feel at home there.

ADDITIONAL GAGS

- I saw a railway passenger explain to the ticket inspector "Yes, I know this is yesterday's ticket. That's how long I had to wait for the train."
- Last Sunday I took things easy, just hung around and stayed put where I was all day. That's the last time I'll use the M25 at weekends.
- The recent train drivers strike led B&Q to advertise a new product, British Rail emulsion – it doesn't run.

- The only punctual thing about our railway is its fare increases.
- Naples is considered to be a dangerous place to visit because of all the muggings there. I drove through the whole of Naples without once leaving the scene of the crime.
- My wife told the travel agent to book us both a round-the-world trip… going in different directions.
- The best thing about our recent holiday is that it's over.
- They're very fussy on cruises. They won't let you drink on an empty wallet.
- I don't think my parents liked me when I was a kid. They gave me my weekly allowance in traveller's cheques.
- The trouble with holidaying in England is the weather. You can be sure when you go for a paddle it'll piddle.
- Las Vegas is the place for the man who has everything…but not for long.
- I thought I'd go to the Casino and leave everything to chance. Instead I just left everything.
- In Las Vegas I started off with a stack of chips as tall as John Wayne. Two hours later, Mickey Rooney!
- Gambling is a way of getting nothing for something.
- After a week in Las Vegas I'm convinced the best throw of the dice is to throw them away.
- They say travel is broadening and it's true. On my last cruise I gained 12 lbs.
- The banks say if you lose your travellers cheques they will replace them. But they wouldn't replace mine. I lost them in Las Vegas playing roulette.
- The very first British Railways train left Euston for Edinburgh way back in August 1952. It's due to arrive there any day now.
- My wife and I take a holiday once every year, to replace our towels.
- When it comes to choosing a holiday I always go by the book. My cheque book.
- I don't need to go on holiday this year. I'm already broke.
- Taxi drivers are very helpful. They'll take you wherever they want to go.
- It's the same every time we go on a cruise. We take along twice as many clothes as we need and half as much money.

- The casino I went to in Las Vegas was so fancy they made me wear a collar and tie to lose my shirt.
- Even the dishwashers in Las Vegas are elegant. It's not surprising. Last week they were customers.
- When the hotel caught my brother taking their towels home he said he was just being helpful. He said he made them dirty, so he's taking them home to wash.
- The hotel was so bad they're offering special rate for any guests staying half a day or longer.
- I've had one of those horrible days when even my digital watch stopped digiting.
- The space alien said "Never mind about taking me to your leader. I've been travelling for 400 light years. Take me to your toilet."
- I took my wife on a cruise for my health. If I didn't she'd have killed me.
- My wife wants to take one of those pay-as-you-go holidays, but I turned her down. We haven't yet finished paying for where we've been.
- I've already seen an advert for space travel. It said "12 major planets in 10 days."
- We're safe. Aliens are not going to invade us. They're waiting till the meek inherit the Earth.
- I'm not saying the trains were running slow, but by the time I got home my wife was already getting remarried.
- The airport Customs Officer opened the large case. Inside was a midget pointing a gun and saying "Close it up and keep your mouth shut."

UGLY

She was so ugly she asked the Beauty Parlour what they could do for her. They gave her 20p and told her to dial-a-prayer. When she walks out of a pet shop the alarm goes off. She's so ugly she loves Halloween. It's the only night of the year she looks natural. As far as looks are concerned I'd say her main appeal would be....for help. On a rating of 1 to 10 she's the 0 in the 10.

I won't say she's ugly but she'd make a powerful antidote to an aphrodisiac. When she walks into a bank they switch off the cameras. Her psychiatrist makes her lay face down on the couch. Immigration made her put someone else's picture in her passport. If her face is her fortune she'd never have to pay income tax. People look at her face and ask if anyone else was hurt in the accident. When you look at her time stands still, because she has a face that could stop a clock. She went to the dog track and six men bet on her. When she was born her parents didn't know whether to buy a cot or a cage.

ADDITIONAL GAGS

- She used to be fat and ugly till she went on a diet. Now she's thin and ugly.
- I'm not saying that woman is ugly, but I wouldn't be at all surprised if she has a Transylvanian passport.
- She's ugly but she loves nature, in spite of what it did to her.
- She's so ugly even the tide wouldn't go out with her.
- She's so ugly, if she looked like that on purpose, it would be an art.
- She's so ugly, at her coming-out party they made her go in again.
- She wears a mudpack that guarantees she'll look beautiful, right until the moment she takes it off.
- She's so ugly men want to play "dress" poker with her.
- She's so ugly, when she undresses at night, Peeping Toms pull down their blinds.

VACATIONS

With the current value of the pound, people booking foreign holidays are getting a lot more than they expected. The lot more is cost. The way things are going, soon the 18 to 30 holiday group won't refer to the age, but just the number of people that can afford them.

ADDITIONAL GAGS

- I heard one travel agent say to a client "For the price you have in mind, sir, I suggest you join the navy.

- At my age travel insurance is expensive. The agent said it should be a hundred quid, give or take a few pounds. It turned out to be a lot more that I was giving and they were taking.
- When I go on holiday now I take half as much luggage and twice as much money.
- When we go on holiday the most expensive thing is my wife.
- When you're on vacation everything goes so fast, especially your money.
- I went to Miami and got a wonderful tan. Then I got the bill and went white again.
- I don't know about you but I can never relax after a motoring holiday. I need a full week just to refold the road maps.
- On holiday I went to a little town in Italy that was so small the bank's only protection was a man at the door with bad breath. The place was that small the town clock was a wristwatch.
- The town was so small I got claustrophobia just driving through it.
- My next door neighbour went skiing in Zermat and came back with two broken legs. His wife caught him kissing the female ski instructor.
- You could tell the lift operator was new. On the way up he stopped three times to ask directions.
- When I told my wife I'd got tickets to Pavarotti, she wanted to know if we were going there for a week or fortnight.
- The way my wife packs, I never know whether we're going on holiday or moving house.
- Some hotels have a gymnasium so you can do your daily exercises. One I stayed in was so posh they had someone do your exercises for you.
- My next door neighbour's such a show off. The stickers on his luggage say "Here, there and everywhere."
- Anyone who believes you can't take it with you has never seen my wife packing for our vacation.
- Last summer the beach in Bournemouth was so crowded I had to find a psychiatrist so I'd have a place to lie down.
- A family holiday is when you take along all the people you need a holiday from.

- I love to go fishing when I take my holiday. Trouble is the fish choose the same time to go on their holiday.
- They say the best time to fish is when it's raining. I did that last week and all I caught was a cold.
- My wife must be a descendent of Noah. When we go on holiday she takes two of everything.
- We stayed at a hotel that was so cheap they stole the towels from us.
- Last time I was on a cruise some of the passengers were so old they were just hanging on by the skin of their tooth.
- The plumber came and our vacation went.
- Last year I had enough holiday money to be able to get away from it all. This year I can only afford to get away from some of it.
- Last year I had enough holiday money to be able to get away from it all. This year I can only afford to get away from some of it.

WEATHER

Like most people in Britain I'm saving for both my holiday and a rainy day. Unfortunately with our British weather those two things usually come at the same time. The weather in The Canaries was really hot. I tell you, I haven't sweated that much since my last tax demand.

Due to our weather the International Winter Olympics will be held in Britain….this summer. The biggest surprise last summer is that we didn't have one. Nothing's reliable these days, especially the weather. I've just come back from a seaside holiday and the only colour in my cheeks is blue.

Yesterday it was so cold snooker players were reaching for their jackets. In fact so cold even Jehovah's Witnesses aren't out on the streets. What's happened to the global warming they promised us? Everything here in Britain is freezing. I took a shower this morning and had to wear a bullet proof vest.

ADDITIONAL GAGS

- There's a book out now telling us to save the rain forests by buying less paper. I did my bit by not buying the book.

- Environmentalists advise us to only use biodegradable dustbin bags which are supposed to break down quicker. That's true. Mine break down the moment I put anything in them.
- The weather forecaster said "Tomorrow there will be some broken clouds, but overnight we'll do our best to repair them.
- The male weather forecaster said "Today there will be high winds, followed by high skirts, followed by me."
- You can tell when the weather's really good. All the kids are outside and all the ants are inside.
- As the man said when he saw Dolly Parton "I'm no weather man but I know a major front when I see one."
- The TV Weather Girl wore such a low cut dress, she not only talked about a cold front, she showed it.
- My air conditioning is guaranteed to keep me cool, until I get the electric bill.
- Lightning never strikes in the same place twice. That's because the same place isn't there after it's been struck by lightning.
- I woke up this morning feeling on top of the world. It was that cold.
- I knew the storm was going to be really bad; they interrupted a commercial to announce it.
- We may complain about the heat in summer, but at least we don't have to shovel it.
- Yesterday then wind was so strong my pet hen laid the same egg six times.
- Africans complain if they don't have any rain for two months. We complain if we DO have rain for two days.
- For summer I bought an automatic air conditioner. Every time it gets really hot it automatically breaks down.
- It rained so much yesterday I saw a drunk in the gutter being rescued by the Salvation Navy.
- I think we're in for a very wet winter. Today I passed the Met. Office and saw them building an ark.
- Rain is what makes flowers grow and taxis disappear.
- They say everything comes to those that wait…..except a taxi on a rainy day.
- It rained twice last week. Once for three days and once for four days.

- I blame the recent floods on those new Indian immigrants. They never stop doing that ruddy rain dance.
- Last month Devon had such a bad flood, I'm surprised the county didn't shrink.
- The global warming situation's taken such hold that Frosty the Snowman's now known as Frosty the Puddle.
- The difference between the Arab spring and the British spring is theirs is much warmer.
- It was so hot yesterday I bought a steak at the supermarket and by the time I got home it was cooked.
- It got so hot my frigid wife almost thawed out.
- She looks her best in cold weather, because if it wasn't for her goose bumps she'd have no figure at all.
- It's got so hot they're thinking of bringing back the cold war.
- In this excessive hot weather I read the Labour Party manifesto. That always leaves me cold.
- It's so cold penguins are now bringing babies instead of storks.
- It was so cold this morning I woke up to find two feet of ice on my bed. They both belonged to my wife.
- They say the sun never sets on the British Empire. Right now the sun doesn't even rise here.
- When I'm abroad I always buy British newspapers, so I can read about the rotten weather back home.
- The best way to ensure rain is to give your garden a good soaking.
- Some days I stay up late to get the weather forecast. On other days I rely on my rheumatism.
- Because of the recent floods I was able to buy a house cheap in Wales. For just £100,000 I got a four bedroom house equipped with double glazing, a fully fitted kitchen, a double garage and an anchor.
- After a strong wind blew off the roof they advertised the restaurant as being topless.
- As the TV weather forecaster said "Tomorrow there's a thirty per cent chance of rain and a fifty percent chance I'm right."
- I spent four hours digging the car out of the snow, only to find it wasn't my car after all.
- When the barometer fell yesterday I was very upset. It fell on my head.

- If feminists had their way all future hurricanes would be named after men.
- Hurricanes named after women are more deadly because when they've left you find have your stuff is gone.
- The weather forecaster says he's 34 years old, but with the wind chill factor he feels more like 56.
- The only good thing about the flood was our house wound up in a better neighbourhood.

WIVES

She claims she has me wrapped around her finger. It started the day I put a ring on it. I guess I should have suspected it when she took the "Just Married" sign off our wedding car and replaced it with "Under New Management." She even refers to our wedding album as her Owner's Manual. Not that she wants to wear the trousers in our marriage. She'd rather wear the diamonds and pearls. She claims to be a woman of simple needs. All she wants is a roof over her head and a man under her thumb.

Like all married couples we often have words. Mind you, hers were said out loud. I don't want you to get the impression I'm a wimp. I even bought a book called "How to Be the Boss in Your Own Home", but I haven't read it yet. She won't let me. My wife says she can read me like a book. Must be why she's always putting me down. She's even bought bathroom towels marked "HERS" and "ITS" I told her what our marriage needs is more spice. She said she'd rather have more space. The only time my wife and I see eye to eye is when I do something right and she stares at me in disbelief. But I must say we're getting closer every day....to murdering each other.

My wife's certainly outspoken. But not by anyone I know. She's what they call a straight talker. She can talk straight through the day and night. She even talks to our plants. I wouldn't mind that, but when we're on holiday she sends them postcards. This morning my wife complained that I never listen to her. At least, I think that's what she said. She accused me of faking deafness. I said "I'll pretend I didn't hear that."

When my wife's out driving she always picks up hitchhikers, which is only fair. After all, she's the one that knocked them down. She never stops changing things in our house. Last month she knocked two rooms into one. Our car was a total write-off. According to my wife, everything's my fault. When she crashed the car she blamed me for letting her drive it.

I surprised my wife on our last anniversary. I remembered it. She kept hinting she wanted something to wear on her finger. So I bought her an Elastoplast. My wife's never satisfied with anything I ever give her. I gave her a book called "One Hundred Chicken Recipes." She threw it away. She said "What's the use? I haven't got a hundred chickens."

My wife's forever on the phone. Her hang-up is she can't hang-up. BT rang and offered me "call waiting" I told them I already have it. Waiting for my wife to get off the phone so I can make a call.

After a few weeks of marriage I felt like a new man. Unfortunately so did my wife. I asked her if, during our 50 years marriage, she'd been completely faithful. She said "Yes. Several times." When we were courting my wife played hard to get. Now she's hard to take. She keeps suggesting we have a second honeymoon. I wouldn't mind that, but she wants a second husband to go on it with.

My wife can be insanely jealous. She even looked at my diary and wanted to know who April, May and June were. I refer to her as the bird imitator, because she watches me like a hawk. She hates me referring to my previous girlfriends. She says my old flames weren't all that hot in the first place.

It was my wife's birthday last week and I had the problem of what to buy a woman who wants everything. She hinted heavily she would like a present that has four wheels and an airbag. So I bought her a Hoover. She loves flowers and my local florist had a sign "SAY IT WITH FLOWERS - £25." So I forked out a fiver and said it in shorthand. My wife hasn't changed a bit in the last fifteen years. She's still the same height, weight and age. Yesterday she was robbed. She spent £20 at the Beauty Parlour. She went in a vision and came out a sight. You've heard of a hostile takeover? Well she had a hostile makeover. She spends a fortune on beauty treatments, but lately they haven't been working. I think she's built up immunity. She puts on so much cream at night, I never know whether she's preparing for bed or to swim the channel. This week she finally decided to dye her hair back to its original colour, but she can't remember what it was.

Give my wife an inch and she immediately starts a diet. She used to be my dreamboat till her anchor dropped and her cargo started shifting. Whenever we eat out my wife always insists on a free meal. Sugar free, nut free, starch free…

Before we were married my wife said she would go through anything for me. So far she's gone through my bank account, my savings, my pension…I used to have a disposable income till she disposed of it. The way my wife spends, the only thing I can put away for a rainy day is an umbrella. I told her the bank returned one of her cheques. She said "Oh good, then I can use it again." In our household it's my wife' job to balance the budget. And mine's to budget the balance.

As soon as we got married she wanted to start making babies. I said "First learn to make salad." My wife says we got married too soon. She wanted to wait till we could afford a live-in cook. It's a pity we didn't. When we first married my wife used to serve me a boiled egg every morning for breakfast. But that soon stopped. She lost the recipe. Last night I asked her what she was cooking for dinner. She said "I don't know. The label fell off the tin."

I know it's a woman's privilege to change her mind, but my wife thinks it's compulsory. She's never satisfied. If she was in the Olympics and won a gold medal, she would ask for it in a different colour. She just can't make up her mind. It takes her so long to dress, by the time she puts one on, it's already out of style. It's the same in the supermarket. It takes her ages to make up her mind what to buy. Yesterday at the fish counter her shopping trolley got clamped. Occasionally my wife does make a final decision, but unfortunately it never tallies with the one she makes after that.

Some people can keep a secret for weeks, months or even years. With my wife you can reckon it on an egg timer. She says wild horses couldn't drag a secret out of her. Unfortunately everything else can. She's on the phone immediately. That's my wife's main trouble. She's great at hanging up the washing, but she can't hang up the phone.

275

My wife said "You want sex this year too? You're an animal!" Before we were married I asked her if we could make love. She said "Over my dead body." Then we got married and I realised she wasn't kidding. She's so frigid every time she opens her mouth a little light comes on.

My wife's so house-proud she not only has the carpet shampooed, twice a month she gives it a cut and blow dry. She says I don't help her with the housework. Not true. I always lift my feet so she can Hoover under them. We used to do the dishes together, but she got annoyed when I said "let's switch roles. YOU wash and I'LL gripe!" Now she's found a novel way to keep all her dishes, pots and pans sparkling clean. She doesn't use them. We eat out a lot which isn't easy with her. Not only does she count the cost, she counts the calories.

My wife's always grumpy in the mornings. She's what you'd call a surly riser. When she lowers her voice you know she wants something. And when she raises her voice, you know she didn't get it. Trouble is, she won't agree she's disagreeable. We have frequent arguments and afterwards she tries to smooth things over. She hits me with the steam iron. I once tried to drown my sorrows, but the lifeguard saved her. However she does occasionally do what I say. Like the time I told her to go to the devil, and she went straight home to her mother.

My wife finds it easy to tell a lie. She says she can tell it the moment I open my mouth. Mind you, we seldom argue because as a couple we share everything. Well, everything except the wardrobe space. When I married her she was a widow. Her first husband was a real wimp. She once tried to contact him through a medium but it didn't work. He was afraid to answer her back.

The only time my wife ever economises is when she puts candles on her birthday cake.

ADDITIONAL GAGS

- I promised my wife a jaguar for her birthday on one condition. She keeps its cage clean.
- She never laughed at my jokes, so I cut her out of my will. Well, anyone who doesn't get my jokes isn't going to get my money.

- I called my wife Angel, because she's always harping on.
- She gave me the ten happiest years of my life. She divorced me in 2005.
- If my wife got what she wanted we'd have had a new washing machine, a new car and a new house. Instead I got what I wanted. A new wife.
- My wife's just joined the Masons. She's a maisonette.
- I have to be honest and admit I'd be lost without my wife. She's the one that works our SatNav.
- My wife's that selfish she once won a holiday in Miami for two and she went there herself twice.
- My wife and I have a lot in common. It's at Edmonton cemetery.
- I met my wife when I popped into a pub for a quick pick-me-up, and she quickly picked me up.
- I took my wife for better or worse, Trouble is the better got worse.
- My wife's very safety conscious. If our house was on fire, she wouldn't let the firemen in the bedroom till they showed their credentials.
- My wife never understood me. Unfortunately the private detective she hired did.
- My wife found a good way to quit smoking. She only had a cigarette after sex.
- My wife's a lousy housekeeper. People think we have green carpets in our living room. Actually, it's moss.
- I should never have bought my wife that waterbed. I came home early one day and found her kissing the lifeguard.
- My wife and I are closer than ever before. Our electric blanket shrank.
- My wife's super cautious about everything. She even looks both ways before crossing her legs.
- My wife and I had a bond between us, but she put it in her name.
- Since my wife became a feminist her favourite dish is Chicken-A-La-Queen.
- Some men prefer a dog to a wife. They're usually just as loving and they don't demand jewellery and a new coat every year.
- My wife's a compulsive shopper. She keeps buying till she finds something she needs.

- She came home from the January sales with two big blisters. One on her foot and the other on her credit card.
- I'm not saying my wife's a fanatic about cleanliness, but she even washes the windows on envelopes.
- Some women cry to get things out of their system. Others cry to get things out of their husband.
- When we go abroad, my wife's so fussy about the water she even boils their ice cubes.
- My gossipy wife came home disappointed from her old school reunion. Everyone turned up, so there was no one to talk about.
- My wife has a great interest in my happiness. So much so, she hired a private detective to find out what's causing it.
- My wife has the same attitude as the government. She never lets being broke stop her spending more.
- I told my wife not to buy me an anniversary present this year. I can't afford it.
- The bank told my wife she was overdrawn by £50. So she wrote out a cheque to cover it.
- My wife laughs at everything we do, which explains why we have no children.
- I now have a lie detector that works without wires. My wife.
- My wife wants to learn to drive and I'm not going to stand in her way.
- My wife stopped me buying a Japanese TV set because she was afraid she wouldn't understand what they were saying.
- I told my wife I'd go to the end of the world for her. She said "Yes, but would you stay there?
- With my luck, if my ship ever did come in it would be full of my wife's relatives.
- My wife wouldn't let me go play golf with my friends. I was under spouse arrest.
- My wife's already planning to have me cremated so she can collect on the fire insurance.
- My wife's so cautious; she won't even sleep on a waterbed without a lifejacket.
- People say I'd be a lousy travelling salesman because the only orders I ever take are from my wife.

- I never put my wife on a pedestal, unless of course, the ceiling needs painting.
- My wife loves to worry. She once answered the phone and there was no one there. She thought it was an obscene phone call from Marcel Marceau.
- When my wife goes shopping she comes home with everything but money.
- I'm not saying my wife nags a lot, but she's he only one I know who too her driving test from the back seat.
- My wife has a very clean mind, which is not surprising since she changes it so often.
- My wife can be outspoken, but so far I've never seen anyone do it.
- My wife will never repeat gossip. So you have to listen carefully the first time.
- My wife and I have a perfect understanding. I don't try to run her life and I don't try to run mine either.
- When she prepares for bed at night, everything either comes off or out.
- My wife always lets me run things. Mostly errands.
- My wife would dearly love to shed 140 lbs. Me.
- Bingo has given me the happiest nights of my life. Especially when my wife is out playing it.
- I wouldn't trade my wife for all the jewels in the world. If anyone wants, they can have her for nothing.
- My wife takes after her father. They both have the same moustache.
- My wife thinks I'm a very versatile man. She says there's nothing I can't do…wrong.
- Before we were married my wife played hard-to-get. Unfortunately for me, she didn't play it hard enough.
- In the Orient, when a wife walks several paces behind her husband it's a sign of respect. If it happens in the West, he's being tailed.
- My wife told the traffic warden "It's alright; I'm using the fifteen minutes I had left over from yesterday."
- My wife complains about everything. In Selfridges yesterday she complained about the Complaints Department.
- My wife believes in sharing duties. When we bathe our newborn baby, she always says the same "You wash I'll dry."

- My wife and I are always arguing. Even when we have the same point of view.
- I didn't mind my wife rearranging the furniture, but she put my bed in the spare room.
- The wife who listens when her husband speaks is probably on the extension.
- My wife not only reads me like a book, she gives a review to all the neighbours.
- My wife's a chronic complainer. She goes on and on about things she says leave her speechless.
- It wasn't till after I married my wife I found out the Japanese make a cheaper model.
- My wife can say more with one look than I can say in a whole book.
- As a family man I have several small mouths to feed and one big mouth to listen to.
- When a wife throws in the towel, it usually means it's time for the husband to do the dishes.
- I used to help my wife with the dishes, but not anymore. I do them myself now.
- My two greatest expenses are the maid who lives in and the wife who eats out.
- My wife's on the phone so much she's developed a cauliflower ear.
- My wife wears a lot of make-up. She's trying to improve Mother Nature, but she's not fooling Father Time.
- My wife's every bit as pretty as she ever was. Only now it takes her a lot longer.
- With my wife I can never speak out of turn because I never get a turn.
- The only time my wife suffers in silence is when the phone's out of order.
- My wife isn't always the boss in our house. Sometimes it's her mother.
- When I first met my wife she was a vision. Now she's more of a sight.
- When I first met my wife she looked good enough to eat. And by God she did! Cost me a fortune in food bills.
- Our marriage has been all give and take. I gave and she took over.

- We had a power failure in our house. My wife lost her voice.
- When I come home late at night my wife always asks me where I've been before she tells me where to go.
- These days the only time my wife and I hold hands is when we're playing cards.
- My wife never does what I tell her. She says she wasn't made to order.
- I think my wife's trying to get rid of me. She even throws a going-away party when I take out the garbage.
- My wife's so stubbornly dogmatic; she won't even listen to the other side of a record.
- My wife's outspoken, but not by many.
- It's easy to tell when my wife's dialled a wrong number. She'll only talk for ten minutes.
- My wife's been missing for our days. I don't know whether she's left me or still out shopping.
- My wife has sinus trouble. "Sinus a cheque for this and sinus a cheque for that."
- My wife always asks my opinion, but only after she's made up her mind.
- My wife's a phonoholic. When I ring from work I can't get her on the phone. And when I'm home I can't get her off the phone.
- My wife's really lazy. When we were courting I swept her off her feet and she's been off her feet ever since.
- My wife's found a new way to save on electricity. She's given up ironing and cooking.
- I married my wife for her looks. Mind you, not the ones she gives me now.
- My wife was furious when she found out I have a will of my own…and she's not listed as the beneficiary
- I haven't seen my wife this happy since she thought our marriage licence might be invalid.
- My wife's got a great way of making a long story short. She interrupts.
- People ask me if my wife and I ever have a difference of opinion. The answer is "Yes, but I never tell her."

- With my wife it's a case of give her an inch and she thinks she's a ruler. I never argue with my wife. I might win, then I'd be in trouble.
- My wife says she wouldn't mind me leaving her, as long as I leave her enough.
- My wife is really pleased I'm not perfect. She loves to nag.
- My wife and I were very happy for twenty years. Then we met.
- My wife's always demanding new things. I call her my gimme pig.
- My wife pays so little attention to me, if I died she wouldn't even be able to identify the body.
- I bought myself a new tie and asked my wife what's best to wear with it. She said "A long beard."
- This fellow's wife had gone missing for a week and the police told him to prepare for the worst. So he went to the charity shop to get all her clothes back.
- My wife has jaded tastes. She just loves jade.
- My wife tried on every shoe in the store and then left barefooted. She decided she didn't even like the pair she went in with.
- I used to be an incurable romantic, but my wife cured me. Talk about frigid, I would say she's like a glacier, but even a glacier moves a little.
- My wife wants four things. A second car, a second holiday this year, a second home and a second job for me so I can pay for them.
- These days the only thing my wife and I are doing together is going broke.
- I owe my success to my first wife. And I owe my second wife to my success.
- My wife is good in the sack. Especially when she puts it over her head.
- My wife and I are not perfect for each other. But then, we're not perfect for anyone else either.
- I took my wife to Echo Canyon, but her voice never got an echo. It was frightened to answer her back.
- I always say, give my wife 22.4 centimetres and she'll take 1.6093 kilometres.
- My wife hates me going anywhere without her. She won't even let me go on an ego trip.

- She turned down my marriage proposal. She said it wouldn't work because she's a Taurus and I'm an idiot.
- These days the only thing my wife and I are doing together is going broke.
- My wife refuses to wear skis. She says they make her feet look too big.
- My wife went to the funeral and was annoyed because she's wasted two quid on a Get Well card.
- My wife's not as young a 29 as she used to be.
- When we first met she played hard to get. Now she's hard to get rid of.
- There was a phone call for me and my wife told them "He's in his second childhood. He can't come to the phone right now, he's on the potty."
- My wife wants me to join Gamblers Anonymous, but I bet her ten to one it wouldn't work.
- My wife wears her wedding ring on the wrong finger because she says she married the wrong man.
- The only way she'd get clothes with an Yves St. Laurent label is by changing her name to Yves St. Laurent.
- She had a very trying day. The Boss was trying, the milkman was trying, the plumber was trying....
- I knew we had guests coming for dinner, I saw Mum watering the soup.
- My wife and I are not perfect for each other, but then, we're not perfect for anyone else either.
- They had a runaway marriage. As soon as the ceremony was over, she ran away.
- My wife got annoyed when I said I liked her alligator shoes. Well how was I to know she was barefoot.
- My wife says our new neighbours are unspeakable and she hasn't stopped speaking about them all week.
- My wife went to the January sales and left me a note which said "Back in six hours or sixty quid, whichever comes first."
- My wife has no sense of economy. Last December she wrote to all our friends saying we weren't going to send them Christmas cards this year.

- My wife and I make a good team. She talks, I listen…she cooks, I eat….I earn, she spends.
- My life is empty without my wife. She took all our furniture with her.
- She says I'm a poor husband, and she should know. She's the one that made me poor.
- Our sex life a case of give and fake.
- The wife told the Marriage Counsellor "We're happiest during the football season. At least then he talks to me during halftime."
- She's what's called a medical phenomenon. Her body's rejected all four husbands.
- My wife didn't speak to me at all yesterday. She's mad at me for something I did in her dream.
- She said she's glad she married me. I had everything she'd want to change in a man.
- After her operation my wife said we'd have no sex for a fortnight. The doctor said it would hurt when she laughs.
- My wife hasn't been home at all today. I think she was recalled by the Beauty Parlour.
- My wife got everything she ever wanted. A roof over her head. A wardrobe full of fancy clothes…and a divorce.
- As soon as my wife found out I had a huge sexual appetite, she put me on a diet.
- When the Marriage Counsellor suggested my wife and I go on a second honeymoon she called him a sadist.
- My wife's so suspicious. This morning she said "You didn't talk in your sleep last night. Are you trying to hide something?"
- My friend says his wife's an angel. He's lucky. Mine's still living.
- The Wright Brothers wives complained they couldn't keep anything up for long.
- His wife didn't mind him pushing her around and talking behind her back. She welcomed it. After all, she was in a wheelchair.
- The husband tells his wife "I've worked out our household budget and one of us has to go."
- My wife and I have call-waiting. We have to wait till our daughter's off the phone to make a call.

- My fat wife insisted we get a new car. She said the old one was getting tight on her.
- We had a big argument over our wedding plans. She wanted someone else for her groom.
- I call my wife Hun because she reminds me of Attila.
- What she liked best about him were the four letters after his name R-I-C-H.
- My wife's always indecisive about where to go our annual holiday. She spent two house with the travel agent who finally said ""I'm sorry, Madam, but they're the only countries so far discovered."
- The chemist told the young bride "We're out of that pill, but these are just as effective. They'll put your husband to sleep.
- She thought she'd found her Mr Right till she realised he was looking for a Mr Right too.
- I well remember our wedding night. It was then only night my wife didn't have a headache.
- She even complained about the wedding cake not tasting as good as her previous weddings.
- She had to slap him twice during their wedding night. He kept falling asleep.
- My wife said on Father's Day I could have breakfast in bed, but only if I slept in the kitchen.
- It was our first date and can honestly say there wasn't a dull moment. It lasted all evening.
- The nearest she ever got to putting me on a pedestal was buying me a pair of platform shoes.
- Nowadays the only time my wife and I communicate is when we're fighting
- You've heard of the Tin Man. Well I call my wife the Tin Woman, because everything she serves is out of a tin.
- My wife never looked at other men. But then, she never looked at me either.
- We've been married 36years, 4 months, five days and three hours, to the penny.
- They tried tap my wife's phone, but it didn't work. She was on for so long they ran out of tape.

- His wife was bored just lying in hospital, so he took her his socks to darn.
- She's so house-proud, once when ransacked our home she wouldn't let the police in till she's tidied everything up.
- My wife and I have so many fights I've just had to spend two weeks in hospital with battle fatigue.
- My wife complains we don't communicate, but it's one of the few pleasures I have left in life.
- My wife's a hypochondriac. She even says she's seasick when she sleeps on a water bed.
- My wife came home so happy because, before he'd sell her cigarettes, the tobacconist asked if she was over eighteen.
- As the diplomatic husband said "How do you expect me to remember your birthday when you don't look any older?"
- My wife says the one regret she has about our wedding is that she didn't keep the bouquet and throw me away.
- She's a very bossy wife. Even at the altar when he said "I do." She said "Oh no you don't."
- My wife says "In our house there's always something not working. Usually it's my husband."
- She always introduces me as her husband, Mr. Wrong.
- My wife's a very careful driver. She always slows down before going through a red light.
- My wife can be very nice when she wants to. Liked the other day she left me.
- I used to put my wife on a pedestal. Now I'm putting her on a budget.
- My wife's so frugal for her thirtieth birthday she only used twenty one candles.
- My wife knows how to drive the car. She just doesn't know how to aim it.
- When I asked my future wife if she likes to do housework, she says she likes to do nothing better. And that's what she does – nothing.
- People think my wife came from an old distinguished family. That's not true. She brought them with her.
- My wife's always gossiping with the neighbours. It's called mouth-to-mouth recitation.

- My wife likes the simple things in life. She says that's why she married me.
- My wife objects to me talking in my sleep, but it's the only chance I get.
- She's a really cruel wife. One day she hid her husband's teeth and for supper served corn on the cob.
- My wife admits most of her arguments are irrational, but she insists they make sense.
- I used to enjoy having peace of mind, till my wife gave me a piece of hers.
- I wasted my money paying for my wife to take a course in domestic science. I thought the advert said "Domestic Silence."
- Husband on phone says "She's not here. She's out recycling money."
- My ex-wife says she's happily dance on my grave. But I've fixed her. I've arranged to be buried at sea.
- Webster started his dictionary after an argument with his wife. Then one word led to another
- Did you hear about the sultan with so many wives, when he takes them out he has to have a stretch camel.
- My wife's never won a slogan competition. She just can't say anything in 256 words or less.
- My wife and I always argue, even when we agree with each other.
- His wife has rekindled his will to live. She's asked for a divorce.
- I asked my wife if she'd call me a handsome man. She said "No. Call your own."
- I changed more times than Pet Clark's age.
- My wife was hinting for a diamond for her birthday. She said she wanted something that would last a lifetime. So I gave her herpes.
- The nightmare was not that my wife left me, but that I woke up and she was still there.
- My wife knows how to keep a secret, like the Arab who found a substitute for oil.
- My wife's so predictable. Every time we have an argument she takes her side.
- I always help my wife with the housework. I stay out of her way.
- The nightmare was not that my wife left me, but that I woke up and she was still there.

WOMEN

They say a woman's beauty comes from within. Mostly within tubes, jars and bottles. It's also true what they say about a woman's face being her fortune. That's what it costs for all those face lifts

Joan Collins once said every woman's goal is to get married. So far she's scored six goals. She's made a charm bracelet out of her old wedding rings. Some women keep their love letters. Others let their love letters keep them. Many women say they prefer shopping to sex, because in shopping if something's too small they can change it for one that's bigger.

I always say you should never put a woman on a pedestal. That's unless you want the ceiling painted. Did you hear about the woman who burned her bra and was arrested for having no means of support?

ADDITIONAL GAGS

- She only wore a bra on Sundays. The rest of the week she was a topless waitress.
- The woman told her husband she was worried because the doctor said she was in good health for her age. She'd lied to the doctor she was ten years younger.
- I love women – when they let me.
- Her chest is so flat if it weren't for goose pimples she'd have no figure at all.
- A feminist believe a Ms. is as good as a male.
- My brother's the only man I know who likes to see women fully covered. He's an insurance salesman.
- There was this newlywed woman so cunning she went to a fortune teller to find out something about her present husband's past that she could use in the future.
- A woman knows she's reached middle age when her corset and shoes pinch her, but men don't.
- Some men really believe a woman's place is in the home and that she should go straight there after work.

- She had six kids just because someone told her she looked good in maternity clothes.
- She followed a recipe that said "Add one tablespoon of water" so she phoned them up to asks if that was level or heaped.
- A woman needs her ears pierced like a hole in the head.
- As far as women are concerned, falsies are the bust money can buy.
- I find it difficult to look a woman in the eye. Especially if she's wearing a bikini.
- When a woman has a love affair she goes into ecstasy. A man goes into details.
- Women wear sweaters to accentuate the positive and corsets to eliminate the negative.
- Some women have their husbands eating out of their hand, just so they can save on dishes to wash.
- The only time some women let their husband put his foot down is when he's shovelling the snow from the footpath.
- Very expensive jewellery can turn some women green. Especially when they see other women wearing it.
- What's said to a man often goes in one ear and out the other. What's said to a woman goes in one ear and out through the telephone.
- Every woman needs two friends. One to talk to and the other to talk about.
- A smart woman is one who knows how to play piano, tennis and dumb.
- She used to look for a man with sex appeal. Now it's cheques appeal.
- She was going to have a facelift, but when she found out what it cost she let it drop.
- Most women are animal lovers. They love a jaguar in their garage, a tiger in their bed, a mink in their wardrobe and a stupid ass to pay for it all.
- Women are now prepared to overlook a man's belly bulge as long as there's also a bulge in his wallet.
- A career woman is one who goes out and earns a man's salary instead of staying home and taking it away from him.
- A woman no longer wants a man who will satisfy her smallest wish. She wants him to satisfy her big ones as well.

- A woman will spend £25 on buying a beautiful slip and then get annoyed when it shows.
- The plain looking woman asked her husband "What do you like most about me, my pretty face or my sexy body?" He said "What I like most is your sense of humour."
- My wife spends like there's no tomorrow. Last week my wife spent £500 on nothing to wear. I think those huge shopping centres are great. If it weren't for them my wife wouldn't get any exercise at all. The only thing she ever watches on TV are the shopping channels. She says she prefers them because they're not interrupted by commercials.
- I became a misogynist just from watching TV commercials and finding that so many women are anaemic, have stringy hair, weigh too much and have rough hands.
- He has a way with women. It's called money.
- Girls used to want to grow up to be secretaries. Now they want to be Home Secretary like Theresa May.
- Girls just used to want to be homemakers. Now they want to run companies that make homes.
- It's estimated that at least ten per cent of industry bosses are effeminate. That's because they are women.
- I asked the young girl what she wants to be when she grows up. She said 38-24-36.
- Women are now more prominent in the workplace than they used to be. Even Jack-In-The-Box has been replaced by Jill.
- She wears Red Riding Hood perfume because she knows it attracts wolves.

WRESTLING

I used to watch all the wrestling matches on TV and didn't realise they were faked till afterwards when they ended and the audience shouted "Author, author!" The referee used to call both wrestlers into the centre and say "Shake hands, go back to your corners, and when the bell rings, come out acting."

One wrestler got disqualified for not sticking to the script. The only wrestling match that isn't fixed is the one in the backseat of a car.

JOKES

Finally in this book we move on from gags to actual jokes, otherwise known as humorous stories. Many speakers like to start and end with a good joke. I must confess to never actually having written a joke and I don't know anyone who has. Jokes either come out of collections in joke books or are passed around from friend to friend.

Assuming you, my reader, are now also my friend, here are some of my favourite jokes I'd like to pass on to you.

During the Olympics in London in 2012 an Englishman, a Scotsman and an Irishman want to get in to watch the games, but they haven't got tickets. They try to buy tickets at the event, but it is completely full. They're told that the only people who can get in now are the actual competitors and they would enter through the Players Gate at the rear of the stadium. All three go round the back and see that the gate is very near to an unfinished building site. The Scotsman has an idea. He picks up a length of scaffolding, slings it over his shoulder and tells the guard at the gate "I'm Angus McTavish, Scotland team- pole vaulter" and is allowed in. The Englishmen has a similar idea. He picks up a small manhole cover, tucks it under his arm and tells the guard "I'm Alistair Smythe, English team – discus thrower. He is allowed in too. That leaves just the Irishman who stands there thinking for a moment before spotting a roll of barbed wire. He picks it up and with it tucked under his arm he tells the guard "I'm Paddy McGinty, Irish team – fencing!"

A businessman wanted to get on the good side of a client and invited him home for a meal. When the meal was over they made idle conversation on a variety of topics such as the weather, traffic conditions, politics and holidays. While they were talking, the businessman's three young sons came running into the room. They were playing noisy games and making a terrible racket. The host's wife shouted to them from the kitchen to be good or they'd get no ice cream for dessert. But that had no effect and they carried on with their noise. "My system is better," their father told his guest. I give George, my seven-year-old eldest son a five pound note and he keeps still." He handed the boy the note and he immediately ceased his noise. "Next" the father said "I give Robert, he's five, a one pound coin and he'll quieten down. The boy was given the coin and stopped his share of the disturbance. "Sounds like a good idea" said the guest, "but what about your youngest son?" The wife who'd been listening to this, shouted from the kitchen "Don't worry about him. He's just like his father – good for nothing!"

The Pope finished his American tour and was sitting in the back of his Popemobile being driven back to Kennedy Airport. It was a long journey and he was bored so he asked the chauffeur if he could take over the wheel for a while. The chauffeur didn't want to argue with his boss, so he stopped the vehicle, climbed into the passenger seat and let the Pope have his way. Not used to driving the Pontiff put his foot down too heavily on the accelerator and was soon doing nearly 90 miles an hour. Suddenly he saw a blue light flashing in his wing view mirror as he was being chased by a traffic cop for speeding. So he pulled over and stopped the car. The cop came over, peered through the window, and said "Just a moment please, I need to call in for instructions. So the policeman got on the phone to his Chief and explained that he had just pulled over a very important person for speeding. He wanted to know what to do. "Is it the Mayor" asked the Chief. "No" said the cop. "This guy's even more important." "Is it the State Governor?" "No, even more important than that." "Well, who the heck is it?" shouted the Chief down the phone. "I'm not sure, sir "replied the cop. "but he's got the Pope as his chauffeur."

The teacher was giving private computer lessons over the phone to a student who'd fallen behind with his studies. She said "The first thing is I need you to right-click on the open desktop." The lad said "OK." "Did you get a pop-up menu?" she asked. "No, I didn't." replied the boy. "OK, right click again", she repeated. "Do you see a pop-up menu now?" "Still no" he replied. The teacher was getting a little impatient but was trying to keep calm "OK Johnny. Can you tell me what you have done up till this point?" "Sure" he said. "You told me to write 'click' and I wrote click."

A couple have been married for many years and suddenly the man finds he is no longer able to perform his duties as a husband between the sheets. He goes to his doctor who tries a few things, but none of them work. "I think it's all in your mind" says the doctor, and refers the man to a psychiatrist. After a few visits the shrink confesses he is at a loss as to how the man can be cured. In desperation he refers him to a witch doctor who claims he can actually help the poor fellow. So he throws some powder on a flame which causes a flash of billowing blue smoke. "This is powerful healing," says the witch doctor "but you can only use it once a year. All you have to do is say '1-2-3' and the important part of your anatomy will rise for as long as you wish." "That's great." Says the patient "But what happens when it's all over?" The witch doctor replies "All your partner has to say is '1-2-3-4' and the swelling will immediately go down. But be warned, after that it will not work again for a whole year." The man goes home, and that night he is excited and anxious to surprise his wife. They get into bed and he says "1-2-3" and just like magic he gets an erection. His puzzled wife turns to him and says "What did you say '1-2-3' for?"

A man takes his pet hamster to the vet and, after examining the creature, the vet pronounces it dead. The man isn't happy with the vet's diagnosis and asks for a second opinion. The vet gives a whistle and in strolls a Labrador dog. The dog nudges the hamster around with its nose and sniffs it a couple of times before shaking its head. "There" says the vet, your hamster is dead." Still not happy, the man asks for a third opinion. So the vet opens the back door and in comes a cat. The cat jumps up onto the table and looks the hamster up and down for a few minutes and then shakes its head. "It's definitely dead, sir." says the vet. The man is finally convinced and says "How much do I owe you?" "A thousand pounds please." Says the vet. The man is shocked. "A thousand pounds just to tell me my hamster is dead?" "No" says the vet. "It's for my diagnosis, the lab report and the cat scan."

A passenger in a taxi leaned over to ask the driver a question and tapped him on the shoulder. The driver let out a blood curdling scream and lost control of the cab. He managed to stop just inches away from a large plate glass shop window. For a few seconds everything was silent. Then the driver apologised. He was still shaking as he said "I'm sorry, but you scared the living daylights out of me." The passenger said "It's me that should be sorry. I didn't realise a mere tap on the shoulder would frighten you so much. There must be a good reason for it." The cab driver said "There is. Today's my first day driving a cab. For the past 25 years I've been driving a hearse."

A middle aged unmarried woman went to confession. She said to the priest "Forgive me, Father, for I have sinned." The priest said the usual thing "Confess your sins and be forgiven." "Well Father," she said last night I invited my boyfriend home for a cup of coffee. Things got out of hand and he made mad passionate love to me seven times." The priest thought about it for half a minute and then told her to squeeze seven lemons into a glass and drink it all in one go. "And will that cleanse me of my sins?" she asked. The priest said "No. But it will wipe that smile off your face."

Two hard drinkers were in a pub downing a whole bottle of whisky between them. They got really merry, dancing and singing at the top of their voices and generally causing a stir. When the pub's landlord complained they said they were celebrating something they had just achieved. "This afternoon we finished a fifty-piece jigsaw puzzle after only six weeks." said one of them. The landlord couldn't believe what he was hearing. "It took the two of you six whole weeks to do one fifty-piece jigsaw puzzle? That's ridiculous! It shouldn't take that long." "It should have taken longer." Said the other drunkard "On the box it said 2 to 4 years."

A woman in her eighties got her name in the newspapers because she was getting married for the fourth time. Her local radio station picked up the story and sent a reporter along to interview her. The reporter asked her what it felt like to get married again at that old age. He pressed her for any stories she could share with the radio listeners. He was particularly intrigued by the fact that her husband-to-be was a funeral director. The old lady thought for a moment and then a smile came to her face as she proudly explained that she had first married a banker when she was in her twenties, then a circus ringmaster when she was in her forties, followed by a priest when she was in her sixties. Now, in her eighties it was to be a funeral director. Then reporter thought that was fascinating and asked why she wedded such a variety of characters. She beamed another big smile as she explained "I married one for the money, two for the show, three to get ready and now four to go."

At Christmas a routine police patrol car was parked outside The Rising Sun public house. The policeman driver noticed a man leaving the pub so intoxicated that he could barely walk. The man stumbled around the car park for a few minutes with the policeman watching his every move. After what seemed like an eternity during which he tried his keys on five different cars, the man managed to find his own car and fell in to it. He was there for about quarter of an hour while a number of other drinkers left the pub and drove off. Finally the man started up the engine of his car and even though it was a completely dry night, he turned on his windscreen wipers, flashed his fog light and sounded his car horn. Then he moved the car forward a few inches and reversed it back into its original space. He remained stationary there as a few more customers got into their cars and drove out of the car park. Finally our man turned on his car's sidelights and drove slowly out onto the street. The police officer, having made notes of his erratic behaviour, drove after him and pulled him over. He immediately made the man stop the car and breathalysed him and was amazed to find it registered no trace of alcohol at all. Dumbfounded, the policeman said "I'll have to ask you to accompany me to the station. This breathalyser equipment must be broken." "I doubt it" said the driving smiling broadly. "Tonight, I'm the designated decoy."

An elderly gentleman had serious hearing problems for several years, so he finally went to see his doctor about it. The doctor was able to have him fitted with a set of hearing aids that restored his hearing back to 100%. He was asked to test them out for a month and then report back for a further audio check. The doctor tested his hearing again and said it was perfect. He said "Your family must be very pleased that you can hear again." The old man said "Oh, I haven't told my family yet. I just sit around and listen to their conversations, especially when they talk about me. As a result, I've changed my will five times!"

Father Murphy walked into a pub in Donegal and said to the first man he met there "Do you want to go to heaven?" The man said "I do, Father." So the priest said "Then leave this pub right now!" Then he approached a second man. "Do you want to go to heaven?" "Certainly, Father" the man replied. Then leave this den of Satan" said the priest as he walked up to Seamus O'Toole. "Do you want to go to heaven?" "No, I don't, Father." Replied O'Toole. The priest looked him straight in the eye and said "You mean to tell me that when you die you don't want to go to heaven?" O'Toole smiled. He said "Oh, when I die, yes, Father. I thought you were getting a group together to go right now."

A middle-aged, mild mannered lorry driver was eating at a transport café just off the busy motorway when three very hefty, leathered young motor bikers walked in and taunted him. The first walked up to the driver and pushed his lit cigarette into his half-eaten pie and then took a seat at the counter. The second walked up to the driver, spat in his cup of coffee and took a seat at the counter. The third turned over the driver's plate of food and then joined his mates at the counter. Without a word of protest, the lorry driver got up and left the café. A short while later one of the leathered louts said to the waitress "He wasn't much of a man, was he?" She said "No. And he wasn't much of a driver either. He just backed his ten ton lorry over your three motorcycles."

A religious man climbed to the top of Mount Sinai to talk to God. When he got there he asked The Almighty "God, what is a million years to you?" And God said "A minute." Then the man asked "Well, what's a million pounds to you?" And God answered "A penny." So the man asked "God, can I have a penny?" And God said "Sure…in a minute."

Paddy, a factory worker wanted a few days off to watch his favourite cricket team play at Lords, but he knew his boss would never agree to it. So he had the idea that if he acted crazy enough. Then his boss would tell him to take a few days off. So he hung upside down from the ceiling and made all sorts of weird noises. His co-worker , Seamus, asked what he was doing and he told him "I'm pretending to be a light bulb so the boss will think I'm crazy and send me home. A few seconds later the boss did exactly that. He told Paddy "You're obviously stressed out from working too hard. Go home and recuperate for a few days." Paddy jumped down and hid a smile as he walked out of the office. Seamus saw this and started to follow Paddy to the door. The boss said "Seamus, what do you think you're doing?" And Seamus said "I'm going home too. I can't work in the dark."

A couple had been married for fifteen years and had three beautiful children. Then, unexpectedly the wife got pregnant. The husband decided he'd be modern and actually attend the birth this time. So he was there at the hospital when she delivered a really ugly baby. He was not only disappointed, he was angry and accusative. He said "We've had three gorgeous kids and now this horrible looking one. Have you been sleeping with another man?" She said "No. Not this time."

A young man attended his grandfather's funeral and, while offering his condolences to the widow asked "Grandma, it's so sad about Granddad passing on, but no one ever told me what the old fellow died from." "He died while we were making love." she said. The young man was astonished. "Making love?" he queried, "But Granddad was 84 years old!" "That's true" she said, "but even so we kept to this ritual of making love every Sunday morning to the sound of the local church bells. In for ding and out for dong. And if it hadn't been for that bloody ice cream van he'd be alive today!"

A middle aged man who hadn't been feeling well went to see his doctor. After a thorough examination of heart, lungs, blood pressure etc., the doctor was grim faced as he announced the result. "I'm afraid I have some very bad news," the doctor said, "You're dying and you don't have much time left." The man was shocked. "Oh, that's terrible!" He said. "Give it to me straight, Doctor. How long have I got?" "I'm sorry to say this, but you only have ten." "Ten what? Months....weeks....what? The doctor drew a breath and said "Nine...eight...seven....."

A couple were making love in the bedroom when they heard a key turning in the lock of the front door. "My God, it's my husband!" cried the woman. "He wasn't expected home till tomorrow. He's very jealous. If he sees you here he'll kill you!" "Should I hide in the cupboard?" asked her frightened lover. "No. He'll find you there. Climb out of the window." So he managed to climb out of the window just before the woman's husband entered the room. "Hello" said the husband. "What are you doing in bed in the middle of the afternoon?" She said "I had this terrible headache, so I thought I'd lie down for a while." The husband was very sympathetic and sat on the bed chatting to her for about quarter of an hour while the other fellow was out on the windowsill freezing. Suddenly he saw a group of runners coming along dressed in their shorts and singlet, so he thought it would be a good idea to climb down and join them. Which he did. While they were running, the head of the group said "Hi, I haven't seen you before. You're new to our group, aren't you?" "Yes" said the lover "I normally go running on my own, but I saw you going by so I thought I'd join you." "You're certainly welcome to" said the group leader. "But tell me, do you usually run in the nude?" "Yes." he sought to explain. "It lets the sun's rays get to my skin. " "That's very commendable" said the leader. "But why are you wearing a condom?" He said "Well, someone said it might rain."

A man went to see a dentist and asked "How much do you charge to take out a tooth?" "A hundred pounds." said the dentist. "That's ridiculous" said the man. "Well," said the dentist "I could cut out the anaesthetic and it would cost only seventy five pounds." "That's still too expensive" said the man. "What can you do for ten pounds?" "For ten pounds I'd have to back out entirely and let one of my new trainee students do it." "That's perfect" said the man. "Book my wife in for next Tuesday."

The salesman dropped in to see a customer. No one was in the office except a big dog emptying two wastebaskets. The salesman thought he was imagining it, until the dog looked up and said "Don't be surprised, Buddy, this is part of my job." The man muttered "Incredible – I can't believe it! I'm going to tell your boss what a prize he has in you, an animal that can talk." The dog pleaded "Please don't. If that swine finds out I can talk, he'll have me answering the phones."

A married couple rushed to the hospital because the woman was in labour. The doctor said to the couple "I have invented a new machine that you might want to try. It takes some of the labour pains away from the mother and gives it to the father." The married couple decided to give it a try. So the doctor hooked the machine up and put it on 10% of pain, then switched it from the woman to her husband who said "I feel okay, turn it up a bit more." The doctor then turned it up to 50% and then husband said "Why don't you put it all on me because I'm not feeling a thing." The doctor was cautious and warned him "This much could kill you if you're not prepared. Undaunted, the husband replied "I'm ready." So the doctor turned the machine up to 100%, but the husband still didn't feel anything. The husband and wife went home happy with the pain free labour. But when they got home they found the postman dead on the front porch.

When Mozart passed away he was buried in a churchyard. A few days later the town drunk was walking through the cemetery and heard some strange noise coming from the area where Mozart was buried. Terrified, the drunk ran and got the priest to come and listen to it. The priest bent close to the grave and heard some faint, unrecognisable music coming from the grave. Frightened, the priest ran and got the town magistrate who also bent his ear to the grave, listened for a moment and said "Ah yes, that's Mozart's Ninth Symphony being played backwards." He listened a while longer and said "There's the Eighth Symphony and it's backwards too. Most puzzling." So the magistrate kept listening. "There's the Seventh...The Sixth...The Fifth..."Suddenly the realisation of what was happening dawned on the magistrate. He stood up and announced to the crowd that had gathered "My fellow citizens, there's nothing to worry about. It's just Mozart decomposing."

A chicken farmer went to a local bar, sat next to a woman and ordered a glass of champagne. The woman perked up and said "How about that? I just ordered a glass of champagne too!" "What a coincidence" the farmer said. "This is a special day for me, I'm celebrating." "This is a special day for me too, I am also celebrating" said the woman. "What a coincidence!" Said the farmer. As they clinked glasses he asked "What are you celebrating?" "My husband and I have been trying to have a child and today my gynaecologist told me I'm pregnant." "What a coincidence" said the man. "I'm a chicken farmer and for years all my hens were infertile. But today they are all laying fertilised eggs. "That's great" said the woman. "How did your chickens suddenly become fertile?" "I used a different cock" he replied. The woman smiled, clinked his glass and said "What a coincidence!"

Henry decided to finally marry his long-time girlfriend. One evening, after they'd returned from their honeymoon, Henry was cleaning is golf shoes. His wife was standing there watching him. After a long silence, she said "Darling, I've been thinking. Now that we are married I feel it's time you quit playing golf. Maybe you should sell your golf clubs." Henry got a horrified look on his face. She said "Darling, what's wrong?" He said "There for a minute you were sounding like my ex-wife." "Ex-wife!" she shouted. "I didn't know you were married before!" Henry said calmly "I wasn't!"

A man and an ostrich walked into a restaurant. The waitress asked, "What will it be?" The man replied "A burger and a coke." "And I'll have the same," said the ostrich. They finish their meal and pay. "That'll be £7.50" the waitress said, presenting the bill. The man reached into his pocket and pulled out the exact amount. This procedure carried on throughout the week till the Friday. "The usual?" asked the waitress. "No," said the man. "Today is Friday, so I'll have steak and a coke." "Me too." said the ostrich. They finish and when the waitress says "That'll be £9.75." the man reaches into his pocket and pulls out the exact amount again. The waitress was dumb-founded. "How is it that you always have the exact amount?" "Well," said the man, "I was cleaning out my attic and I found a dusty old lamp. I rubbed it and a genie appeared." "Wow!" said the waitress. "What did you wish for?" "I asked that when I needed to pay for something, the exact amount would appear in my pocket." "That's amazing!" Said the waitress. "Most people would ask for a million pounds. But what's with the ostrich?" "Well," said the man. "I also asked for a chick with long legs."

A tourist drove his car into a ditch in a desolate area. Luckily, a local farmer came to help with a big strong horse named Buddy. He hitched Buddy up to the car and yelled "Pull, Nellie, pull!" Buddy didn't move. Then the farmer hollered "Pull, Buster, pull!" Buster didn't respond. Once more the farmer commanded "Pull, Coco, pull!" Nothing happened. Then the farmer nonchalantly said "Pull, Buddy, pull!" and the horse easily dragged the car out of the ditch. The motorist was most appreciative and very curious. He asked the farmer why he called his horse by the wrong name three times. The farmer said "Oh, Buddy is blind and if he thought he was the only one pulling, he wouldn't even try."

A woman saw a little old man rocking in a chair on his porch" She said "I couldn't help noticing how happy you look. What's your secret for a long happy life?" "I smoke three packets of cigarettes a day," he said. "I also drink a case of whisky a week, eat fatty foods and never exercise." "That's amazing," said the woman. "How old are you?" He said "Twenty six."

A Swiss man, looking for directions, pulls up at a bus stop where two Americans are waiting. "Entschuldigung, koennen Sie Deutsch sprechen?" he asks. The two Americans just stare at him. "Excusez-moi, parlez vous Francais?" he tries. The two continue to stare. "Parlare Italiano?" No response. "Hablan ustedes Espanol?" Still nothing. The Swiss guy drives off, extremely disgusted. The first American turns to the second and says "Y'know, maybe we should learn a foreign language" "Why?" says the other. "That guy knew four languages and it didn't do him any good."

A father and son who had lived in a remote jungle all their lives came to London on a visit. They were amazed by just about everything they saw. When they stood in their hotel lobby they were especially amazed by the two shiny, silver walls that could move apart and back together again. The boy asked his Dad "What is this, Father?" The father, never having seen a lift before, responded "Son, I have never seen anything like this in my life. I don't know what it is." While the boy and his father were watching wide-eyed, an old lady in a wheelchair rolled up to the moving walls and pressed a button. The walls opened and the lady rolled between them into a small room. The walls closed and the boy and his father watched small circles of lights with numbers above them light up. They continued to watch as the circles started to light up in the reverse direction. The walls opened up again and a beautiful 24-year-old woman stepped out. Then the father turned to his son and said "Go get your mother!"

A fellow went into a restaurant and immediately made a pest of himself by complaining about where he was seated, the menu and the service. "Look at my glass," he shouted at the waitress. "It's empty! What do I have to do to get some water?" The waitress leaned over and whispered in his ear "Why don't you set fire to yourself?"

A Rabbi heard great things about the taste of pork, but as it wasn't kosher he knew he couldn't be seen eating any part of a pig. One day he had to travel to Brighton to attend a synod of Rabbis and he thought this might provide the perfect opportunity for him finally to give pork a try without anyone knowing. So that day he set off early and stopped off halfway to Brighton in Crawley. He went to a high street restaurant there where roast pig was on the menu. The Rabbi ordered that dish and while waiting for it, another Rabbi that he knew also stopped off at the same place for a meal. He recognised the first Rabbi and came over to join him at the table. He'd hardly had time to sit down when the waiter arrived with the plate of roast pig with the traditional apple in its mouth. The second Rabbi was understandably shocked and his colleague had to think really fast. He said "What a generous restaurant this is. All I ordered was an apple and look what it came with."

The leader of a committee collecting money for deserving charities remembered hearing that during the previous year a local businessman had anonymously won over a million pounds in the national lottery, so he went along to visit the man to try to get a generous donation. He said "I heard through the grapevine about your lucky windfall. Congratulations. I feel sure you'd like to share some of your good fortune by giving a part of it to charity." The businessman looked the man straight in the eye and said "Did your grapevine also tell you that I have both a mother and father in a nursing home which charges a thousand pounds a week each for their keep? Did it tell you I have a brother who's desperately trying to give up being an alcoholic and has just been admitted to the very expensive Priory Rehabilitation Clinic? Did it tell you that my sister's husband died last year leaving her and her four children destitute with no money to pay the mortgage and are about to have their house repossessed? "No," said the visitor feeling a bit guilty. "Well," said the businessman. "If I'm not giving to them, why should I give to you?"

The owner of a large chain of furniture stores was in bed fast asleep when, at three o'clock in the morning the phone rang. It woke him up and, not best pleased he got up and answered it. A voice at the other end said "My name's Fred Conway and I'm one of your customers. I bought a leather sofa and two matching armchairs at your Manchester branch and I want to tell you how pleased I am with them." The store owner was still sleepy and though a bit annoyed was quite polite. He said "I appreciate the compliment. Did you buy them today?" "No," said the man "I bought them four months ago." Now the store owner was getting angry. He said "You bought the furniture four months ago! Why on earth are you waking me up at three in the morning to tell me about it?" The customer said "It just arrived."

A British couple got married and planned their honeymoon for a couple of weeks in Hawaii. Playfully on the plane they got into a little argument about how Hawaii is pronounced. He was sure it was Ha_v_aii and she insisted it was Ha_w_aii. She said he should be man enough to admit he was wrong and he said "No, it's you that's got it wrong. But we'll settle this when we get there. When they got off the plane they decided to ask the first person they met. It was an old man with a beard. The husband said "Excuse me, sir. Would you mind telling me how you pronounce the name of this lovely island?" The man said "It's Ha_v_aii." "See," said the husband to his bride, I told you." Then he turned to the man and thanked him. To which he replied "You're velcome."

A husband passed away and his wife was so distraught she went to see a spiritualist. He told her her husband was fine and that he was looking forward to being reunited with her in the distant future. "Is there anything he needs?" she asked. The spiritualist went into a short trance and then he said "Your late husband says he'd like a packet of cigarettes." "I'd be only too glad to send them to him" the wife said. "But did he give an address?" "No" said the man. "But he didn't ask for matches."

A wife who'd never played a round of golf in her life decided she'd let her husband give her her first lesson. They got out on the first tee and he told her "If you look straight ahead, you'll see a flag. Try to hit the ball so it gets as close as possible to that flag." The wife hits a fantastic drive. Unbelievably it lands less than a foot from the cup. "Now what do I do?" she asks. Her husband said "The object it to putt the ball into the cup." She said "NOW you tell me!"

This American fellow desperately wanted to be a famous actor and he firmly believed that a really good actor tries to live whatever part he's ask to play. One day he got an audition to play the part of Abraham Lincoln in a new play. So he did his research and read everything he could find about Lincoln. He bought a replica of the clothes Lincoln wore including the black stovepipe hat, black cloak, red sash and even the large black boots. He wore all this when he went off to the audition. Unfortunately he didn't get the part. But worse than that, on the way home he was assassinated.

A famous tea manufacturer decided it was time it had a new advertising gimmick so it asked its advertising agency to come up with a good idea. The Creative Head thought about it for a while then came up with an idea they all liked. He was going to go to Rome and talk the Pope into doing a television commercial for tea. After all, he thought, everyone listens to what the Pope has to say. So the Creative Head arranged to have a personal audience with the Pope. He said "Your Excellency, my client is prepared to give you half a million pounds for just doing a ten second commercial. All you have to do is say 'Give us this day our daily tea." The Pope said "I'm sorry, I just can't do that." "We'll make it three quarters of a million." The Pope still said no. "Alright", said the ad man, "A million pounds, but that's our final offer." The Pope didn't even consider it. He still refused to make the commercial, so the visitor left. On the way back to England he turned to his secretary and said "I'm surprised he turned down my offer of a million pounds just to advertise tea. That's a lot of money. I wonder what the bread people are paying him.

One dark night a couple were making love on a park bench. They were getting all hot and bothered when a policeman came along. He heard their gasping and moaning and shined his torch on them. "You can't do that here." He said "It's against the law. You're arrested. I'm taking you to the police station. Nest morning they are up before the judge who said "This is a serious charge. You both know the law. Why did you make love in the park?" "Well, your honour," explained the husband, "this woman is my wife." "Well," said the judge, "that's different. As she is your wife, I'll dismiss the case." As they were leaving the court, the policeman that charged them stopped them to apologise. "I'm very sorry" he said. I didn't know it was your wife." "Neither did I" said the man, "Until you shined that torch on us."

After the last drop of rain had fallen on Noah's Ark and the sky was blue again, Noah lowered the gangplank and called all the animals and told them to go forth and multiply. They all did except the snakes. "Didn't you hear me?" Noah asked. "I said go forth and multiply. The male snake said "We can't. We're adders."

A Frenchman, a Scotsman and an Englishman were discussing their individual success as ardent lovers. Pierre, the Frenchman said "Last night I covered my wife in champagne and she screamed for ten minutes." "That's nothing at all" said Jock, the Scot. "I covered my wife in a cream made up of malt whisky and sherry brandy and she screamed for almost an hour." "I can go one better," claimed the Englishman. "On my wife I rubbed chicken fat. It was three hours before she stopped screaming." The other two looked at him in disbelief. They said "How did you manage that?" He said "I wiped my hands on the bedspread."

A disappointed salesman for Coca Cola returned from a sales trip to Israel. His boss demanded to know why he failed to sell one single bottle of coke to the Israelis. So the salesman explained the problem. "I was very confident I would make a good sales pitch, but I don't speak their language" he said. "So I made up three posters. The first poster had a man lying in the hot desert sand, totally exhausted and fainting. In the second poster the man is drinking our Coca Cola. And in the third, our man is totally refreshed. I pasted these posters in every public place I could find." "That should have worked." Said the boss. "Why didn't it?" "Because" said the salesman "I forgot. The Jews read from right to left."

About the Author

During his half century career as an International radio and TV comedy writer, Brad Ashton has enjoyed the reputation of being an exceedingly fast gag writer. He supplied laugh lines to comedians in eleven different countries. Among the British stars he wrote for were Tommy Cooper, Les Dawson, Dick Emery, Frankie Howerd, Bruce Forsyth, David Frost and Bob Monkhouse. Even the great Groucho Marx employed him as Head Writer for his TV series *Groucho In Britain*. One of Brad's earlier books *How To Write Comedy* is still used at some universities as a text book for their Creative Writing courses.